Text-e

Text-e

Text in the Age of the Internet

Edited by

Gloria Origgi

English-language edition first published 2006 by
PALGRAVE MACMILLAN
Houndmills, Basingstoke, Hampshire RG21 6XS and
175 Fifth Avenue, New York, N.Y. 10010
Companies and representatives throughout the world

PALGRAVE MACMILLAN is the global academic imprint of the Palgrave Macmillan division of St. Martin's Press, LLC and of Palgrave Macmillan Ltd. Macmillan® is a registered trademark in the United States, United Kingdom and other countries. Palgrave is a registered trademark in the European Union and other countries.

ISBN-13: 978–1–4039–4883–0
ISBN-10: 1–4039–4883–6

This book is printed on paper suitable for recycling and made from fully managed and sustained forest sources.

A catalogue record for this book is available from the British Library.

Library of Congress Cataloging-in-Publication Data
Text-e. English
    Text-e : text in the age of the Internet / edited by Gloria Origgi.
        p.   cm.
    Original title: Text-e : le texte à l'heure de l'Internet.
    Essays commissioned by the Centre Georges Pompidou for a virtual trilingual symposium which took place on the Web site www.text-e.org from October 2001 to March 2002.
    Includes bibliographical references and index.
    ISBN 1–4039–4883–6
    1. Written communication—Social aspects.   2. Internet.
    3. Communication and technology.   I. Origgi, Gloria, 1967–
    II. Centre Georges Pompidou.   III. Title.
    P211.7T4913 2005
    302.2′244—dc22   2005051164

10   9   8   7   6   5   4   3   2   1
15 14 13 12 11 10 09 08 07 06

Printed and bound in Great Britain by
Antony Rowe Ltd, Chippenham and Eastbourne

Contents

Foreword

This book is the result of an adventure which took place over five months. Every two weeks, between October 2001 and March 2002, a prestigious lecturer spoke from the virtual lectern of a web symposium devoted to discussing the effects of digital media on our relations with the world of reading and writing. As is the rule in this kind of public event, the lecturer then willingly participated in a debate with the audience, but, with this exception, that the 'audience' had no more material reality than did the lectern, the lectures and debates being held entirely online, on the website *www.text-e.org*, designed for the purpose.

As for the organisers of the first virtual symposium, the adventure had begun eighteen months earlier, when in response to an invitation issued by the Studies and Research department of the Bpi on the topic of 'Screens and networks: towards a new relationship with the written word', a group of researchers proposed putting into effect, not a study, but a 'research-action'. It was suggested that a symposium be organized entirely online, making use of the same technologies that were proposed as the topic for collective research. The NICTs (New information and Communication Technologies) would thus be at one and the same time the theme, the medium and the context for the symposium.

This innovative project naturally attracted the interest of the Bpi. Experimenting, innovating in the field of access to knowledge and diffusion of ideas, is one of the fundamental missions of this multi-media library, which since its creation has been offering its users a wide and constantly updated choice of documents, delivered through various media. The NICTs arose both as an opportunity to enrich this offering and as a question: What might be the cultural mission of the library in this new context? Like other major libraries, the Bpi tries to design original digital offerings which exemplify the library's own information identity. This library is not in charge of preserving ancient documents and does not possess any patrimonial collections in the strict sense of the word. However, its location in the Pompidou Centre, a symbol of modernity, and its vocation as a source of new ideas, has enabled the Bpi to establish itself as a centre of excellence over the years. With the support of this 'current' inheritance, the Bpi plans to build up a digital library which will focus on the second half of the twentieth century, and on the evolution of ideas, society and the arts.

The virtual symposium was thus perfectly in tune with our concerns and our programme. One of the issues at stake in the symposium was to encourage subject experts and theorists to take part in the dialogue, as well as researchers and information professionals. This principle guided the choice of the ten invited lecturers and the wish to open the discussion to any interested persons. Mounting the operation itself rested with a mixed combination in the form of collaboration between an international team of researchers at the Institut Jean Nicod (CNRS, Paris), a public establishment – the Bpi, and a Franco-American company GiantChair Inc, which specializes in helping publishing houses, libraries, universities and academic communities to implement new methods of publishing and distribution. The combination was not an obvious one, but the mixture at once gave an international dimension to the operation.

The symposium was trilingual and it is important to recognize the work of the two 'moderators', Noga Arikha and Gloria Origgi, who brilliantly undertook the challenge of animating the online polyglot debate. The demonstration was put before UNESCO, which gave its support. Thanks to the generosity and expertise of the GiantChair company, for which we are deeply grateful, the symposium was enriched by an experiment in digital publication, with the lectures themselves available as e-books offered free of charge to participants on the website. There is no doubt that many visitors to the site discovered on this occasion that it is easy to download an e-book to one's computer without owning a special device and that this kind of publication opens up new possibilities – indeed, one of the objectives of the experiment was to 'popularize' this new resource, and this seemed successful.

Quite naturally, from the very beginning of the project it was envisaged that the proceedings of the debates should be published digitally but without giving up a printed edition as a permanent record. We are, indeed, convinced that far from being competing, digital and printed environments are complementary. The results of the survey we undertook on text-e and the practices of writing and reading confirmed this view. Most of the people interviewed told us that they had read the debates on screen but needed to print out the ten major contributions before going through them. The publication of the 'proceedings' of the debate – the ten 'conferences' and selected items of commentary, does not mark the end of this collective adventure. On the contrary, it enables it to continue and you the reader will, more than ever, be able to take part.

GÉRALD GRUNBERG
Director of the Bibliothèque publique d'information

Acknowledgements

The authors first presented their work as part of a virtual trilingual symposium organized on the web site *www.text-e.org*. This book can convey only a part of the lively discussion that took place on the web. I would like to thank all the participants to the discussion, and in particular Noga Arikha, who moderated with me the debate on line in three languages for five months and greatly contributed to the project's overall quality. Texts and discussions are available here in English thanks to the efforts of an outstanding team of translators: Noga Arikha, Deborah Kan Furet, Stash Luczkiw and Garry White.

Introduction

Gloria Origgi

This collection of essays on the impact of the Internet on texts, intellectual life, research, communication and culture was commissioned by the Centre Pompidou in Paris for a trilingual symposium which took place over five months on the web site *www.text-e.org*. The essays were discussed on line in a public forum accessed from three continents and a dozen countries. Its success and the wealth of ideas it brought out signal how timely the event was and the relevance of the themes around which the discussions were centred. Each text grapples with a theme. Together the essays form a coherent, accessible survey of what the Internet is doing to our reading and writing practices.

The Internet is often compared to the invention of writing and printing because of the revolutionary cultural and cognitive shift it has incited. Many volumes have been written on this phenomenon, but it has rarely been analysed in any systematic way by thinkers and writers whose intellectual lives have been transformed by it. In general, the digital revolution is studied in either highly technical, monothematic or oversimplified postmodern terms. This collection of reflections is conceived in response to this lack, in an attempt to approach the subject in an interdisciplinary and accessible way.

The world of text production – publishing, journalism, humanistic academies – has reacted to the digital era with consternation. The challenge was enormous, disrupting professions that have traditionally been humanistic rather than technical in their modes of creating, producing and distributing texts. The clear advantages of digital production have obviated any possible defence of the old methods of production, but at the same time the direction of innovation has been confusing. Possible solutions have competed in a cacophony of standards and models of production, becoming increasingly unrealistic. Even today it is still hard to imagine what the standard formats for reading and diffusing texts will be in ten years, as in the world of culture there are various coexistent support systems and technologies. Notwithstanding the confusion, one cannot deny that our everyday manner of working on texts has changed. The practices are no longer the same, and the modes of information exchange, support systems and timing have all undergone a profound and irreversible transformation. The texts gathered here are reflections upon these changes.

Participants include: a historian, Roger Chartier; two philosophers, Roberto Casati and Gloria Origgi; a cognitive scientist, Stevan Harnad; a journalist, Bruno Patino; a historian and writer, Theodore Zeldin; a publisher, Jason Epstein; an anthropologist, Dan Sperber; a novelist and semiologist, Umberto Eco; a team of librarians and another team of experts. Texts are written for a general, heterogeneous public, and present a 'state of the art' analysis of the relationship on the Internet between writing, reading, information, conversation, publishing, memory, authorship. They include personal accounts (such as Bruno Patino's experience as editor of the on-line edition of *Le Monde*), venturesome predictions (such as Dan Sperber's description of the end of writing in a near future) and provocative proposals (such as Stevan Harnad's case for free access on the Web to all scientific information).

In Chapter 1, Roger Chartier argues that our very notion of a 'book' is put in question by digital books. The screen can erase the traditional boundaries of a text and transform the way we receive it by dissociating its content from its support, thereby changing our perception of the 'order of discourse' such as it has historically been conceived in our culture.

In Chapter 2, Roberto Casati resumes the issue of the impact of forms on content by asking the ontological question: 'What is a book?' Books are physical as well as mental entities, objects through which social practices are realized. Are we talking of the same thing when we talk of a physical book and a digital one? Which relevant properties do we need to replicate in the virtual world in order to have a digital object that enters the same mental and social networks of a real book?

Chapter 3 is devoted to a defence of liberating access to peer-reviewed scholarly articles on line. According to Stevan Harnad, it is the failure to make the distinction between what he calls 'give-away' work (refereed scientific and scholarly research papers) and 'non-give-away' work (books, magazines, software, music) that is delaying the inevitable transition of the give-away work to what would be the optimal solution for scholars and scientists: that is, open access to the refereed articles through author/institution self-archiving.

In Chapter 4, Bruno Patino brings his personal experience at *Le Monde* to explain the new job of the Internet journalist. The Internet is probably unique in that, for the first time, a new medium has been created without generating a new language. What is available to the reader on the Internet is content that appears in a format which is already familiar: texts and audiovisual files. While a global network is now a reality, a multimedia language proper to Internet remains, at best, an aspiration. How can a journalist adapt his practices to this new media? The Internet makes it possible to treat news in a novel way, giving it a new context and a new relationship with time and memory.

In a conversation with Gloria Origgi (Chapter 5), Theodore Zeldin suggests a very different picture of technological change. The Internet does not change the world. It is the awareness of our new needs and goals that creates a new vision of the world, a vision that can help us understand what we want out of the Internet.

In Chapter 6, Jason Epstein, one of the most innovative publishers in the twentieth century, bets on the 'print on demand' model of distributing books in the digital era while acknowledging that various book supports will continue to coexist. But the 'book business' will be radically affected by the change of expertise needed for the publishing of texts and the managing of rights.

A team of librarians pursue the topic of the change of expertise in Chapter 7 by asking, 'What is a library in the numerical age?' In an institution traditionally devoted to the written word and to its memory, the advent of unstable and potentially infinite information could put into question the very nature of the library.

In Chapter 8, Dan Sperber tackles the thorny issue of the future of writing skills. The production of texts will increasingly involve speech-to-text technologies. Writing is at the basis of teaching and a necessary condition for access to the modern world, but it will become a secondary technique like stenography or calligraphy. Reading, however, won't be replaced in the same way. What is the future of our relation to texts? Still read but no longer written?

In Chapter 9, the usability experts Stefana Broadbent and Francesco Cara present a survey of their observations of hundreds of users interacting with websites and draw some conclusions, based on the rigid architecture of the first-generation websites, about the crash of the New Economy.

In Chapter 10, Gloria Origgi interviews Umberto Eco, who presents his views on authorship, intellectual authority and the future of the copyright. Can experts play the role of information-filters in the Google era?

Finally, in Chapter 11 Gloria Origgi presents a 'state-of-the-art' overview of the transformations of research practices in the academy. Although the Internet is now an unavoidable tool for research, most of the fears and hopes about the production of scholarly texts have revealed themselves to be unsubstantiated. We are still looking for publishers for our manuscripts and still need to publish papers in peer-reviewed journals for our academic careers. The digital era we were dreaming of only ten years ago was too far removed from the world we were used to, and we have faced a conservative reaction in the practices and policies of information access. But we are still at the dawn of a much more radical transformation concerning the 'division of cognitive labour' in the society of knowledge.

Notes on the Contributors and Discussants

The contributors

The Bpi team consists of Angélique Bellec, Eliane Bernhart, Agnès Camus-Vigué, Danièle Chatel, Claire Dartois, Isabelle Dussert-Carbone, Christophe Evans, Françoise Gaudet, Gérald Grunberg, Philippe Guillerme, Bernard Huchet and Emmanuèle Payen.

Stefana Broadbent and Francesco Cara are consultants on usability of cognitive ergonomics for various international groups. They have applied the tools of cognitive science to the study of the Internet. Francesco Cara is now at Nokia for studies in human–computer Interaction and Stefana Broadbent works at Swisscom.

Roberto Casati is a philosopher and researcher at the CNRS in Paris. His many works include *Holes and Other Superficialities* (with Achille Varzi), *Parts and Places* (with Achille Varzi), and *The Discovery of the Shadow*. He writes regularly on science for the cultural supplement of the Italian daily *Il Sole 24 Ore*.

Roger Chartier is a French cultural historian, specializing in the history of the book, particularly in the Enlightenment and the French Revolution. His books include *A History of Reading in the West* (with Gugliemo Cavallo), *On the Edge of the Cliff: History, Language and Practices, Culture écrite et société: l'ordre des livres*, and *Les origines culturelles de la révolution française*.

Umberto Eco is Professor of Semiotics at the University of Bologna, as well as a best-selling novelist. He has worked on medieval aesthetics, semiotics, philosophy and literary criticism. His novels have been translated the world over.

Jason Epstein is one of the most brilliant publishers of the twentieth century. He founded Anchor Books in 1952, launching the paperback, was co-founder of the *New York Review of Books* (1963), founded the

Library of America in 1980 and conceived of the *Reader's Catalog*, a precursor of Internet bookshops. He has published a series of articles in the *New York Review of Books* on the transformation of publishing and, recently, published a memoir, *Book Business*.

Stevan Harnad is a cognitive scientist. He founded the journal *Behavioral and Brain Sciences*, one of the most prestigious publications in the cognitive sciences, as well as the Web journal *Psycholoquy*, backed by the American Psychological Association. He also directs the COGPRINTS project, an electronic archive of cognitive science papers. He is a front-line leader in the debate on the liberation of all scientific and academic peer-reviewed articles on the Web.

Bruno Patino is director of the online edition of the French daily *Le Monde – Le Monde Interactif*. He began his career as correspondent for *Le Monde* in Santiago, Chile. He directed the literature section at Hachette in 1997 and became a member of the directorate of *Le Monde* in 1999.

Dan Sperber is an anthropologist, philosopher and linguist, working on the relationship between cognitive science and social science. His books include *On Anthropological Knowledge: Three Essays, Relevance* (with Deirdre Wilson) and *Explaining Culture*.

Theodore Zeldin is a noted historian and Professor at St Antony's College Oxford. His in-depth knowledge of France is illustrated in his *A History of French Passions 1848–1945* and in *The French*. He is the author of the best-selling *An Intimate History of Humanity*, and more recently of a book on *Conversation*, from BBC radio lectures.

The discussants

Patrick Altman is editor and consultant in France for various projects in e-publishing.

Noga Arikha is a historian of ideas. She teaches at Bard College, NJ. With Gloria Origgi she was the moderator of the virtual symposium *www.text-e.org*

Chris Armstrong is Managing Director at Information Automation Limited and at the Centre for Information Quality Management, involved in research on the use of electronic information resources in higher education.

Agnès Amus-Vigué is a sociologist. She works at the *Service Etudes et Recherches* of the Bpi, Paris.

Colette Bergeal is Chief of Electronic Services at Bpi, Paris.

François Bon is a writer who was trained as an engineer. His first book, *Sortie d'Usine*, was published in 1982. In 1997 he founded the Internet literature site which became *www.remue.net*.

Bernard Conein is Professor of Sociology at the Université de Lille III, France.

Stephen Downes works at the Institute for Information Technology's e-Learning Research Group and is known for his daily research newsletter, *OLDaily* (*Online Learning Daily*).

David Goodman is Biological Science Bibliographer at the Princeton University Library.

Michael John Gorman is a historian of science, and director of the Arkimedia initiative in Dublin and of the Athanasius Kircher correspondence web project.

Jack Kessler is a journalist and editor of *FYI France* at *www.fyifrance.com*

David Klemke prefers not to give biographical details.

Fabienne Martin studies linguistics at the Université Libre de Bruxelles.

Cory McCloud is CEO of GiantChair.com

Richard Minsky is an artist and an author based in New York. He is founder of the Center for Book Arts.

Gloria Origgi is a philosopher and researcher at CNRS, Paris. Along with Noga Arikha she was the moderator of the text-e online experiment.

Serge Pouts-Lajus is consultant and researcher at the OTE *Observatoire des technologies pour l'éducation en Europe*, which he founded in 1988 with Eric Barchechath.

David Prater is a Melbourne-based writer and researcher. His main areas of interest include the changing nature of authorship, future roles for copyright and e-books.

Jean-Michel Salaün is Professor at the Ecole Nationale Supérieure des Sciences de l'Information et des Bibliothèques (*Enssib – www.enssib.fr*). He also runs the Institute for digital document sciences (*Isdn – isdn.enssib.fr*).

Arthur Smith leads the IT group at the American Physical Society editorial office, publishing the *Physical Review* journals, and other journals and online physics information resources.

Lorre Smith is Librarian for Digital Library Initiatives at University at Albany, State University of New York.

Thierry Soubrié teaches applied linguistics at the Stendhal University in Grenoble, France.

Peter Suber is Professor of Philosophy at Earlham College and editor of the *Free Online Scholarship Newsletter*.

Jean Tardif is President of the international association PlanetAgora.

Michael Ullyot does academic research and university teaching in Toronto.

Rob Walker is Director of the Center for Applied Research in Education, Norwich *http://www.uea.ac.uk/care*

1

Readers and Readings in the Electronic Age

Roger Chartier

Se habla de la desaparición del libro; yo creo que es imposible.

Jorge Luis Borges

In 1968, in a celebrated essay, Roland Barthes associated the all-powerfulness of the reader with the death of the author. Dethroned from his former sovereignty by language, or rather by 'multiple writings from several cultures, all in a dialogue with one another, in parody and protest', the author gave up his preeminence to the reader, this '*someone* who, in one field, gathers together all the traces which constitute the written'. Reading was here the place where plural, mobile and unstable meaning was drawn and where texts, regardless of their nature, acquired their sense.[1]

Death of the author, transfiguration of the book

This affirmation of the birth of the reader was followed by the diagnosis of his death. There were three main kinds of diagnosis. The first looked to transformations in reading practices. On the one hand, statistical information gathered in surveys on cultural behaviour has conclusively shown – although this may not signify a drop in the overall percentage of readers – a reduction at least in the proportion of 'heavy readers' in each age category, particularly in that of adolescent readers. Observations based on editorial policies have reinforced the belief in the existence of a reading 'crisis'.[2] While fiction is not spared, this crisis is most cruelly felt in the areas of the social and human sciences. The effects are comparable on both sides of the Atlantic, even if the primary causes are not quite the same. In the United States, the essential factor is the drastic reduction in the acquisition of *monographs* by university libraries whose budgets are eaten up by subscriptions to periodicals which in some cases reach considerable prices – between US$10,000 and $15,000 dollars a year. Hence the reticence of university publishers to publish works that are considered too specialized: doctoral theses, monographic studies, scholarly works, and so on.[3] In France and, no doubt, more widely in Europe, a similar prudence, which limits both the number of titles published and the number of copies per title is a consequence of a shrinking buying public – which does not only consist of academics – and a drop in sales.

The death of the reader and the disappearance of reading tend to be thought of as the inevitable consequence of the civilization of screens, of the triumph of images and electronic communication. It is the latter diagnosis that I would like to discuss in this essay. The screens of our century are indeed of a new breed. Unlike cinema or television screens, they bear texts – not only texts, certainly, but also texts. The old opposition between, on the one hand, the book, the written and reading, and, on the other, the screen and images, has been replaced by a new situation in which a new medium for written culture and a new form for the book are now possible. Hence the very paradoxical link between the omnipresence of writing in our societies and the obsessive theme of the disappearance of the book and the death of the reader. In order to understand this contradiction, we need to look back in time and evaluate the effects of previous revolutions in the media of written culture.

In the Fourth century of the Christian era, a new form of book imposed itself, at the expense of the one that had been familiar to Greek and Roman readers. The codex – a book composed of pages folded, assembled and bound – progressively but inexorably supplanted the scrolls which, up until then, had borne written culture. The book's new material form ensured that once impossible practices, such as writing while reading, leafing through a work or locating a particular passage, became common-place. The codex form profoundly transformed the use of texts. The invention of the page, the precision conferred by foliation and indexing, the new relationship between the work and the object which transmits it paved the way for a new relationship between readers and books.

Is it the case that we are on the brink of a similar transformation and that the electronic book will replace or is already replacing the printed codex such as we know it in its various guises, as book, journal, or newspaper? Perhaps. In the decades to come, however, there will most probably prevail a coexistence – not necessarily a peaceful one – between these two book forms and the three modes of inscribing and communi-cating texts: manuscript writing, printed publication, electronic texts.

This hypothesis seems more plausible than the laments about the irremediable loss of written culture or the unbridled enthusiasm which announced the imminent advent of a new era of communication. This probable coexistence requires that we think about the new ways in which fields of knowledge will be constructed, and about the reading modalities enabled by the electronic book. The latter neither can nor should substitute one medium with another, in the case of works conceived and written in codex form. It has been said that 'form has an effect on meaning'.[4] Electronic books thus reorganize the way in which we rely on sources to demonstrate arguments. Writing or reading this new type of book necessitates the transformation of the criteria we use for evaluating the credibility of any discourse, particularly learned discourse. Historians have recently begun looking at the various, shifting techniques used to confer credibility to knowledge and at their effects, through the cases, for example, of quotations, footnotes[5] or what Michel de Certeau, echoing Condillac, has called the 'language of calculations'.[6] These established ways of proving the validity of an analysis are profoundly modified once arguments cease to be attached to a linear and deductive logic and are instead open, fragmented and relational (as they are in electronic texts)[7] and once the reader can consult the documents (such as archives, images, words or music) which are the objects or instruments of research.[8] In this sense, the revolution in the modalities of production and transmission of texts is also a fundamental epistemological shift.[9]

With the advent of the codex, written works were constructed on the basis of their material form; for example, texts previously contained in several scrolls were now divided into books, parts or chapters of a unique discourse, all contained in a single work. Similarly, the possibilities as well as the constraints of the electronic book call for the reorganization of the necessarily linear and sequential structure of present-day books, still dependent on the codex form. The electronic format of hypertext and hyper-reading modifies the relation between images, sounds and texts linked up electronically in a non-linear manner, and makes possible a virtually unlimited number of connections between texts.[10] In this borderless textual world, *links* are the key through which textual units, fragmented for ease of reading, can be joined together.

It is thus the very notion of 'book' which is put in question by electronic texts. In printed culture, one tends to associate a type of discourse with a type of text and its intended use. The order of discourse is thus based on the material medium, be it letter, newspaper, journal, book or archive. This is not the case in the digital world where all texts, regardless of their nature, are read in the same medium (the computer screen) and in the same forms (generally those decided on by the reader). A 'continuum' is thus created in which no differences remain between the various textual genres or repertoires, now similar in appearance and equivalent in authority. The disappearance of the criteria which once allowed one to distinguish, classify and order discourse has bred much anxiety.

Properties and ownership of texts

The concepts and technical tools used to designate some electronic texts as 'books' therefore need to be analysed. The reorganization of the world of digital writing is a necessary condition for the introduction of paid on-line access and for the protection of the author's moral and economic rights. These conditions are based on the necessary, albeit conflictual alliance between publishers and authors, and will probably lead to a profound transformation of the electronic world such as we know it. Security systems aimed at protecting some works or databases, and made more efficient by e-books, will probably multiply and, therefore, fix, freeze and seal texts published electronically.[11] It is a predictable evolution: the 'book' and other digital texts will be defined in opposition to the free and spontaneous electronic communication which allows everyone to circulate their thoughts and works on the Web. This division, it is true, could lead to the economic and cultural hegemony of powerful multimedia and computer companies; but more positively, it could help establish an order of discourse which would take into account the major differences between, on the one hand, spontaneous texts released onto the Web, and on the other, vetted, edited writings. The authority of any given text whose provenance and status are clearly stated would thus be assessed on the basis of the modality of its 'publication'. Such a system is needed if one is to counter the indiscriminate nature of the 'information' obtained by most search motors.[12]

Another element could, in the long term, turn the world of digital technology on its head. It arises out of the possibility of detaching the transmission of electronic text from the computer (PC, portable or 'e-book'), through the creation of electronic ink and 'paper'. Researchers at MIT have been developing a technique whereby any object (including the book as we still know it) would be capable of becoming the medium for an electronic book or an electronic library, provided it is equipped with a microprocessor or that it is downloaded from the Internet, and that its pages receive the electronic ink which allows different texts to appear successively on the same surface.[13] Electronic texts could thus be emancipated from the constraints inherent to the screens we are familiar with. This would break the bond (a source of profit for some) between the trade of electronic machines and on-line publishing.

Even without imagining this still hypothetical future, one may wonder whether the electronic book in its current form will be able to attract or produce readers. The long history of reading clearly shows that revolutions in the order of practice always lag behind, and are often slower than, revolutions in technology. New ways of reading did not follow immediately from the invention of printing. Similarly, the intellectual categories which we associate with the world of texts will endure with the new forms of book. It might be useful to remember that, after the invention of the codex and the disappearance of the scroll, the 'book' – here denoting ordered discourse – often corresponded to the textual matter previously contained in a scroll.

Moreover, the electronic revolution, which at first seems universal, can also deepen, rather than reduce, inequalities. A new 'illiteracy' could emerge, no longer defined by the inability to read and write, but by the impossibility of gaining access to the new forms of transmission of writing – which, to say the least, do not come free. An electronic correspondence between authors and readers – now transformed into co-authors of a book kept open through their comments and interventions – allows for an author–reader relationship, close in kind to that to which some ancient authors aspired, but hard to achieve with the printed book. A more immediate, more dialogic relationship between the work and the reading of the work is an attractive prospect, but it should not make us forget that the potential readers (and co-authors) of electronic books are still very few. The gap remains great between the obsessive presence of the revolution and the reality of reading practices which are still attached to printed objects and which make only very partial use of the possibilities bred by digital technology. We have to be lucid enough not to take what is virtual for a reality already here with us.

What is original, and perhaps worrying about our period is that the different revolutions in written culture which, in the past, had been disjointed, are now happening simultaneously. The electronic text revolution is at once a revolution in the technology of the production and reproduction of texts, a revolution in the medium of writing, and a revolution in reading practices. It is characterized by three main traits which profoundly transform our relationship to written culture. First, the electronic representation of writing radically modifies the notion of context and, as a result, the very process of the construction of meaning. The physical contiguity of different texts gathered in one book or in the same periodical here gives way to their mobile distribution, programmed into the architecture of databases and digitized collections. Second, the electronic representation of writing redefines the material characteristics of works because it dissolves the visible link between the text and the object which contains the text, and because it gives the reader, and no longer the author or the publisher, control over the composition, the arrangement and appearance of the textual units that are to be read. It is thus the whole system of perception and handling of texts which is utterly changed. Finally, when reading on screen, the contemporary reader returns somewhat to the posture of the reader of Antiquity. The difference is that he reads a scroll which generally runs vertically and which is endowed with the characteristics inherent to the form of the book since the first centuries of the Christian era: pagination, index, tables, etc. The combination of these two systems which governed previous writing media (the volumen, then the codex) results in an entirely original relation to texts.

Given these transformations, electronic texts could turn into a reality the old but never fulfilled fantasy of complete knowledge. Like the library of Alexandria, they promise the universal availability of all texts ever written, of all books ever published.[14] As with the practice of commonplace rhetoric in the Renaissance,[15] they call on the collaboration of the reader who can now write in the book himself, entering the wall-less library of electronic writing. As with the Enlightenment project, they delimit an ideal public space where, as Kant believed, there must be a free, unrestricted and all-inclusive deployment of the public exercise of reason, which 'one engages in as a *scholar* for the whole of the *reading public*' and which authorizes each citizen 'in his quality of scholar, to comment publicly, that is to say in writing, on the faults of the old institution'.[16]

As was the case in the age of printing, but more forcefully so even, the era of the electronic text is fraught with major tensions between different imaginable futures: the proliferation of separate communities, defined by their use of new technologies; the grip of powerful multimedia companies on the constitution of digital databases and the production or circulation of information; or the establishment of a universal public, defined by the participation of each of its members in the critical examination of exchanged arguments.[17] The free and immediate communication at a distance made possible by the Web might give birth to any one of these situations. It could lead to the loss of common references, to the compartmentalization of groups and the exacerbation of idiosyncrasies. It could also bring about the hegemony of a single cultural model and destroy diversity. On the other hand, however, it might also lead to the growth of a new form for the constitution and communication of knowledge, adding to the transmission of established sciences the collective construction of knowledge through the exchange of expertise and wisdom, in the manner of the correspondences or the periodicals of the old Republic of Letters.[18] If it takes everyone on board, the new encyclopaedic navigation could bring about the realization of universality, the hope for which has always been present in the effort to embrace the multitude of things and words within the order of discourse.

For this to happen, however, the electronic book has to define itself over and against current practices, in which rough texts are placed on the Web which neither have been thought out in relation to their new form of transmission, nor have undergone an editing process. To plead for the use of new technology in the publication of knowledge is therefore to warn against the laziness bred by electronic technology and to encourage a more rigorous control over cultural and individual exchanges. The uncertainties and conflicts with regard to epistolary civility (or incivility), language conventions and relations between public and private sectors as they are redefined by the use of electronic mail all point to this need.[19]

Libraries in the digital age

The new medium of writing does not mean the end of the book or the death of the reader. The very reverse might be true. However, it does require a redistribution of roles within the 'economy of writing', the competition (or complementarity) between various media and a new relationship, material as much as intellectual and aesthetic, with the world of texts. One may wonder whether electronic texts might ever be able to construct on the basis of written exchanges a public space in which each and everyone can participate. Neither the alphabet, in spite of the democratic qualities which Vico attributed to it,[20] nor printing, in spite of the universality which Condorcet recognized in it,[21] succeeded in doing this.

How, then, are we to locate the role of libraries within these profound transformations of written culture? With the possibilities that new technology allows, our young century can perhaps hope to overcome the contradiction which has always haunted our relationship with the book in the West. The dream of the universal library is the expression of the desire to seize and accumulate the totality of all texts ever written, of all knowledge ever built. But disappointment has always accompanied this expectation of universality since all collections, however rich, can only ever result in a partial, flawed version of the exhaustiveness required to fulfil this wish.

This tension can be understood in the context of the very long duration of attitudes towards writing. It is a tension founded on the fear of loss or lack. It has governed all actions geared at saving the written heritage of humanity: the quest for ancient texts, the copying of the most precious books, the printing of manuscripts, the construction of great libraries, the compilation of the 'libraries without walls' that are encyclopaedias, the collections of texts and catalogues.[22] Given that texts can always disappear, one has had to gather, fix and preserve them. But another peril threatens this never-ending task, that of excess. The reproduction of manuscripts and, later, of printed books was perceived as a terrible danger very early on. Proliferation can become chaos, and abundance can hinder knowledge. Instruments capable of sorting, classifying and ordering are required for the control of excess. Various people have been participating in this ordering process: the authors themselves who judge their peers and their predecessors, the powers at be which censor and subsidize, the publishers who publish (or refuse to publish), the institutions which consecrate and exclude and the libraries which preserve or ignore.

Faced with this double anxiety and with the need to navigate between loss and excess, the library of tomorrow – or of today – can play a decisive role. Admittedly, the electronic revolution has seemed to signify its demise. The communication of electronic texts makes the universal availability of the written heritage conceivable, if not possible; libraries no longer need be the sole centres for the conservation and communication of this heritage. Every reader, wherever he is reading, could receive any one of the texts which make up this library without walls, situated nowhere in particular, where all books would be present in ideal, digital form.

This dream is far from unattractive. But it must not lead us astray. The electronic conversion of all texts whose existence does not originate with computers must in no way entail the downgrading, neglect, or, worse, destruction of the manuscripts or printed matter which bore them in the first place. More than ever, perhaps, one of the essential tasks of libraries is to collect, protect, catalogue and make accessible the written objects of the past. If the works that they have transmitted cease to be communicated, or even preserved in anything other than electronic form, the risk is great that the past's textual cultures, embodied as they are within the objects – the books – which have transmitted them, will no longer be intelligible to us. The library of the future therefore must sustain the knowledge and currency of written culture, in the forms it has taken in the past and still takes, for the most part, in our day.

Libraries will also have to be instruments assisting new readers in finding their way in a digital world where differences between genres and uses of texts are invisible and where the authority of all texts seems equivalent everywhere. Libraries can be attentive to the needs or confusions of readers and can play an essential role in the teaching of the instruments and technology that less expert readers need in order to master the new forms of writing. Just as the presence of the Internet in schools does not in itself dissipate the cognitive difficulties inherent in learning how to write,[23] so the electronic communication of texts does not by itself transmit the knowledge required to understand and use them. Quite the contrary, the reader–navigator of digital technology is at a high risk of getting lost in textual archipelagos without beacon or harbour. The library can be both of these.[24]

Another role for the libraries of tomorrow could be that of reconstituting the sociability around the book, which has been lost. The long history of reading teaches us that, over the centuries, reading became a silent and solitary practice, and broke itself further and further away from the shared conviviality of writing which once helped unite families, friendships, scholarly societies or militant groups. In a world where reading is defined in terms of a personal, intimate and private relationship with the book, libraries (paradoxically, perhaps, since in the medieval era they required of readers that they be silent) must protect written patrimony and intellectual and aesthetic creation. As Walter Benjamin pointed out, the techniques of the reproduction of texts or images are not in themselves good or bad.[25] Whether it is historically true or not, this observation shows the extent to which one technique can be used in a variety of ways. Nothing constrains technical devices to play a single, predetermined role. This is an important point, given the ongoing debates about how the ever-increasing electronic dissemination of discourse will affect the public realm.[26] In a future which is already our present, these effects will be what we collectively make of them, for better or for worse. This is the responsibility we all share in today.

Notes

1. Roland Barthes, 'La mort de l'auteur' (1968), in Roland Barthes, *Le Bruissement de la langue: Essais critiques IV* (Paris, 1984), pp. 63–9.
2. Hervé Renard and François Rouet, 'L'économie du livre: de la croissance à la crise', in *L'Edition française depuis 1945*, ed. Pascal Fouché (Paris, 1998), pp. 640–737. See also Pierre Bourdieu, 'Une révolution conservatrice dans l'édition', *Actes de la Recherche en Sciences Sociales*, 126–27, March 1999, pp. 3–28.

3. Robert Darnton, 'The New Age of the Book', *The New York Review of Books*, 18 March 1999, pp. 5–7.
4. See D.F. McKenzie, *Bibliography and the Sociology of Texts*, The Panizzi Lectures 1985 (London, 1986), p. 4; French translation: *La Bibliographie et la sociologie des textes* (Paris, 1991), p. 30.
5. Anthony Grafton, *The Footnote: A Curious History* (London, 1997).
6. Michel de Certeau, *Histoire et psychanalyse entre science et fiction* (Paris, 1987), p. 79.
7. For the new argumentative possibilities offered by the electronic text, see David Kolb, 'Socrates in the Labyrinth', in *Hyper/Text/Theory*, ed. George P. Landow (Baltimore and London, 1994), pp. 323–44, and Jane Yellowlees Douglas, 'Will the Most Reflexive Relativist Please Stand Up: Hypertext, Argument and Relativism', in *Page to Screen: Taking Literacy into the Electronic Era*, ed. Ilana Snyder (London and New York, 1988), pp. 144–61.
8. For an example of the possible links between historical demonstration and documentary sources, see both the print and electronic versions of Robert Darnton's article 'Presidential Address. An Early Information Society: News and the Media in Eighteenth-Century Paris', *The American Historical Review*, 105, 2000, pp. 1–35 and *AHR* web page, http://www.indiana.edu/~ahr/
9. For examples in theoretical physics, see Josette F. de la Vega, *La Communication scientifique à l'épreuve de l'Internet* (Villeurbanne, 2000), in particular pp. 181–231; for philology, see José Manuel Blecua, Gloria Clavería, Carlos Sanchez and Joan Torruella, eds, *Filología e Informática: Nuevas tecnologías en los estudios filológicos* (Bellaterra, 1999), and Jean-Emmanuel Tyvaert, ed., *L'Imparfait: Philologie électronique et assistance à l'interprétation des textes* (Reims, 2000).
10. For definitions of hypertext and hyperreading, see J.D. Bolter, *Writing Space: The Computer, Hypertext, and the History of Writing* (Hillsdale, NJ, 1991); George P. Landow, *Hypertext: The Convergence of Contemporary Critical Theory and Technology* (Baltimore and London, 1992); new edition: *Hypertext 2.0 Being a Revised, Amplified Edition of Hypertext: the Convergence of Contemporary Critical Theory and Technology* (Baltimore and London, 1997); Ilana Snyder, *Hypertext: The Electronic Labyrinth* (Melbourne and New York, 1996); Nicholas C. Burbules, 'Rhetorics of the Web: Hyperreading and Critical Literacy', in *Page to Screen*, pp. 102–22, and Antonio R. de las Heras, *Navegar por la información* (Madrid, 1991) pp. 81–164.
11. Jean Clément, 'Le e-book est-il le futur du livre ?', in *Les Savoirs déroutés. Experts, documents, supports, règles, valeurs et réseaux numériques* (Lyon, 2000), pp. 129–41.
12. See Daniel Schneidermann, *Les folies d'Internet* (Paris, 2000), in particular Chapter 11; on the mostly revisionist sites found by search engines on the Holocaust, see pp. 145–56.
13. Pierre LeLoarer, 'Les substituts du livre: livres et encres électroniques', in *Les Savoirs déroutés*, pp. 111–28.
14. Luciano Canfora, *La Biblioteca scomparsa* (Palermo, 1986); French translation: *La véritable histoire de la bibliothèque d'Alexandrie* (Paris, 1988) and Christian Jacob, 'Lire pour écrire: navigations alexandrines', in *Le Pouvoir des bibliothèques: la mémoire des livres en Occident*, ed. Marc Baratin and Christian Jacob (Paris, 1996), pp. 47–83.

15. On the technique of commonplace rhetoric in the Renaissance, see Francis Goyet, *Le 'sublime' du lieu commun: l'invention rhétorique à la Renaissance* (Paris, 1996); Ann Blair, *The Theater of Nature: Jean Bodin and Renaissance Science* (Princeton, 1997); Ann Moss, *Printed Commonplace-Books and the Structuring of Renaissance Thought* (Oxford, 1996).

16. Immanuel Kant, 'Beantwortung der Frage: Was ist Aufklärung? Réponse à la question: Qu'est-ce que les Lumières?', in *Qu'est-ce que les Lumières?*, ed. Jean Mondot (Saint-Etienne, 1991), pp. 71–86.

17. These different possibilities are discussed in Richard. A. Lanham, *The Electronic World: Democracy, Technology and the Arts* (Chigago, 1993); Donald Tapscott, *The Digital Economy* (New York, 1996) and Juan Luis Cebrían, ed., *Cómo cambiarán nuestras vidas los nuevos medios de comunicación* (Madrid, 1998).

18. Ann Goldgar, *Impolite Learning: Conduct and Community in the Republic of Letters, 1680–1750* (New Haven and London, 1995).

19. On electronic mail, see Josiane Bru, 'Messages éphémères', in *Ecritures ordinaires*, ed. Daniel Fabre (Paris, 1993), pp. 315–34; Charles Moran and Gail E. Hawisher, 'The Rhetorics and Languages of Electronic Mail', in *Page to Screen*, pp. 80–101, and Benoît Melançon, *Sevigne@Internet. Remarques sur le courrier électronique et la lettre* (Montréal, 1996).

20. Giambattista Vico, *La Scienza Nuova*, ed. Paolo Rossi (Milan, 1994); French translation. *La Science nouvelle* (1725; Paris, 1993).

21. Condorcet, *Esquisse d'un tableau historique des progrès de l'esprit humain* (Paris, 1988).

22. Roger Chartier, 'Bibliothèques sans murs', in Roger Chartier, *Culture écrite et société: l'ordre des livres (XIVe–XVIIIe centuries)* (Paris, 1997), pp. 107–31.

23. Emilia Ferreiro, 'Leer y escribir en un mundo cambiante', *26° Congreso de la Unión Internacional de Editores* (Buenos Aires, 2000), pp. 95–109.

24. Robert C. Berring, 'Future Librarians', in *Future Libraries*, ed. R. Howard Bloch and Carla Hesse (Berkeley, Los Angeles and London, 1995), pp. 94–115.

25. Walter Benjamin, 'The Work of Art in the Age of Mechanical Reproduction' (1936), in Walter Benjamin, *Illuminations: Essays and Reflections*, ed. Hannah Arendt (New York, 1969), pp. 217–51.

26. Geoffrey Nunberg, 'The Place of Books in the Age of Electronic Reproduction', *Representations*, 42, 1993, pp. 13–37.

Discussion

Is this a revolution?

Chartier talks about the novelty of our situation, pointing to a concurrent revolution 'in the technology of the production and reproduction of texts, a revolution in the medium of writing, and a revolution in reading practices'. Something else is novel: we are in possession of conceptual and theoretical tools, argumentative practices and varieties of discourse that inform the way in which we make intellectual sense of new technologies, just as these new technologies allow for the proliferation and intensified communication of these concepts, theories and discourses (*Text-e* is one example). The result is what might be a real, but equally an illusory integration of technology with intellectual content. For the question remains, as Chartier's text shows and in spite of the discussions opened yesterday, of whether or not our computer-age children really will think and write differently from the way in which their parents do simply because of a technological revolution. Those who grow up with bedtime stories still like linear stories. Once education and technology are brought together, then we might have an intellectual revolution similar to that of Gutenberg, beginning with a real increase in literacy.

Noga Arikha

Temporal scales of change

Roger Chartier writes: 'The gap remains great between the obsessive presence of the revolution and the reality of reading practices which are still attached to printed objects and which make only very partial use of the possibilities bred by digital technology. We have to be lucid enough not to take what is virtual for a reality already here with us.' To which I might add: and lucid enough not to take the reality already here for the future of the virtual. A problem that is in fact esssential to a reflection upon the effects of the new technologies is how to distinguish between temporal scales and put them into relation with one another without extrapolating one from the other. A few questions, for Roger Chartier in particular:

(1) Is there indeed a major technological revolution from which we might expect radical effects, especially in the realms of social and cultural communication, but without predicting in how much time? (Are we talking in terms of years or generations?)

(2) What is the time-scale we might project for the effects that we are seeing today – the more or less radical or marginal changes in the domain of general reading and writing practices? Must we necessarily come to the conclusion that the effects of digital technologies will remain, as they still are today, marginal? (I am persuaded of the contrary – this sort of extrapolation seems to me to be as futile as that of so many commentators, who have forgotten the financial bubble of the railroads in the nineteenth century, about the stock market crisis of new technologies – which were, in the end, not so revolutionary as all that.)

(3) To understand the social and cultural impact of new technologies, shouldn't we also study their cognitive impact on individuals, an impact which varies radically according to age? The spread of personal computers and the Internet began less than twenty years ago. The Web is no more than ten years old. Today's adult generations have acquired their cognitive routines in a world only marginally affected by the new technologies. They are, for the most part, the mediocre and even reticent transmitters of these technologies. If truly radical changes are to be anticipated, they will come with the generations for whom these technologies are as ordinary as running water or electricity.

Dan Sperber

Material culture of the electronic text

Text on the Internet has been described as an infinitely renewable resource. Infinitely renewable resources pose obvious problems to authors seeking reward and copyright protection.

Clearly, differences between electronic forms produce significant differences in the socially embedded practices of reading. The electronic book does not exist as something stable, closed and unproblematic. Rather, each version of the electronic book encodes a model of its ideal reader, and these models are produced in a struggle in which market forces are extremely significant.

Far from denying the sociability of the text, analysis of the differences, technical and superficial, between different forms of electronic book might bring us a greater understanding of virtual communities of readers.

Michael John Gorman

The immaterial book

Michael raises an interesting point which may lead to a reflection around the nature of the transformation of a 'text' or 'manuscript' into a book. While the Internet is filled with texts, it feels comparably void of books. One of the roles of the publisher is to help transform an author's manuscript into a polished book. Behind every material book sitting on our bookshelves lurks an immaterial master text, an abstract literary entity. A published paper book is simply one physical manifestation of the author's (and publisher's) work. When a 300-page hardback becomes a 400-page paperback, the master text is simply being retooled to fit into a different mould. We can think of each physical book as being a different-sized screen onto which the Platonic master copy of the text is being projected. Whereas I recognize the apparent multiplicity of the texts to which Michael refers, I care to see this as an illusion that can disappear or reappear as easily as the flame casting the shadow. Today we may be seeing the text cast upon Adobe or Microsoft's screens, tomorrow it maybe Palm or Gemstar. The goal is to make it so that the author and the publisher only have to produce the master text once, and then that same source can be cast into a multiplicity of moulds, many of which are yet to be invented. And just as the consumer chooses today between paperback or hardback, the reader of an e-book chooses a preferred format. If the paper of one's personal printer is the preferred format, then so be it. Without publishers, we would walk into bookstores to find a bunch of 'texts' floating around in a mass chaos, much as when we're swimming around in tens of pages of responses to a Google search. Whether the final 'screen' onto which a reader chooses to read books is a computer screen or a sheet of paper, the quality of the content is at least partially dependent on the decision by an editorial group to transform the text into a book. Today's current efforts are relatively early attempts to help the publishing industry offer their quality book content to consumers who would like to receive their books in an immaterial manner, for various individual (subjective) reasons. Some people are attracted to the immediate access, especially those who may be geographically distant from a source of the paper book, and are just using the 'e' format as a means of tele-transporting the book to their printer. Others may actually have a preference for reading on a screen, perhaps in order to gain portability (laptops, Palms, PocketPCs, dedicated reading devices). Personally I end up reading most of my books on my PalmVx, not necessarily because it is the best reading experience, but simply because I always have it with me with several good books in it, and its form factor is so amenable to having it in your hand very often, that it just ends up being the most frequently read object around me when I'm away from my desk (and thus when I have time to enjoy a book, versus all of the many texts (web-pages, articles, e-mails, etc.) that I read during the course of a day behind my computer screen). And I can sure appreciate the difference: a well edited book is like a well edited film, it makes all the difference. And this is where we come back to the materiality of the immaterial book. Publishers cannot afford to finance these transformations of raw texts into edited books if there is not a notion of commercial exchange. The immaterial nature of the e-book should not change this centuries-old threesome between the reader, publisher and author. Whether the book is projected onto pre-bound paper, or upon the virtual paper of an e-book reader, the work and careers that are necessary to create a quality book-reading experience still exist and need to be compensated. We have no problem paying $10 to see a movie or $3 to rent a video. Why should we question paying $8 to purchase a quality book-reading experience? And without protected access, it appears next to impossible to protect the inherent value of the (e-)book, versus the millions (billions?) of free texts comprising the Internet.

Cory McCloud

Back to the oral tradition

It seems to me that Roger Chartier does not reach back far enough in his search for the precursors and constituents of the on-line age. In many ways, it is restoring the mode and even the tempo of the interaction of human minds to those of the oral tradition. Oral/aural interactions occur at around the speed of thought, to which the brain is optimally adapted, at least in its real-time, on-line functions. Reading, and especially writing, were always solo, off-line functions, in the Codex as well as the Gutenberg age. The speed of interaction was reduced orders of magnitude by the sluggish turnaround time of handwriting and even print, although their scale and scope, and of course their all-important permanency and accuracy, were incomparably enhanced by the new scripted tradition.

But now, in the post-Gutenberg galaxy of on-line skywriting/reading, the dialogic cycles of interaction among human minds have at last been returned to something much closer to the speed of thought, yet retaining and even hyperextending the power and advantages of the lapidary medium. Chartier writes: 'the "book" and other digital texts will be defined in opposition to the free and spontaneous electronic communication which allows everyone to circulate their thoughts and works on the Web. This division...could help establish an order of discourse which would take into account the major differences between, on the one hand, spontaneous texts released onto the web, and on the other, vetted, edited writings". That dynamic communication (but not its global scale) is a throwback to the oral tradition. The static digital book, whether on-paper or on-line, drastically constrained the freedom and spontaneity. But the possibility of skyreading – appending graffiti to everything that appears in the digital skies – can breathe interactive life into the dead pages of books, opening on-line dialogues with the written word even after the author is deceased. None of this has anything to do with the orthogonal dimensions of published/unpublished or vetted/unvetted, which are, and always have been, merely quality-control tags sign-posting the corpus, whether on-paper or on-line.

'Virtual books' – digital peripherals that simulate as much as we want to retain of the look and feel of books – are not advances but throwbacks. It is not at all clear how many of those familiar features of books are really optimal and how many are merely habitual. But there is no doubt that what is really revolutionary about e-texts is their navigability and interactivity and not their papyromimetic capacity. Until and unless book authors elect to give away their texts as the authors of refereed research do (and I doubt they ever will: why should they?), the similarities between on-paper and on-line books will far outweigh their differences (insofar as trade matters are concerned).

He writes then: 'An electronic correspondence between authors and readers – now transformed into co-authors of a book kept open through their comments and interventions – allows for an author–reader relationship, close in kind to that to which some ancient authors aspired but hard to achieve with the printed book. A more immediate, more dialogic relationship between the work and the reading of the work...'. True, except that most of what self-appointed commentators have to say will hardly be worth hearing, any more than it was in the oral medium. Quality-control signposting (by qualified experts, where necessary) will continue to be our guide, as it was in the Gutenberg age. Most of the virtual chatosphere will be a global graffiti board for trivial pursuit, the Gaussian distribution of human verbiage being what it is.

Stevan Harnad

Roger Chartier's paradox

Roger Chartier proposes a paradox that has important implications for future discussions: the omnipresence of writing accompanies the disappearance of books and readers. One way to resolve the paradox is to point out the coexistence of a plurality of reading media and methods. As for electronic books, coexistence seems in fact to define the present state of affairs where the very poor functional qualities of electronic books (limited interactivity, bad quality of screens) ensure a lasting coexistence with a predominance of printed books as long as the e-book remains the sole alternative to books. The disappearance of the book and its replacement by electronic texts are predicated on the separation of the notion of the book and the reader from writing and graphic operations. This is something that Goody and Olson have already noted apropos of non-alphabetic writings such as proto-writings. In this case one must relativize the notion of book and reader. Two arguments go in this direction. One is historical: not only the historical plurality of forms of reading that have coexisted with book-form, but the existence of writing with interpretations of graphic signs which are very far from what one calls reading. An anthropological argument: the notion of book and reader seem, at first glance, to be cultural (or at least relational) categories that allow us to group together the artefacts and the disparate mental and physical operations associated with these artefacts. In a word, it is possible that the book might disappear but it is also possible that the categories of book and reader do not allow us to understand the graphic operations which are realized on screens. In the same way, the interactive and dynamic properties alluded to by Steve Harnard are not easily integrated into a book/author/reader configuration. The fact that this configuration is our principal mode of understanding the graphic signs in our cultures relativizes its application to new cognitive technologies.

Bernard Conein

Roger Chartier: reply

The observations and critical comments that followed my text seem to require that we pursue three main themes of investigation.

(1) The first theme concerns the growing tension between, on the one hand, malleable, mobile and open electronic texts, and, on the other, the intellectual, aesthetic or legal categories with which all works are described, which establish the rights (and profits) of authors and publishers to an original work bearing an author's name, and which are applicable with

regard to individual texts. Michael John Gorman remarked on the difficulty of ensuring within the 'infinitely renewable resource' of the Internet the recognition of 'reward and copyright protection' as required by authors and publishers, and on the tendency of current legislation to focus on literary property. Both these points clearly show up a contradiction and indicate how resistant are notions which have defined works since at least the eighteenth century to a world where texts would circulate free of any individual appropriation, stable boundaries or market value. This resistance might lead to the eventual coexistence of two 'economies' of electronic writing, the one unshackled by the constraints of a past that still is our present, the other able to reconstitute with new technical, legal and conceptual tools the order of discourse which allows for authors to be owners and for publishers to be entrepreneurs.

I do not mean here to condone the limitation or censorship of access to texts. One should not confuse the analysis with its object. My text describes what I think is happening in the digital world, given the needs of electronic publishers (who want to profit from their activity) and the needs of authors, who want their work to be recognized and protected. It is possible to dream of another order of discourse, as Michel Foucault sometimes did, where there is neither author, nor intellectual property, nor remuneration of written work. But this dream is so antipodal to the policy of attribution, publication and identification of texts which governs our perceptions that it cannot become a reality in the near future – at least, it could not possibly become the dominant feature of the world of electronic texts.

(2) Another theme, which has often been discussed here, is the relationship between oral communication and electronic writing. Some participants are tempted to believe that electronic writing can bring about a return to the immediacy and interaction of oral communication; so Stevan Harnad entitled his (very critical) comment 'Back to the oral tradition'. There are indeed good reasons to compare oral communication with writing, whether it is electronic or not. Some are historical reasons: for example, in old Spanish, the verb 'leer' is generally used to mean reading out loud, and the verb 'oir' is used to mean reading. Other reasons are theoretical and have something to do with Derrida's notion of 'archiécriture'.

For my part, however – and in this sense I follow Jack Goody – writing, whatever its form and support, cannot be equalled to oral communication. Writing objectifies the text, which can be communicated in the absence of its author, ordered, manipulated (for better or for worse) or re-used. The irreducibility of oral communication to writing is shown up by the very limited success of all the techniques that have been devised to transcribe the voice, such as tachigraphy, brachigraphy, stenography and so on. The written order – linear or relational – defines a mode of relation to the text which is not that of the order of oral communication, even if the illusion of instantaneousness remains in electronic exchanges; indeed, such exchanges always suppose the reading of a text that is engraved, can be archived and is mediated by distance. This relation to the written word cannot be considered the equivalent of the act of listening to an ephemeral, untouchable word that disappears as soon as it has been spoken. This is why I do not believe in the view that electronic communication is a 'throwback to oral tradition'.

One conclusion to the exchanges in this discussion is that we need to reconsider the connections between the various kinds of texts, the various modalities of reading and the variety of supports of texts – manuscripts, print, or electronic edition. The electronic form accelerates and increases the efficiency of reading where what is being read is a delimited textual unit belonging to an alphabetic or thematic set but so far it is (and might remain) disconcerting for the reading of texts that require one to see the work as one unitary, coherent whole and that demand a prolonged familiarity in order to be understood. It is true that electronic support is not the only form that makes prolonged, continuous reading difficult: think of anthologies of chosen pieces, or of photocopied fragments. But, to heed one of the best specialists of new technologies, Antonio Rodriguez de las Heras, it is precisely the digital text's capacity to resist its inherent tendency to fragmentation, disjunction and division that will determine the extent to which it can appropriate for itself genres of texts that do not consist of juxtaposed units of information. That is one way of answering the questions Dan Sperber asked me. First, I do believe that the entry into a new textual world is a 'major technological revolution' that transforms, for the first time simultaneously, the techniques of transmission of the written word, the morphology of textual supports and the modalities of reading. Second, it seems to me (although historians do not make good prophets) that, for many decades, the coexistence of different modalities of inscription, communication and reception of the written word will define an order of discourse which is unstable, changing and uncertain but which is also governed by the tension between inherited categories, incorporated practices and new possibilities.

(3) A third angle of thought should consider, as Noga Arikha invites us to do, the way in which the proliferation of discourses on new technologies (such as those we are engaging in here in this forum) are a constitutive element of this very revolution. This is not an entirely new phenomenon.

The invention of printing also generated numerous discourses, some enthusiastic (think of *Pantagruel*), others anxious or sceptical (in Lope de Vega's *Fuenteovejuna*, a graduate from Salamanca realizes, disillusioned, that the new art has not given birth to a new St Jerome or a new St Augustine). But it is clear that the present revolution is more provocative than that of Gutenberg, which did not radically change the morphology of the book or the gestures of readers used to the codex since the first centuries of the Christian era. This might explain the rash of discourses aimed at taming a transformation more radical than that of the mid-fifteenth century. I believe that there is a dearth of precise investigations into the practices and effects of the new modes of publication and appropriation of texts.

These investigations should be deployed in two directions. In one, there could be some research on the various forms of 'putting on screen', using the questionnaire and techniques developed by studies on the actual materiality of texts, which are based on the material bibliography and the sociology of texts as defined by Don McKenzie. It will dissolve the illusion according to which texts can be reduced to their semantic content, as if the forms of their inscription, both in the (real or metaphorical) thickness of the work and on the surface of the page or screen had no importance in the process that gives them a meaning. This is why I warned against the idea that the supports of one 'same' text could all be equivalent, and why I defined libraries as the irreplaceable sites where texts in their different, simultaneous or successive states should be preserved and available for transmission. But this requirement does not imply that we should abandon or reduce the digitalization of manuscript or print collections. Another direction for research concerns, as Dan Sperber points out, the specific cognitive effects of electronic texts and of the digital world, as well as their use, which differ according to social environment and age, and also according to the reading and writing environment of the reader. François Bon, who gives free access to his site in the 'book studio' and who publishes works in a traditional way, exemplifies the practices and divisions that we invent today – or, rather, that are invented by those who have the possibility, still a privilege, of entering a new textual world that is not without cost.

Roger Chartier

2
What the Internet Tells Us about the Real Nature of the Book

Roberto Casati

The so-called 'virtual world' is often described with the help of metaphors derived from ordinary discourse on perception and action. This should not be surprising, since virtual objects were partly conceived on the basis of these metaphors. Yet, it is not a given that these metaphors are appropriate; one might need to begin using different concepts and eventually to invent new ones, more appropriate to the phenomena they describe. It might even happen, as I shall show, that these new concepts will themselves be used in situations described by the discourses on perception, action and social behaviour in a way that so far seems perfectly natural, but that, in turn, might reveal itself to be entirely inadequate. One could use these new metaphors, born as they are of new practices and new usages, for the reinterpretation of the non-virtual world. The subject of this piece is the metaphysics of the book. I shall look at the way in which the Web frees it from our inadequate conception of it. This emancipation, strangely, seems to involve an economic liberation.

Let us look at the 'recycle bin' icon on the computer desktop. What this icon represents is not a recycle bin. In actual fact, it is not even an icon: it only represents the bin indirectly. Instead, this is the image of a sensitive field which activates a particular object. The activated object itself obviously is not a bin, and, if one looks carefully, it does not look much like one.

A recycle bin contains documents in the form of bits of paper. There is no order in there. The first bit to land in the bin ends up more or less at the bottom. A bin may contain things of a completely different kind than a document, and one never even thinks of reorganizing it.

The virtual 'bin' stores data. It behaves intelligently, keeps a record of what has been thrown away, has an unlimited capacity for content, allows for the limited (re)use of the objects it contains, and so on. One can reorganize the bin.

Actually, one may begin to think that this is not at all a recycle bin, but a proper archive. Or a limbo. And the metaphor of a limbo, with all its redemptive ramifications, is very different from the metaphor of a bin. In a philosophical investigation, one can have rather discordant intuitions even about rather common objects, and even about rather basic concepts. With slightly more complex objects (and with much more complex objects, such as books) one is in great difficulty as soon as one tries to describe them with the precision that is necessary in certain contexts such as the legal and economic ones. The philosopher often does nothing else than weigh up these intuitions. What is a book? An ambiguity is inherent in this question:

My book weighs a kilo.   My book is inspired by yours.

Is the book that weighs a kilo the same thing as the book that is inspired by yours?

A. It is the same thing. There is only *one* book on the shelf.

B. It is not the same thing. I can destroy the book that weighs a kilo without destroying the book that is inspired by yours. The book that is inspired by yours could remain in my mind; it is a mental-book, a text. It could be printed on lighter paper and give birth to an object-book that weighs half a kilo.

This might look like an exercise in metaphysics. But it so happens that the issue of understanding what *kind* of thing a book is has given food for thought to the experts of on-line publication, who have tried to define the *ontology* of the numerical heir of the book, the e-book. In 2000, the Open eBook Forum (OEBF, a consortium which includes publishers such as McGraw Hill and Random House, producers of software such as Adobe and Microsoft, computer constructers such as IBM and new electronic publishing houses like iBooks) published a programmatic document to open the discussion on the ontology of the e-book.

In the preceding paragraph my use of the word 'e-book' was ambiguous; this intrinsic ambiguity points to the nature of the problem in which the OEBF is interested. It is an ontological ambiguity. An 'e-book' can signify either:

The machine that receives the text.	the text sent on to the machine.

And of course the same ambiguity holds good for 'book'. In the case of the e-book, the ambiguity is more vivid still. The e-book-machine can receive an infinity of e-book-books. The uncertainty with regard to the two notions prevails in the OEBF document, and this might pose difficulties in the project of establishing an ontology, instead of helping define a standard for it. We shall see that this indecision does necessarily need to be resolved.

When I say that I have read a book or remember it by heart, I am talking about the immaterial content. But if I say that I burned it, it is the physical support that I am referring to. If, on the other hand, I say that I have *sold* the book, I leave open the two possibilities. Now, we can take the question about the nature of the book further precisely by asking ourselves what place it occupies in human transactions, and especially in commercial transactions. *What is it that one is selling when one sells a book?* In an article published in 1785, Immanuel Kant discussed the issue of the copyright. His idea is simple. Some ways of *copying* a text are a form of piracy, while others are not.

My publisher prints many copies of my book and sells them, and he is not a pirate.	My neighbour prints many copies of my book and sells them, and he is a pirate.

What is the difference? According to Kant, books generate a right to stop anyone else from copying them or reading them in public, and this right can be ceded to a publisher against payment. But where does this right come from? For Kant, it arises out of the very nature of the book, which is not a thing like other things. To produce a book is not like producing a chair – unless the chair is a signed object. Kant was concerned with finding a good justification for copyright because he noticed that remuneration for words and ideas was not self-evident. If words and ideas are commodities, they are strange ones indeed. Let us stay for a moment with this comparison between ideas (and the words that express them) and chairs.

1. If I build a chair and give it to you, the chair leaves with you. For this reason it is easy to sell and buy chairs: the transfer of the object can recapitulate the transfer of the rights I have with regard to the object.

2. When you buy my chair, you can do whatever you want with it. In particular, you can resell it.

1. If I sing a song to you, neither text nor music leave me when they reach your ears. For this reason it is difficult to understand how one can sell a song.

2. When I sell my book to you, you may give it to a friend or burn it, you can even sell it to a second-hand bookstore, but you cannot make copies of it and sell it in your turn. The invention of the copyright has turned the sale of an abstract product into that of a concrete product – a record, a printed volume, a photograph. The trick here is that the transfer of rights is limited.

There is an assumption in this book-protecting mechanism that cultural contents are a commodity – albeit a commodity of a strange kind. We know, however, that this does not have to be the case. If no one were willing to pay for songs there would be no sense in trying to sell them or in inventing ways of selling them. There have always been cultural contents that were never sold: songs improvised during a walk, drawings given away, books printed at the writer's own cost, love letters, anecdotes told during a conversation. Why pay for songs and books? Maybe because they have an intrinsic value? No: if we were all to become illiterate, books would no longer have much worth. A putative value depends on external circumstances. How can one know the value of a cultural content? Again, a comparison will help.

'Concrete' products, such as chairs, are subject to laws of the market which allow one to value them in relation to other concrete products. If I compare the price of a chair to the price of a match, the resulting information concerns the relative value of the chair and of the match, within a specific context. If, for example, the chair costs ten pounds and the match costs a hundred thousand pounds, I might conclude that there is a penury of matches and an excess of chairs. Pricing systems function with regard to physical objects just as they do with regard to pools of information. (We know, however, that the system can be twisted, especially in situations where the market is not free. In a planned economy pricing systems do not tell us much, since the match can cost a hundred thousand pounds and the chair ten pounds even if there is an excess of matches and a penury of chairs.)

Cultural products have never been really subject to the free market. For the market of cultural products, distortion is the norm. In effect, the mode of their selection, the marketing which promotes them to the public, the presence of innumerable mediators between author and reader, not least the bookseller who chooses what to display, the pressure of institutions, whether academic, ecclesiastic (think of the imprimatur) or governmental (think of books by famous politicians published with the tax-payer's money and distributed in schools), the shortage or partiality of reviewers – all these elements prejudice any attempt at obtaining reliable information about the value of cultural products from the observation of their commercial life. For example, academic publishers tend to request subsidies for publication, or the guarantee that the author's students will 'adopt' the book; they may also ask the author to buy a certain number of copies. Their publishing guidelines are dictated by the traffic of favours between members of reading committees, or more simply, by cultural fashions. Cultural contents are not like chairs because their economy has no connection to the free market, and it cannot reflect their value. For a counter-example, think of your bookseller's reaction if you were one day to return a book to him, demanding reimbursement because its contents had disappointed you.

At this point, we can bring in the Web, and turn to a series of examples that, I hope, should help explain what I mean when I suggest we redefine objects and functions belonging to the pre-Web world according to what we can learn from the Web-world. Let us take the case of a producer of cultural contents, a research scientist.

I could want to publish a text with a publisher, but I would have to wait for months, await the scrutiny of a reading committee which might possibly be hostile to my research, for the most varied reasons. Moreover, I can be sure that the text will be read only by those who have been charged for access to the book, which will eventually be sold out and out of print.

When I publish a specialized research article on my Web site, I hope for a non-restricted access to it, indeed for the widest possible access, free of charge. I wish for my article to be read and for a response on the part of the readers.

Given such a choice, I should not hesitate to publish on the Web. Authors of scientific papers are tired of private and institutional filters to their work, and so they inevitably tend to publish straight on the Web. Here, on the Web, it is possible to assess the work in a real sense; and indeed, a constant assessment is what takes place, not by private or institutional mediators but by consumers, who affect it in a similar, but also significantly different way from the price system. I would like to propose three models for the assessment of on-line contents.

Model 1: visits (*salon.com*)

Consumers judge 'concrete' products by buying them.

On the Web, cultural contents are *voted* for by visits to the pages most liked. The number of hits gives the measure of the extent to which the page is appreciated.

There have been cases in which on-line magazines (such as *salon.com*) fired those journalists whose articles did not get enough hits. What is interesting about the on-line world is that it is possible to obtain visitor figures that are more precise than those of any other media. Television channels, which use highly sophisticated recording systems, could not even hope to achieve the kind of precision yielded by visitor counters. These are capable of identifying individual computers with extremely simple programmes that are available to anyone who builds a website. This precision is the on-line writer's bogeyman. Until now, his or her article was judged only by editors; now, its readers give their direct vote.

Two sorts of problems emerge here. One, is it desirable to entrust assessment directly to readers? And two, how reliable is an assessment based on visitor figures?

Is it desirable to entrust assessment directly to readers?

There is always someone deciding what is good and what is bad to read; editorial teams make choices. The test case is that of an excellent paper, with excellent analyses, but read by no one. Should one keep it alive only in order to defend an abstract idea of what is worth reading? To want to do so can lead to cultural paternalism and to the invention of ideal readers who *should* be interested in certain things. The point is that one does not really know what 'excellent' means; nor does one know what are the criteria according to which ideal readers are defined. Counting visits to a page obviates this situation: visits are the currency which allows demand to be measured in the realm of cultural products, where until now such quantitative evaluation has been traditionally resisted and therefore hard to apply. There is even the new possibility of a *comparative* evaluation, which might generate some surprises: an article signed by a famous writer could turn out to be less liked than the one written by a young unknown.

How reliable is an assessment based on visitor counts?

A reader can very well have visited a page without having read an article; he or she could have read it distractedly, or read it and not liked it at all. But even if what the visits measure *exactly* is unclear, one has to suppose that readers have an idea of what they want to read and that they visited a particular page for the sake of satisfying their own desire to read. This gives a rough estimate of a text's value. But is there a way of correcting the distortions of this rating system? Clearly, one cannot ask readers to give a summary of what they read in order to check that their judgement is informed rather than plucked out of thin air; but one could ask them to vote for pieces by expressing an opinion ('Did you like this? Yes/No'). The argument, however, might not impress a publisher. Indeed, it is possible that readers will loathe a piece, while the publisher's main goal is simply to make sure the paper is read. A special button could be set up to enable readers to answer a more precise question, such as 'Were we right to publish this piece?' if not 'What is the value of this piece in the context of the journal's other contents?' In this case a piece on the dying art of lacing could be rehabilitated in the context of an issue which contains another – probably more visited – piece on the summer adventures of a celebrity performer. One could also imagine a system of reviews (which would themselves be reviewed – and indeed the visitors have the possibility of rating the reviews on *amazon.com*). But there is a deeper problem. The vote-visitor mechanism is potentially irresponsible insofar as there is nothing at stake for readers when they vote-visit. In a future (that many hope, and others fear is not far off) in which there will be a way of charging for on-line contents, a subscription might simply amount to the purchase by the reader of a power to vote for or against pieces. Writers would then be paid directly by the readers: here the readers' action would be responsible, since it would have a price.

There is, however, a second way of obtaining information about a content's quality on the basis of visit counters.

Model 2: links (*google.com*)

Consumers judge 'concrete' products by buying them.	On the Web, cultural contents are voted for. How? By the *creation of a link* to the page one has liked.

Let us return to the case of the academic researcher who has to choose between publishing his own text on line or sending it to a journal. Journal reading committees are obsolete as soon as the texts published on the Web are judged by the readers, who create links to the pages they like. The system tends to generate a virtuous circle.

If I create a link to pages judged good by readers of my page, my page will be given a positive assessment by these readers and will in turn receive many links.	If, instead, I publicize mediocre sites on my page, no one will vote in its favour.

Honesty and competence are recompensed. A page that receives positive votes acquires an authority it transmits to its own links. I am not calling here for a *new* way of analysing cultural phenomena or of evaluating cultural products: I am only *describing* the democratic reality of the Web, one which exists already. A search engine like Google exploits the information contained within the link structure. Links from site A to site B are interpreted as votes for site B. This seems reasonable: if one wants visitors to one's site A to know that the best site on football (or on gamma waves) is B, one will vote for B by creating a link to it. If site A contains many useful links, other sites, at some point, will vote for it, and the authoritativeness it so acquires will be passed on to its links. Google collects the results of such votes. Why should one trust (enough) in the result? For the same reason as that for which we trust (enough) price tags in a shop. Behind those web-pages, there are individuals who exert their judgement, just as behind the price tags there are consumers who acquire the products. We are all mini-experts. Google envisions the Web as one great system of votes. This system is similar, in the end, to the pricing system, which informs us as to the relative value of products. The main difference between publishing cultural contents on the Web rather than through other means (books or television, say) is that the Web contains a huge amount of immediately accessible information about the value of the published products (a bit like feedback).

Scenario: But this means the death of cultural contents transmitted outside the realm of the Web. One would immediately assume these to be valueless. If publishers do not take on the risk of making the texts of their authors available on the Web, free of cost and unabridged, they will end up in a marginal economic niche.

I would welcome a research programme on the link system which could study its informational potential, its possible distortions and the corrections to these distortions. It seems to me that much too little attention has been dedicated so far to this aspect of the Web's structure.

Model 3: the expert's opinion (*about.com*)

There is an alternative, of course: *the expert opinion-filter*. Various experts, including Umberto Eco, have been defending the expert's role as a guide through the mass of information on the Web. Eco has dealt in particular with the issue of access to the Web in schools, although his argument can be applied to many other types of cultural transmission. This argument seems solid: 'There are no instruments available to teach how to select information. One does not know how to distinguish between serious and crazy sites. The site of a nazi criminal like Eichmann could end up becoming the same thing as that of Mother Theresa of Calcutta.' Filters are useful: there is too much material on the Web. 'Until now the role of the Church and of scientific institutions was to filter and reorganize knowledge and information. Although these intermediaries restrict my intellectual freedom, they ensure that the community has filtered what is essential... I insist on the need for a filter external to the Web, whether it applies to schools, books or newspapers' (*Libération*, 1 July 2000). Again, filters are useful: almost everything is available on the Web, but without a good guide, one gets lost.

A highly important distinction might not be noticed here. Eco speaks of two types of filters.

Filters of the first type – let us call them negative filters – *forbid access* to objectionable pages.	Filters of the second type – let us call them positive filters – *select* only pages considered *commendable.*

But there is no reason why one filter should do both things. Eco seems to suggest that the need (in the end quite understandable) for negative filters could help make the case for positive filters. A positive filter, according to Eco, is an expert, or an institution external to the Web. The expert compiles – for example – a page that contains links to other sites worthy of a visit. (A site like *about.com* uses exactly this principle.) The site gains credibility because the expert who compiles it is authoritative.

A problem arises here. How does one get to a credible site? I trust Eco, but does Eco know all the sites? It could be that a site unknown to Eco delivers more authoritative information than that delivered by a site Eco knows. And how do I get to Eco? Of course the state can set up educational portals. But if negative filters are a reasonable reaction to our vulnerability to bad contents, positive filters which tell us whom we should read are a much more doubtful idea. Other scholars, like Omar Calabrese, have pronounced themselves in favour of officially certified sites. Does this not seem a strange idea? Just think of what the governmental approval of officially certified publishers would mean in the context of the book trade.

Google is not an expert – in fact it is ignorant and it acts blindly. But it comes close to the perfect librarian described by Musil in *The Man Without Qualities*: in order to do his job well, he should know next to nothing. Furthermore, one could simply argue that there are no experts on the information available on the Web.

But why prefer link-votes to experts? The link-vote system can be distorted just like the price system. In fact, within the link system everyone is considered a mini-expert. Why prefer so many mini-experts to one great expert-filter? Would it not be better to trust such an expert? No. If I may use a metaphor, expert-filters are to the vote-link system what planned economies are to the market. The fate awaiting expert-filters on the Web is that of planned economies. In five years all new knowledge will pass through the Web. And if they are of no use on the Web, where else do we need experts?

Here one may tie together the threads of the discussion on these three models. *The Web and the link-economy make the nature of cultural contents explicit. On the Web, contents become what they are, abstract entities that are difficult to fit into the copyright system. This derives from the specific nature of judgements based on feedback.*

Let us return to the book and to the nature of the book. We have seen that cultural contents are evaluated as soon as they become immaterial within the Web, and this throws light on something that the paper book masks. But what can we expect, and how profound will be the changes affecting the *channels* of culture? The next example will tell us.

In 2000, Stephen King priced *Riding the Bullet* at two and a half dollars. You can purchase it (only on the Web), download it onto your computer or e-book reading device, and send a chapter to a friend by e-mail. Gripped from the very first lines on, that friend will then not hesitate to click on the button that will enable her to have the complete version, in turn paying two and a half dollars.

Scenario: The paper book is intoning its swan song. Unless it turns out that the paper book is *irreplaceable*.

Let us see. The boring objections to the possibility of transferring print production to e-books usually appeal to a number of facts:

One can tear away a page from a book and send it to a friend.	The e-book cannot be taken apart without there incurring significant damage to its functionality.
If a book falls it is not damaged.	
Books do not risk going dead in the middle of Chapter 3.	Since it is high-tech, it is liable to various risks of breakage or malfunctioning.

The 'functioning' of a book only depends on the reader, no maintenance is required.	There is no agreement yet on what the standard for e-books should be.
A book is ergonomically perfect, it is an object that never ages.	The hardware of e-books and the text formatting can be changed very quickly (think of how much computers and documents.doc have changed over the past ten years).

These details are interesting, but mere smoke when compared to the much more serious problems that are, in my view, too frequently over-looked. Just as with paper books, we can shift the discussion now to questions around the *functional role* of the e-book within the chain of social relations: for example, to the ways in which the author (and his or her publisher) can be protected from copyright violations. But we can go further and try to redefine the social ties created by the circulation and electronic sale of cultural contents.

I can give a book as a present. No one ever gives as a present an introductory chapter of a book in order to get the friend to read the whole thing.	I would find it terribly rude for a friend to send me by e-mail the first chapter of a text by King or whoever else along with a button to click to acquire it.
I can sell the book to a second-hand shop.	I cannot lend an e-book without depriving myself of the hardware.
I can *lend* the book to whomever I want without depriving myself of the pleasure of reading a thousand other books in my library.	The idea of a loan is hard to carry out in the world of e-books. And the idea of a book that I cannot lend (or resell) after reading it does not make me feel much sympathy for the author.

The idea that the author defends himself with software seems to me to signify that he thinks of me as a potential pirate – not exactly the image of the reader I thought he had in mind when writing his text.

One can see that, once broadened in this way, the discussion on the nature of e-books forces us to think again about their eventual use. The field has been electrified by the sale of a few bestsellers, but it still has no precise place in the world of transmission of contents. Despite its impact on the media, electronic content that is sold rather than free has had difficulty in establishing itself. There might be an issue of cost here.

Contentville.com sells for $12 the electronic version of a novel which costs $17 in its bound version. The saving this represents does not seem very significant. It is sometimes thought that the difficulty of selling electronic content is due to the lack of appropriate gadgets on which to read it (it is true that the e-book reading devices on sale nowadays are a bit primitive), but this does not seem quite accurate. One American family out of three has access to the Internet and can download a book onto the house computer without having to acquire a new gadget.

To summarize. Social norms and rules have crystallized around the book over the centuries and have protected it. This is not an expression of nostalgia but a fact, inherent in the function of the book, which is to ensure the circulation of ideas at a low cost and in a format whose advantages include not only the ease with which it is consulted physically but also the possibility of transmitting it to others or copying it, of using it repeatedly, of giving it away: the book is an object of exchange and communication. We do not yet know how to replace these social practices surrounding the book. The e-book is actually a hybrid product, somewhere between book and portable computer; it was born when someone looked at a book and wondered: 'How can I make this book electronic?' The result was to create something influenced by the past and not to think in terms of new technologies, which create machines that are completely integrated and capable of treating information of all kinds. It is necessary to understand this and to invent something new; otherwise the e-book will be a gadget amongst a thousand others. Paper books, then, will resist as long as it they serve certain functions: culture is a highly complex phenomenon, connected not only to means of transmission but also to social practices. *And to try to tie electronic content down to the book metaphor means not to take advantage of the various possibilities it opens up.*

Let us accept the double nature of the book. Numerical format frees the content, but the paper book is a perfect object. How can one resolve this antinomy? It is not so certain that one has to resolve it. The market could stabilize with a dual object. Authors will make their unabridged texts available on the Web, and for free. Will you read the book on line? Perhaps yes, perhaps no.

But books still make great presents. By clicking on a button, and by paying two and a half dollars at the on-demand printer-distributor, your friend will receive a much appreciated paper-bound volume.

Scenario: Try this thought experiment and imagine this scene. Millions of people publish books each year at their own cost (fattening up a particular category of pay-for-yourself publishers). Millions of people simply want to publish, or to make public their own cultural products. Nowadays they can do exactly that on the Web, and for free; hundreds of million of other people can read these books for free, without paying two dollars and a half. Of course, Stephen King is Stephen King, and an amateur scribbler is an amateur scribbler. But big numbers are big numbers. The choice between two and a half dollars for the super-famous Stephen King and zero dollars for a beginning author (who might have been pointed out to me by an aficionado, maybe in a small, but – thanks to a links page – accessible market niche), repeated millions of times in one day, simply becomes a choice between two and a half dollars and zero dollars. Free is free, especially if what I receive is a screen page and not a volume endowed with weight.

Another problem:

| Payable contents should be protected | Free contents cannot be pirated. |

If the market of cultural products tilts towards electronic contents, it will have to literally take account of the fact that, in the electronic world, free contents do not have competitors. Which means that priced must be free if they are not to disappear. Which means that priced contents disappear, and with them, publishers, agents and authors who live off royalties. Moreover, the figure of the author living off his royalties is a recent phenomenon and there is no reason to believe that it is an everlasting institution. This scenario can give rise to others. In order to avert the disappearance of cultural commerce, one could forbid the publication of free content by buying all providers; or impose, monopolistically, the purchase of a hundred books along with the purchase of a computer, as does a certain kind of software.

Copyright? It will continue to exist, in a 'lighter' version, because an author may well be glad that people are reading his or her book for free, but not that someone else is profiting from it on the author's back. (This view of authorial behaviour may seem optimistic, but the alternative would be that everyone believes they are Stephen King, capable of making a fortune with their books, which is completely unrealistic.)

Again, the Web makes the nature of cultural contents explicit. Here contents become what they are, abstract entities, difficult to frame within the notion of copyright.

A reader's ethic

I now would like to look at the reader's perspective and to tell a story with a political slant which demonstrates just how much the old conception of books will have to be revised in the light of a profound reflection on cultural contents.

In 2000, three hundred francophone writers signed a petition addressed by a number of publishing houses and corporations to the French ministry of culture. The signatories were well-known French figures – Bernard-Henri Levy, Tahar Ben Jelloun, André Comte-Sponville, Jean Ziegler, and others – whose cause was rather odd: it was to attack public libraries. Libraries, they said, were acting as pirates by allowing their readers to read books for free. A reader who borrowed a book from a library did not buy it and so was reading at the expense of other people, without rewarding the author for writing the work and the publisher for taking the risk of publishing it. The petition called for the state to find a way of making sure a fee was paid to authors and their publishers every time a book found its way off the library shelf.

There are clear figures here. 300 million books are bought in French bookshops every year; 150 million are lent by libraries. Divide this by the six and a half million public library members and you get an average of twenty three books a year per user (or one book every two weeks). Now request from each user *c.* €15 per year, and divide the proceeds, allowing 30 per cent to the authors and the remaining amount to the publishers.

There are objections to this reasoning. The figures are approximate: how many of the 150 million books lent every year generate royalties for the author? Authors would surely lose less money if publishers settled their royalties with monthly rather than annual payments. And how can one count all the times a library book has been signed out? In order to simplify what is a technically complicated exaction, one could, it has been suggested, remunerate all authors whose books can be found on library shelves, without taking account of loan frequency. This suggestion, however, seems to invalidate one of the very points of the petition. Why should an author read by no one receive as much as an author whose book is taken out often? The injustice suffered by the second author cannot be put right, and it is hard to understand what justice is being done by the first. One is overlooking, too, the fact that having a library at one's disposal allows for the correction of another injustice, this one committed against the reader-client. Why should one buy books blindfold? Libraries are the only way we have of reading a book, finding it unsatisfactory, and returning it, at no cost.

But beyond the economic aspects of the issue, lies a moral problem which bears discussion. The moral addressees of the petition signed by the three hundred authors are not libraries or ministers of culture, but readers. This represents the unilateral breach of a subtle, almost invisible trust which connects authors and readers in the republic of letters. In fact, in their view, all readers who enter a library become criminals. And all loans end up as criminal acts – including the simple loan of a book to a friend.

If I consider legally liable all those who download bits of my music from the Web at no charge, I would logically have to call the police each time someone played that piece to his friends, or when two people exchanged a CD (without copying it). But of course this is absurd. It would certainly be unacceptable for a pirate record company to gain income from contents without having asked the author permission to do so. But there is a big difference between pirated contents, exchanged contents and free contents, and one has to make sure that regulations aimed at stopping the circulation of pirate contents do not harm the other two.

When social pacts are broken, so are the behaviours associated with them. Some authors have asked libraries to make clear that their books were not to be loaned out. I cannot imagine anything more strange for an author – a red tag telling the reader: do not read me.

In conclusion: the liberated book and its dual nature

The Web allows us to understand what constitutes contents; it has liberated contents economically and metaphysically. It makes explicit their criteria of identity precisely by virtue of the character of the circulation and sale of contents in electronic form. This holds for *all* contents, and not only those one finds on the Web, because the most profound feature of the nature of contents is their amenability to transmission.

There is a wide grey area, however, and one will have to establish strict norms for the regulation of competition, necessary to stop a concentration of providers. One has to prevent the purchase of many providers by one giant publisher which would get hold of its clients' Web pages and forbid them to publish contents free of charge. This would be an encroachment on the right to free speech. The Internet allows users to go straight to the contents of interest to them; if there is a risk here of creating a 'culture on demand', the risk is minimal, given the huge amount of data one has access to. The user's autonomy is what enables one to dodge the filtering of information, which in theory should only improve the quality of our knowledge but which actually represents the retrograde defence of a caste of intellectuals who try to impose themselves as the only possible point of access to knowledge.

In this text, I have argued that no problem will arise out of the book's transformation, because the two conceptual poles made out of the physical book, on the one hand, and of the immaterial book, on the other (and its evanescent digital incarnation), can coexist perfectly well within a dual product. We will pay for the physical aspects of the book, but we will also make sure that its immaterial aspects circulate.

Discussion

Old books

Roberto Casati partly bases his case for the free distribution of information on the Web and his scepticism of the e-book format on the notion that a book's contents do not need the support of the traditional codex format, or of anything resembling it, in order to play the role of a book – defined as a 'cultural commodity'. Books are indeed non-exchangeable goods; their value as objects is entirely dependent on the value of their contents. Furthermore, as he says in order to demonstrate the book's intrinsically dual nature, when I sell or give away a cultural commodity such as a story or a song, I am not thereby depriving myself of the good I am selling or giving away, as I would be if I were selling or giving away a chair. One might say that I am merely, in the best of cases, transmitting its value.

Yet no one has yet identified, say, the blurb on a cornflakes packet or the visitor pamphlets containing the history and map of a monument as anything resembling a book. We all know that a book must be a unitary object with a subject-matter, a cover and an ordered textual sequence – or a collection of images or graphs and texts – edited, one hopes, with commitment and flair, 'patronized', so to speak, by the publishers and produced with some degree of care, whose pricing reflects the production value of the paper, ink and binding as well as the place of the book's author and contents on the offer-demand scale. The separation of book-content from book-object that Casati believes must derive from his ontological analysis of 'the book', provocative as it is, might not be as evident as it seems if one tries to actually focus on the value of a book. The story might begin to change once distribution is brought in, although the cost involved in distributing a book should ideally reflect the amount of effort its 'patrons' have deemed worth putting into the task, that is, it should have something to do with the ascription of some kind of value. With the Web, no such effort is needed. But what does that really say about the nature of the book whose contents can be circulated for free?

One may argue that the book market depends, for its orientation, on prizes and critics and such like, indeed that these structures defined the market in an essential fashion, and in a way not that dissimilar to the various search engines offered by the Web – Google included. The need to delimit fields of knowledge and structures within these fields is evidently at the root of the invention of the codex, and, beyond, of writing itself. The question then arises, yet again, of whether or not a field of knowledge, a story, a text that could be described as a 'book' rather than a pamphlet, is really that detachable from its format. The free circulation of contents on the Web most definitely changes the map of knowledge and facilitates the exchange of information. The Internet itself has already given rise to a flurry of books, complete with cover and table of contents, whose ideas are newer – although rooted in a historical continuum – than the book format itself. For how long will this continue to be the case?

Noga Arikha

A definition for today

I have already argued elsewhere that the physical aspect of a book is only important in so far as it describes a means by which an author's work may be communicated easily. Arikha's definition of a book as 'a unitary object with a subject-matter, a cover and an ordered textual sequence – or a collection of images or graphs and texts – edited, one hopes, with commitment and flair, "patronized", so to speak, by the publishers and produced with some degree of care, whose pricing reflects the production value of the paper, ink and binding as well as the place of the book's author and contents on the offer-demand scale' is predicated on the *need* for a physical object and so includes reference to a cover and paper, ink and binding. It is thus circular in nature and self-denying.

I think that today we use the term book to distinguish from the cornflake blurb, or letter, or journal article, or any other form of written communication, something that is essentially weightier, probably longer, and almost certainly editorially more significant. A book may be a monograph, a textbook, a novel, a manual, a handbook, a collection, a reference work, a directory, an almanac, an encyclopaedia or a catalogue (although electronically these last few might also be databases!). In physical form, the book may be a paperback or a hardback, of almost any size, full-colour or monochrome, printed on a whole variety of paper types, and so on. My point is that there is almost no set of physical attributes that could automatically be assumed when one hears mention of 'a book'. The need for a physical or material entity through which to lay hold of the essential essence of the book (its *raison d'être*: its content) was obvious until about ten years ago – how else to communicate or publish that content?

Now, the 'unitary object' view does not seem appropriate in either aspect of the phrase. In this networked age, there is no need for a physical presence (and so, perhaps 'object' is not the right word), and a text is rarely unitary (the same electronic original may appear, and appear differently formatted, on many diverse screens simultaneously). As Casati notes, the definition does not fit an e-book, but this is simply because it encompasses too much: the book is defined by attributes that are physical, intellectual, managerial, qualitative and economic. If we are to define a book, which of these are essential to the true purpose of a book? Not, I would suggest, those that are grounded in historical necessity or those which relate only to the publishing or marketing process – these are desirable to assure quality but not necessary to define the product as a book. This leaves us with 'a medium for communicating substantive literary or scholarly text'. As Ernst Mayr says in *The Growth of Biological Thought*: 'definitions are temporary verbalizations of concepts, and concepts – particularly difficult concepts – are usually revised repeatedly as our knowledge and understanding grows.'

Chris Armstrong

Of books and blurbs

What makes a book different from an e-book, what makes a book different from the blurb on a cornflakes box? – asks Noga Arikha, among other things. Let me answer somewhat deviously. What is the nature of the text that I wrote for *Text-e*? It was presented on the website *www.text-e.org* as an html text, as a word text, and as an e-book. When you download and open it as an e-book, you see a cover, an advertisement page, and the text itself in a format that looks very much like a book. You do not scroll down the text, you 'turn' 'pages'. You may even print it out and actually turn the pages. When you open it as an html document, you move up and down the text. In the e-book case, it is clearly the intention of the e-book designer to make what appears in your screen as similar as it gets to a book. Surely it makes us think of a book more than a blurb on the cornflakes container. Yet if we look closely at similarities and differences and average them, it seems clear that the old book and the cornflakes blurb are way more similar to each other than the old book and the e-book.

Let's take Arikha's tentative definition of a book (but I have already expressed scepticism at the possibility of defining anything) that reads: 'We all know that a book must be a unitary object with a subject-matter, a cover and an ordered textual sequence – or a collection of images or graphs and texts – edited, one hopes, with commitment and flair, "patronized", so to speak, by the publishers and produced with some degree of care, whose pricing reflects the production value of the paper, ink and binding as well as the place of the book's author and contents on the offer-demand scale.' If we use this definition we see that most of it is perfectly satisfied by the blurb and the book, but not by the e-book!

Roberto Casati

Books and digital economy

Casati manipulates juridical and economic categories in a rather loose way and I was not particularly convinced by the steps of his argument. But here, I will discuss only his conclusion. In this last, he suggests that in the future the economy of the book will be a dual one: on the one hand, there will be the paper-book, which will be sold, and on the other, the digital book which will circulate freely. The idea of a dual economy is interesting but its second component must also find a stable form of financing. I would like briefly to explain why, in my opinion, this is indeed the direction in which we are headed, but also why the winning formula for the digital book economy is not forthcoming. This sort of dual economy exists in other cultural domains: the marriage – stormy but in the end harmonious because complementary – between movies and television is a good example. Of course, we are talking about a different type of cultural good, but we are wrong in not searching for the key to its digital future in the history of the book. The first (movies) is sold by the piece, whereas the logic of the second (television) is based principally upon an economy of attention (ratings, advertisements or subscriptions). The economy of the Web, which is based not on the scarcity of its content, but, on the contrary, its abundance, cannot be an economy of attention. The means to realize this have yet to be found and will undoubtedly remain inaccessible for a time. This is for two, closely related reasons: on the one hand, the founding principles of the Web make the commercialization of its content very difficult. The W3C consortium is very effective in defending its original principles, especially that of a 'peer to peer' medium and at the same time, those of an availability and equality of tools for everyone. This somewhat contradictory *doxa* has been and remains extremely fecund. It was the basis for the explosion of the

Web. On the other hand, the market of containers (machines, software, networks) is not yet saturated. This is the source of the sector's economic value. As long as these manufacturers have not reached a plateau, it is unlikely that the producers of content will be able to make money in this network. Since the goal is to sell technique, the content is merely a marketing ploy. There again, the history of other media and situations is comparable (for example, radio prior to the 1920s). These two reasons are complementary. We must not forget that if the W3C consortium defends ideas that are justly considered to be politically egalitarian, it is, paradoxically, at the same time financed for most part by the principal manufacturers of containers who have a stake in the longest possible duration of the Internet explosion.

Jean-Michel Salaün

Books and networks: a concrete problem

In response to Roberto Casati's paper, I would like to submit to collective analysis a very timely and concrete case, combining books and networks. Over several years, a French public television channel presented a weekly show called *A Century of Writers*. When the show went off the air, Channel FR3 put its archives – some fifty-odd dossiers on authors such as Blanchot, Gracq, Duras, Caillois and many others, on line. These archives included explanatory texts, excerpts of interviews, photos, reproductions of manuscripts, and a few links. Two months ago, the station, since this site was not its purpose, did away with its archives, making us aware of how important this virtual resource had become in presenting and introducing major works. For certain authors, like Gracq, Proust, Céline, Koltès, there are materials on other sites. For others, such as Blanchot or Duras, there is nothing.

I, myself, for example, put some links between the archives of this show and my websites and on-line documents on Koltès and Beckett, links which are obviously henceforth blocked. I had also archived nine photos of Duras, but without complementary texts.

Here is where the excellent analyses of Roberto Casati come in: in the realization that we have already entered a phase of necessary complementarity between books and virtual resources, which does not annul the physical need for books, and thus publishing, but makes the network tool an autonomous, reactive, multi-level field which increases the reader's silent dialogue with the book: in a literal sense, as one finds more and more things on the Internet, associated with the book – and that applies to our 'classics' of the twentieth century as well as for books which have just come out, and more and more audio resources, lectures, interviews.

For the show *A Century of Writers*, a petition, LITOR, has called for the reconstruction of these archives. This is a good sign, since we are thus made aware of the reciprocal and multi-level interest for a domain – contemporary writing – which is still very fragile. And that warms the heart.

But I also have the impression that one must draw two consequences from this: on the Web today, we are very far from having access to enough on-line resources on twentieth-century literature (that is: research, analysis, presentation and popularization resources) on works which are still protected – there is a common task of making these things available which must be prolonged and intensified, as Patrick Rebollar has done for Claude Simon or Victor Segalen, but we must beware, all the same, of the 'absence makes the heart grow fonder' syndrome: the archives of this show had the merit of covering a vast field of authors, but the material, with some exceptions (like Blanchot, for example, or Koltès) was limited to a biography, a few photos, a complementary text...

What is presented on the Corti Press site on Julien Gracq, or on the site of 'Kafka's Project', the amazing international work of Detlef Wilske, the ambitious choice of the 'Portable Little Library' of the Ministry of Foreign Affairs (Des Forêts, Bataille, Sarraute...) or the site on Céline which provoked the wrath of the IMEC and Gallimard for a few 72 x 72 mm photos taken from their archives... are just a few examples of sites which are much more interesting than those proposed by FR3. My question, in echo of Roberto Casati's paper, is why is it that no public organization has ever undertaken this work of archival protection, which I consider vital for the French language and culture?

Even in the case of an author as important for contemporary research and for teaching as Georges Perec, on-line resources are left to private initiative (the principal site on Georges Perec is the work of a young bank manager) and the work of Perec, happily, is entirely protected. We are no longer in danger of being without studies and resources on Perec, including the Web, in our work today.

To track down Nathalie Sarraute, for example, we need to go on the web site of Télérama to hear her voice (6 audio excerpts, with Sarraute reading *Tropismes* or her last works), to the MAE for a critical presentation, and a few sites like remue.net or Christine Genin's 'Labyrinth' to bring all the links together. And the few excerpts which we put on line on a site like the one I run (*www.remue.net*), since it seems important to us to have a resumé of Nathalie Sarraute's aesthetic approach, constitute a hacker's approach in terms of artistic rights to literary property... All this necessary and innovative research rapidly bumps up against the frontiers explored by Roberto Casati.

François Bon

The concrete, the present and the future

François Bon's discussion had the merit of being very concrete and so instead of merely producing abstractions, it brought them back to their empirical base. While insisting on the difficulties and obstacles posed by the use of the Web in the literary domain, his comment illustrates wonderfully the fact that new and pretty exciting practices and objects have appeared in this domain. The obstacles about which Bon spoke are across paths which, ten years ago, did not even exist.

We thus once more encounter the problem of the temporal dimension already evoked in the discussion of Roger Chartier's text. If we think about the potential of the Web without a care for present difficulties, one could have – legitimately, I think – a revolutionary vision of the future, but in that case, it is important not to project onto the present a possible or even probable future which will come off without a hitch. If one considers the present state of affairs, the risk is, on the contrary, to project present deceptions onto the future. I say this not because of a penchant for the reasonable, but because these two types of unwarranted projections can both give rise to counterproductive practices – a mistrust, a reticence which would push one to flush out the limitations, naivety, or unwanted effects of almost everything that is done on the Web and to minimize the creativity and potential for self-correction of so many initiatives or, alternatively, a joyous headlong rush which sometimes innovates brilliantly, but too often ends up in badly done things, to the joy of sceptics. In short, we risk an absence of reflection on the processes that could lead our present babbling to cultural practices that are radically new and truly good.

When Roberto Casati suggests – I am simplifying – that the Google search engine, by classifying sites in terms of the number of links to these sites on the Web, could advantageously replace the experts – editorial committees of journals, etc. – to determine which texts and more generally, which sites are worthwhile, he engages in a futuristic provocation without specifying what steps must be taken. First of all, those who conceive the search engines seek to classify sites according to criteria of pertinence to the user, and, in this way, the technique of Google is but a first step in what is undoubtedly the right direction. It gives, for example, the same classification for all users whereas what is relevant for one user is not necessarily so for another. One could imagine that search engines will evolve toward increasingly refined and accurate ways of identifying what is relevant to each user, to the point where, in fact, it will be only marginally interesting to know that a certain Savant Cosinus or that this or that Theodule Committee felt that such and such an article was important, or that such and such a book was extraordinary, that such a tune was sublime and that certain others were not.

If we thus wish to do more than complain or prophesy, we must associate reflection with innovative practices, as François Bon has done, but I would also like him to share with us not only his experiences with the obstacles he encountered, but the experiences that motivated and guided him. I would also like Roberto to tell us how he sees the passage from the state of things today to that which he predicts and applauds: is it enough to watch and let things happen, or are their obstacles to be overcome and dangers to avoid and thus reasons to act?

Dan Sperber

Between Dr Cosinus and Google

Dan Sperber asks me to be more specific about the potential of the system of evaluation used by Google. I would begin by saying that all the students with whom I work (including PhD students) begin their research with Google. This is a fact which must be verified and, if confirmed, would give us something to think about. On two specific points: (1) Since Google does not appear to show any sensitivity to context, the wise user ought to enter more specific research criteria when not satisfied. This would make for a closer relation between Google's response and the relevance of the question posed. (2) The intermediate step between the arbitration of an editorial committee and scientific evaluation by search engine is constituted by the indexing of pages by experts (note that the notion of expert used here does not presuppose the possibility of measuring expertise independently of the indexing). Suppose that I publish an article on-line and that Cosinus makes a link to my page. If my article is good, and Cosinus is an expert, sooner or later the system of indexers on the Web will discover this, by making a link to Cosinus' page (thus recognizing him as an expert by rewarding him with an indexation). A page that has been the object of many links is a page that transmits its weight to its own links towards other pages. My article thus receives a rating that gives it a higher rank. Once again, one can imagine many distortions of this system, but they do not seem very original compared to distortions of other systems of evaluation.

Roberto Casati

3
Skyreading and Skywriting for Researchers: A Post-Gutenberg Anomaly and How to Resolve It

Stevan Harnad

*There will be a profound and fundamental dividing line in the post-Gutenberg galaxy, between non-give-away work (books, magazines, software, music) and give-away work (of which the most important representative is refereed scientific and scholarly research papers). It is the failure to make this distinction that causes so much confusion, and that is delaying the inevitable transition of the give-away work to what is the optimal solution for scholars and scientists: that the annual 2,000,000+ articles in all 20,000+ refereed journals across disciplines and languages and around the world should be offered free on line through author/institution self-archiving: **http://www.eprints.org**. This chapter tries to show how questions about copyright, peer review and other controversial issues can be clarified if the give-away/non-give-away distinction is made.*

A post-Gutenberg anomaly

(1) A brand-new PhD recipient proudly tells his mother he has just published his first article. She asks him how much he was paid for it. He makes a face and tells her 'nothing', and then begins a long, complicated explanation.

(2) A fellow-researcher at that same university sees a reference to that same article. He goes to their library to get it: 'It's not subscribed to here. We can't afford that journal. (Our subscription /licence/loan/ copy budget is already overspent.)'

(3) An undergraduate at that same university sees the same article cited on the Web. He clicks on it. The publisher's website demands a password: '*Access denied*: Only pre-paid subscribing/licensed institutions have access to this journal.'

(4) The undergraduate loses patience, gets bored, and clicks on *Napster* to grab an MP3 file of his favourite bootleg CD to console him in his sorrows.

(5) Years later, the same PhD is being considered for tenure. His publications are good, but they're not cited enough; they have not made enough of a 'research impact'. Tenure denied.

(6) Same thing happens when he tries to get a research grant. His research findings have not had enough of an impact: not enough researchers have read, built upon and cited them. Funding denied.

(7) He decides to write a book instead. Book publishers decline to publish it: 'It wouldn't sell enough copies because not enough universities have enough money to pay for it. (Their purchasing budgets are tied up paying for their inflating annual journal subscription /license/loan costs ...).'

(8) He tries to put his articles up on the Web, free for all, to increase their impact. His publisher threatens to sue him and his server-provider for violation of copyright.

(9) He asks his publisher: 'Who is this copyright intended to protect?' His publisher replies: 'You!'

What is wrong with this picture? (And why is the mother of the PhD whose *give-away* work people cannot steal, even though he wants them to, in the same boat as the mother of the recording artist whose *non-give-away* work they can and do steal, even though he does not want them to?)

Five essential post-Gutenberg distinctions

In order to understand what is wrong with the picture, one must first make five critical distinctions. If one fails to make any one of these distinctions, it will be impossible to make sense of the picture or to resolve the anomaly, an anomaly completely unique to the on-line era of 'scholarly skywriting' in the 'post-Gutenberg galaxy'.

1. Distinguish the non-give-away literature from the give-away literature

This is the most important post-Gutenberg distinction of all. It is what makes this small refereed research literature (c.20,000 refereed journals, c.2,000,000 articles annually) anomalous – fundamentally unlike the bulk of the written literature: Its authors do not seek, nor do they receive, royalties or fees for their writings. Their texts are author give-aways. The only thing these authors seek is research 'impact', which comes from accessing the eyes and minds of all potentially interested fellow-researchers everywhere, now, and any time in the future.

The litmus test for whether a piece of writing falls in the small give-away sector of the literature or the much larger non-give-away sector is: 'Does the author seek a royalty or fee in exchange for his writings?' If the answer is *yes* (as it is for virtually all books and newspaper or magazine articles), then the writing is non-give-away; if the answer is *no*, then it is give-away.

None of what follows here is applicable to non-give-away writing, but the non-give-away model is the one that most people have in mind for all of writing. So it is not surprising that the small fraction of writing that the more general model does *not* fit should seem anomalous.

2. Distinguish *income* (arising from paper *sales*) from *impact* (arising from paper *use*)

Unlike all other authors, researchers derive their income not from the sale of their research reports but from the scholarly/scientific impact of their reported findings, i.e., how much they are read, cited, and built-upon by other researchers. Hence all fee-based access-barriers are income-barriers for research and researchers, restricting their potential visibility, impact and uptake to only those (institutions, mainly) who can and do pay the access fees.

As most institutions cannot afford the access fees to most refereed research journals, this means that **most research papers cannot be accessed by most researchers**: Currently, all that potential impact and uptake are simply lost.

Note that although researchers do not derive income from the sale of their refereed research papers ('imprint income'), they do derive income from the impact of those papers ('impact income').

The simple reason why researchers, unlike non-give-away authors, do not seek imprint-income for their refereed research is that the access tolls for collecting imprint-income are barriers to impact-income (research grants, salaries, promotion, tenure, prizes), which is by far the more important reward for researchers, most of whose refereed papers are so esoteric as to have no imprint-income market at all.

3. Distinguish between copyright protection from *theft-of-authorship* (plagiarism) and copyright protection from *theft-of-text* (piracy)

These two very different aspects of copyright protection have always been conflated, because it is the much larger and more representative non-give-away literature that has always been the model for copyright law and copyright concerns. But copyright protection from theft-of-authorship (plagiarism), which is essential for both give-away and non-give-away authors, has nothing at all to do with copyright protection from theft-of-text (piracy), which non-give-away authors want but give-away authors do *not* want. One can have full protection from plagiarism without seeking any protection from piracy.

4. Distinguish *self-publishing* (vanity press) from *self-archiving* (of published, refereed research)

The essential difference between unrefereed research and refereed research is quality-control (peer review) and its certification (by an established peer-reviewed journal of known quality). Although researchers have always wished to give away their refereed research findings, they still want them to be refereed, and certified as having met established quality standards. Hence the self-archiving of refereed research should in no way be confused with self-publishing, for it includes as its most important component the on line self-archiving, free for all, of refereed, published research papers.

5. Distinguish unrefereed *preprints* from refereed *postprints*

Eprint archives, consisting of research papers self-archived on line by their authors, are not, and have never been, merely 'preprint archives' for unrefereed research. Authors can self-archive therein all the embryological stages of the research they wish to report, from pre-refereeing, through successive revisions, till the refereed, journal-certified postprint, and thence still further, to any subsequent corrected, revised, or otherwise updated drafts (post-postprints), as well as any commentaries or responses linked to them. These are all just way-stations along the scholarly skywriting continuum.

The optimal and inevitable for researchers

- The entire full-text refereed corpus on line
- On every researcher's desktop, everywhere
- 24 hours a day
- All papers citation-interlinked
- Fully searchable, navigable, retrievable
- For free, for all, forever

All of this will come to pass. The only real question is 'How soon?' Will we still be *compos mentis* and fit to benefit from it, or will it only be for the *Napster* generation? Future historians, posterity, and our own still-born scholarly impact are already poised to chide us in hindsight.

What can the research community do to hasten the optimal and inevitable? Here are some recent concepts that may help.

Two useful categories, one new distinction, and one new ally

Subscription /site-licence/pay-per-view: the impact/access-barriers

Subscription tolls (and their variants: site-licence and pay-per-view tolls) are the access-barriers, hence the impact-barriers, for researchers and their give-away research. Subscription is the journal publisher's means of recovering costs and making a fair profit. High costs were inescapable in the expensive and inefficient on-paper Gutenberg era; but today, in the on-line post-Gutenberg era, continuing to do it all the old Gutenberg way, with its high costs, must be clearly seen as merely the optional add-on feature (for this give-away literature only: not for the royalty/fee-based literature!) that it has become, rather than as the obligatory feature it used to be.

Beware of the language of obligatory 'value-added', with which the peer-reviewed literature must, by implication, continue to be inextricably wrapped. The only *essential* service still provided by journal publishers (for this anomalous, author-give-away literature in the post-Gutenberg era) is peer review itself.

The rest – on-paper versions, PDF on line page images, deluxe on line enhancements – are all potentially valuable features, to be sure, but only as take-it-or-leave-it options. In the on-line era there is no longer any necessity, hence no longer any justification whatsoever, for continuing to hold the refereed research itself hostage to subscription tolls and whatever add-ons they happen to pay for.

Beware also of any attempt to trade off subscription for licence or licence for pay-per-view: pick your poison, all three are access-barriers, hence impact-barriers, and hence all three must go – or rather, they must all now become only the price-tags for the add-on, deluxe *options* that they buy for the researcher and his institution, but no longer also for the peer-reviewed *essentials*, which can henceforth be self-archived for free for all.

Quality-control and certification: peer review

Peer review itself – the system by which qualified experts control and certify the quality of the work of their fellow-experts – is *not* a deluxe add-on for research and researchers: this quality-control service and its certification is an essential. Without quality control, the research literature would be neither reliable nor navigable, its quality uncontrolled, unfiltered, un-signposted, unknown, unaccountable, unusable.

But the peers who review it for the journals are the researchers themselves, and they review it for free, just as the researchers report it for free. So it must be made quite clear that the only real quality-control cost is that of implementing the peer review, not actually performing it. Estimates as in Odlyzko, 1998[1], as well as the real experience of on-line-only journals (e.g., *Journal of High Energy Physics, http://jhep.cern.ch/; Psycoloquy, www.cogsci.soton.ac.uk/psycoloquy/*) have shown that the quality-control implementation cost is quite low – about 10 per cent of the total amount that the world's institutional libraries (or rather, the small subset of them that can afford any given journal at all!) are currently paying annually *per article* in subscription tolls.

Once the 90 per cent subscription add-ons become optional, the essential 10 per cent quality-control cost could easily be paid out of the 100 per cent subscription savings – if ever the world's libraries decide they no longer need the add-ons. (The other 90 per cent savings can be used to buy other things, e.g., books, which are not, and never will be, author give-aways.)

Separating (a) quality-control *service-provision* from (b) e-print *access-provision* (and from (c) optional add-ons)

Researchers need not and should not wait until journal publishers voluntarily decide to separate the provision of the essential quality-control service from all the other optional add-on products (on-paper version, publisher's pdf version, deluxe enhancements) before their give-away refereed research can at last be freed of all access- and impact-barriers.

All researchers can free their own refereed research now, virtually overnight, by taking the matter into their own hands; they can self-archive it in their institutional e-print archives: *http://www.eprints.org*. Access to the e-prints of their refereed research is then immediately freed of all subscription barriers, forever.

Interoperability: the Open Archives initiative

Papers self-archived by their authors in their institutional e-print archives can be accessed by anyone, anywhere, with no need to know their actual location, because all e-print archives are compliant with the Open Archives Initiative meta-data tagging protocol for interoperability: *www.openarchives.org*

Because of their Open Archives-compliance, the papers in all registered e-prints archives can be harvested and searched by Open Archive services, such as Cite-Base and the Cross Archive Searching Service, *http://arc.cs.odu.edu/*, providing seamless access to all the e-prints, across all the e-print archives, as if they were all in one global, virtual archive.

The subversive proposal

Eight steps will be described here. The first four are not hypothetical in any way; they are guaranteed to free the entire refereed research literature (c. 20,000 journals annually) from its access/impact-barriers right away. The only thing that researchers and their institutions need to do is to take these first four steps. The second four steps are hypothetical predictions, but nothing hinges on them: the refereed literature will already be free for everyone as a result of steps 1 to 4, irrespective of the outcome of predictions 5 to 8.

Step 1: universities instal and register Open Archives-compliant e-print archives (*www.eprints.org*)

The e-prints software is free and is being open-sourced. It in turn uses only free software; it is quick and easy to install and maintain; it is Open Archives-compliant and will be kept compliant with every Open Archives upgrade: *http://www.openarchives.org/*.

e-prints archives are all interoperable with one another and can hence be harvested and searched as if they were all in one global, searchable, 'virtual' archive of the entire research literature, both pre- and post-refereeing.

Step 2: authors self-archive their pre-refereeing preprints and post-refereeing postprints in their own university's e-print archives

This is the most important step; it is not sufficient to create the e-print archives. All researchers must self-archive their papers therein if the literature is to be freed of its access- and impact-barriers. Self-archiving is quick and easy; it need only be done once per paper, and the result is permanent, and permanently and automatically uploadable to upgrades of the e-print archives and the Open Archives-protocol.

Step 3: universities subsidize a first start-up wave of self-archiving by proxy where needed

Self-archiving is quick and easy, but there is no need for it to be held back if any researcher feels too busy, tired, old or otherwise unable to do it for himself: library staff or students can be paid to 'self-archive' the first wave of papers by proxy on their behalf. The cost will be negligibly low per paper, and the benefits will be huge; moreover, there will be no need for a second wave of help once the palpable benefits (access and impact) of freeing the literature begin to be felt by the research community. Self-archiving will become second-nature to all researchers once its benefits have become palpable.

Step 4: the give-away corpus is freed from all access/impact barriers on line

Once a critical mass of researchers has self-archived, the refereed research literature is at last free of all access- and impact-barriers, as it was always destined to be.

Hypothetical sequel

Steps 1 to 4 are sufficient to free the refereed research literature. We can also guess at what may happen after that, but these are really just guesses. Nor does anything depend on their being correct. For even if there is no change whatsoever – even if universities continue to spend exactly the same amounts on their subscription budgets as they do now – the refereed literature will have been freed of all access/impact barriers forever.

However, it is likely that there will be some changes as a consequence of the freeing of the literature by author/institution self-archiving. This is what those changes might be.

Step 5: will users prefer the free version?

It is likely that once a free, on-line version of the refereed research literature is available, not only those researchers who could not access it at all before, because of subscription-barriers at their institution, but virtually all researchers will prefer to use the free on-line versions.

Note that it is quite possible that there will always continue to be a market for the subscription options (on-paper version, publisher's on-line pdf, deluxe enhancements) even though most users use the free versions. Nothing hangs on this.

Step 6: will publisher subscription revenues shrink while library subscription savings grow?

But if researchers do prefer to use the free on-line literature, it is possible that libraries may begin to cancel journals, and as their subscription savings grow, journal publisher subscription revenues will shrink. The extent of the cancellation will depend on the extent to which there remains a market for the subscription -based add-ons, and for how long.

If the subscription market stays large enough, nothing else need change.

Step 7: will publishers downsize to providers of quality-control service+optional add-ons products?

It will depend entirely on the size of the remaining market for the subscription options whether and to what extent journal publishers will have to downsize to providing only the essentials: the only essential, indispensable service is quality-control.

Step 8: will quality-control service costs be funded by author-institution out of reader-institution subscription savings?

If publishers can continue to cover costs and make a decent profit from the subscription-based optional add-ons market, without needing to down-size to quality-control provision alone, nothing much changes.

But if publishers do need to abandon providing the subscription products and to scale down instead to providing only the quality-control service, then universities, having saved 100 per cent of their annual subscription budgets, will have plenty of annual windfall savings from which to pay for their own researchers' continuing (and essential) annual journal-submission quality-control costs (10 per cent); the rest of their savings (90 per cent) they can spend as they like (e.g., on books – plus a bit for e-print archive maintenance).

Post-Gutenberg copyright concerns

There is a great deal of concern about copyright in the digital age, and some of it may not be easily resolvable (e.g., what to do about the pirating of software and music). But none of that need detain us here, because digital piracy is only a problem for non-give-away work, whereas we are concerned here only with give-away work. (Again, failing to make the give-away/non-give-away distinction leads only to confusion and to the misapplication of the much bigger and more representative non-give-away model to the anomalous give-away corpus, which it does not fit.)

The following digital copyright concerns are relevant to the non-give-away literature only.

Protecting intellectual property (royalties)

This is as much of a concern to authors of books as to authors of screen-plays, music, and computer software. It is also a concern to performers who have made digital audio or video discs of their work. They do not wish to see that work stolen; they want their fair share of the gate-receipts in return for their talent and efforts in producing the work.

But the producers of refereed research reports do not wish to have protection from 'theft' of this kind; on the contrary, they wish to *encourage* it. They have no royalties to gain from preventing it; they have only research impact to lose from access-blockage of any kind.

Allowing fair use (user issue)

'Fair use' is another worthy concern. It has to do with certain sanctioned uses of non-give-away material, such as all or parts of books, magazine articles, etc., often for teaching purposes; in general, the producers of these works do *not* wish to lose their potential royalty/fee-income from these works.

The producers of refereed research reports, in contrast, wish to give their work away; hence fair-use issues are moot for this special give-away literature.

Preventing theft of text (piracy)

The producers of refereed research reports do not wish to prevent the theft of their texts; they wish to facilitate it as much as possible. (In the on-paper era they used to purchase and mail reprints to requesters at their own expense!)

Preventing theft of authorship (plagiarism)

The following digital copyright concern is relevant to all *literature, both give-away and non-give-away.*

No author wants any other author to claim to have been the author of his work. This concern is shared by all authors, give-away and non-give-away. But it has *nothing whatsoever* to do with concerns about theft-of-text, and should not be conflated with such concerns in any way. Give-away work need not be held hostage to non-give-away concerns about theft-of-text under the pretext of 'protecting' it from theft-of-authorship. (Unfortunately, many journal publishers try to formulate and use their copyright transfer agreements for precisely this purpose, and authors need to become aware of it.)

Guaranteeing author give-away rights

The following digital copyright concern is relevant to the give-away *literature only.*

Apart from the protection from plagiarism and the assurance of priority that all authors seek, the only other 'protection' the give-away author of refereed research reports seeks is protection of his give-away rights!

(The intuitive model for this is advertisements: what advertiser wants to lose his right to give away his ads for free, diminishing their potential impact by charging for access to them!)

Well, there is no need for the authors of refereed research to worry about exercising their give-away rights, for they can do it, legally, even under the most restrictive copyright agreement, by using the following strategy.

How to get around restrictive copyright legally ('Harnad/ Oppenheim strategy')

1. Self-archive the pre-refereeing preprint

Self-archiving the preprint is the critical first step. Before it has even been submitted to a journal, your intellectual property is your own, and not bound by any future copyright transfer agreement. So archive the preprints (as physicists have done for ten years now, with over 150,000 papers, and cognitive scientists have done for three years now, with over 1000 papers). This is a good way to establish priority, elicit informal feedback, and keep a public record of the embryology of knowledge.

[Note that some journals have, apart from copyright policies, which are a legal matter, 'embargo policies', which are merely policy matters (non-legal). Invoking the 'Ingelfinger (Embargo) Rule', some journals state that they will not *referee* (let alone publish) papers that have previously been 'made public' in any way, whether through conferences, press releases, or on-line self-archiving. The Ingelfinger Rule, apart from being directly at odds with the interests of research and researchers and having no intrinsic justification whatsoever – other than as a way of protecting journals' current revenue streams – is not a legal matter, and unenforceable. So researchers are best advised to ignore it completely, exactly as the authors of the 150,000 papers in the Physics Archive have been doing for ten years now. The 'Ingelfinger Rule' is under review by journals in any case; *Nature* has already dropped it, and there are indications that *Science* may soon follow suit too.]

2. Submit the preprint for refereeing (revise, etc.)

Nothing changes in author publication practices; nothing needs to be given up. Submit your preprint to the refereed journal of your choice, and revise it as usual in accordance with the directive of the editor and the advice of the referees.

3. At acceptance, try to fix the copyright transfer agreement to allow self-archiving

Copyright transfer agreements take many forms. Whatever the wording is, if it does not explicitly permit on line self-archiving, modify it so that it does. Here is a sample way to word it (*http://cogprints.soton.ac.uk/copyright.html*):

I hereby transfer to [publisher or journal] all rights to sell or lease the text (on-paper and on line) of my paper [paper-title]. I retain only the right to distribute it for free for scholarly/scientific purposes, in particular, the right to self-archive it publicly on line on the Web.

Some publishers (about 10 per cent) already explicitly allow self-archiving of the refereed postprint (e.g., the American Physical Society: *ftp://aps.org/pub/jrnls/copy_trnsfr.asc*). Most other publishers (perhaps 70 per cent) will also accept this clause, but only if you explicitly propose it yourself (they will not formulate it on their own initiative).

4. If 3 is successful, self-archive the refereed postprint

Hence, for about 80 per cent of journals, once you have done the above, you can go ahead and self-archive your paper.

Some journals (about 20 per cent), however, will respond that they decline to publish your paper unless you sign their copyright transfer agreement verbatim. In such cases, sign their agreement and proceed to the next step.

5. If 3 is unsuccessful, archive the 'corrigenda'

Your pre-refereeing preprint has already been self-archived since prior to submission, and is not covered by the copyright agreement, which pertains to the revised final ('value-added') draft. Hence all you need to do is to self-archive a further 'corrigenda' file, linked to the archived preprint, which simply lists the corrections that the reader may wish to make in order to update the preprint to the refereed, accepted version.

Everyone chuckles at this point, but the reason why it is so easy is that this is the author give-away literature. No *non*-give-away author would ever dream of doing such a thing (archiving the prepublication draft for free, along with the corrigenda). And copyright agreements (and copyright law) are designed and conceived to meet the much more representative interests of non-give-away authors and their much larger body of royalty/ fee-based work. Hence this simple and legal expedient for the special, tiny, anomalous, give-away literature has no constituency anywhere else.

Yet this simple, risible strategy is also feasible, and legal (Oppenheim, 2001[2]) – and sufficient to free the entire current refereed corpus of all access/impact barriers immediately!

What *you* can do *now* to free the refereed literature on line

Researchers: self-archive all present, future (and past) papers

The freeing of their present and future refereed research from all access- and impact-barriers forever is now entirely in the hands of researchers. Posterity is looking over our shoulders, and will not judge us flatteringly if we continue to delay the optimal and inevitable needlessly, now that it is clearly within our reach. Physicists have already shown the way, but at their current self-archiving rate, even they will take another decade to free the entire Physics literature (*http:// www.cogsci.soton.ac.uk/~harnad/Tp/Tim/sld002.htm*) – with the Cognitive Sciences (*http://cogprints. soton.ac.uk*) 39 times slower still, and most of the remaining disciplines not even started: *http://www.cogsci.soton.ac.uk/ ~harnad/Tp/Tim/sld004.htm*

This is why it is hoped that (with the help of the eprints.org institutional archive-creating software) distributed, institution-based self-archiving, as a powerful and natural complement to central, discipline-based self-archiving, will now broaden and accelerate the self-archiving initiative, putting us all over the top at last, with the entire distributed corpus integrated by the glue of interoperability (*http://www.openarchives.org*).

As to the past (retrospective) literature: the Harnad/Oppenheim preprint+corrigenda strategy will not work there, but as the retrospective journal literature brings virtually no revenue, most publishers will agree to author self-archiving after a sufficient period (6 months to 2 years) has elapsed. Moreover, for the really old literature, it is not clear that on-line self-archiving was covered by the old copyright agreements at all.

And if all else fails for the retrospective literature, a variant of the Harnad/Oppenheim strategy will still work: Simply do a revised second edition! Update the references, rearrange the text (and add more text and data if you wish). For the record, the enhanced draft can be accompanied by a '*de*-corrigenda' file, stating which of the enhancements were *not* in the published version.

(And of course the starting point for the revised, enhanced second edition, if you no longer have the digital text in your word processor, can be scanned and OCR4d from the journal; by thus distributing it, authors can do for their own work for-free what JSTOR *http:// www.jstor.org/* is only able to do for the work of others for-fee.)

Universities: install e-print archives, mandate them; help in author start-up

Universities should create institutional e-print archives (e.g., *CalTech*) for all their researchers. They should also mandate that they be filled. It is already becoming normal practice for faculty to keep and update their institutional CVs on line on the Web; it should be made standard practice that all CV entries for refereed journal articles are linked to their archived full-text version in the university's e-print archive.

For researchers who profess to be too busy, tired, old, or inexpert to self-archive their papers for themselves, a modest start-up budget to pay library experts or students to do it for them would be a small amount of money very well invested. It will only be needed to get the first wave over the top; from then on, the momentum from the enhanced access and impact will maintain itself, and self-archiving will become as standard a practice as email.

But what needs energetic initial promotion and support is the first wave. If (a) the enhanced access of their own researchers to the research of others and (b) the enhanced visibility (Lawrence, 2001[3]), and the resulting enhanced impact of their own research on the research of others are not incentive enough for universities to promote and support the self-archiving initiative energetically, they should also consider that it will be an investment in (c) a potential solution to their serials crisis and the possible recovery of 90 per cent of their annual serials (subscription) budget.

(Note that the success of the self-archiving initiative is predicated on the same Golden Rule on which both refereeing and research them-selves are predicated: If we all do our own part for one another, we all benefit from it. Give in order to receive...)

Libraries: maintain the university e-print archives; help in author start-up

Libraries are the most natural allies of researchers in the self-archiving initiative to free the refereed journal literature. Not only are they groaning under the yoke of the growing serials budget crisis, but librarians are also eager to establish a new digital niche for themselves, once the journal corpus is on line. Maintaining the e-print archives, and facilitating the all-important start-up wave of self-archiving (by being ready to do 'proxy' self-archiving on behalf of authors who feel they cannot do it for themselves), will be a critical role for libraries to play.

Libraries can also facilitate a stable transition through their collective, consortial power (SPARC: *http://www.arl.org/sparc*), providing leveraged support for publishers who are prepared to commit themselves to a timetable for downsizing to the essentials only (the peer review service, to the author/institution). And individually they can also be preparing in advance for the restructuring that will come if their subscription savings grow; about 10 per cent of their annual savings will need to be redirected to cover their university's own authors' quality-control charges per paper. The remaining 90 per cent is theirs to use in any way they see fit!

Students: Stay the course! Surf! The future is optimal, inevitable and yours!

Students are well-advised to keep doing what they do naturally: favour material that is freely accessible on the Web. This will not net them very much of the *non*-give-away literature, but it will put consumer pressure on the give-away research literature, especially as these students come of age, and become researchers in their turn.

Publishers: concede realistically on self-archiving and be prepared to separate essential quality-control service costs (to the author-institution) from optional add-on product costs (to the reader-institution)

Publishers should concede graciously on self-archiving as the American Physical Society (APS) has done and not try to use copyright or embargo policy to prevent or retard it. Such measures are in direct conflict with the interests of research and researchers, they are destined to fail, they can already be legally circumvented, and they only make publishers look bad.

A much better policy is to concede on the optimal and inevitable for research, and plan on the possibility of separating the provision of the essential quality-control *service* to the author-institution (peer review implementation charges, per paper) from the provision of all other add-on products (e.g., on-paper version, on-line version, other added-values), which should be sold as options, rather than used to try to keep holding the essentials (the refereed final draft) hostage to subscription tolls.

There will still be a permanent niche for journal publishers. What remains to be seen is whether that will entail downsizing to quality-control service-provision alone, or whether there will also continue to be a market for subscription-based add-ons even after the refereed drafts are available free through the e-print archives.

Government/society: mandate public archiving of public research worldwide

Government and society should support the self-archiving initiative, reminding themselves that most of this giveaway research has been supported by public funds, with that support explicitly conditional on making the research findings public (*http://www.sciencemag.org/cgi/content/full/281/5382/1459*). In the post-Gutenberg galaxy there is no longer any need for that public accessibility to be blocked by subscription toll-barriers.

The beneficiaries will not just be research and researchers, but society itself, inasmuch as research is supported because of its potential benefits to society. Researchers in developing countries and at the less affluent universities and research institutions of developed countries will benefit even more from barrier-free access to the research literature than will the better-off institutions, but it is instructive to remind ourselves that even the most affluent institutional libraries cannot afford most of the refereed journals! None have access to more than a small subset of the entire annual corpus (*http://fisher.lib.virginia.edu/arl/index.html*). So free access to it all will benefit all institutions (Odlyzko, 1999, 2002[4]).

And on the other side of barrier-free access *to* the work of others, all researchers, even the most affluent, will benefit from the barrier-free impact of their own work *on* the work of others. Moreover, a freed, inter-operable, digital research literature will not only radically enhance access, navigation (e.g., citation-linking) and impact, hence research productivity and quality, but it will also spawn new ways of monitoring and measuring that impact, productivity and quality (e.g., download impact, links, immediacy, comments) and the higher-order dynamics of a citation-linked corpus that can be analyzed from preprint to post-post-print, to yield an 'embryology of knowledge' (Harnad and Carr, 2000[5]).

Notes

1. A.M. Odlyzko (1993) 'The economics of electronic journals', in Ekman, R. and Quandt, R. (eds) *Technology and Scholarly Communication* (University of California Press).
2. C. Oppenheim (2001) 'The legal and regulatory environment for electronic information', Infonortics. *http://www.infonortics.com/publications/legal4.html*
3. S. Lawrence (2001) 'Online or Invisible?', *Nature*, 411(6837): 521.
4. Cf. A.M. Odlyzko (1999) 'Competition and cooperation: libraries and publishers in the transition to electronic scholarly journals', *Journal of Scholarly Publishing*, 30(4) (July), pp. 163–85; and A.M. Odlyzko, 'The rapid evolution of scholarly communication', *Learned Publishing*, 15(1) (January 2002).
5. S. Harnad and L. Carr (2000) 'Integrating, navigating and analyzing e-print archives through open citation linking (the OpCit Project)', *Current Science*, 79(5): 629–38.

Discussion

Will evaluation be reserved for journals?

If we agree with Stevan Harnad's suggestions, which I am willing to do enthusiastically, the only essential role that will remain to scientific journals will be the evaluation of articles. On-line publication of a journal will be all but redundant with institutional and departmental archives, and will only be justified by its contribution to maintaining a coherent image of the journal and drawing attention to the articles it will have selected, and all this at a reasonable cost. Paper publication will be to scientific journals what bound and numbered vellum editions are to the book: if there are buyers, why not, but nothing important depends on it. But if their only essential function is peer-review, why must the institutions that conduct this be exclusively or even mainly journals issued or copied from current paper journals, with their material dependence on publishers, their institutional structures, their periodicity, their concern with durability, etc. Of course, current journals are, from the outset, the best at playing this role of organizing and evaluating since they are experienced at it. But useful competition could come from individuals or groups that would organize the evaluation in another way and perhaps according to other criteria.

Organize the evaluation another way. This could be done by renouncing, purely and simply, periodicity and by 'publishing' (that is, granting approval) article by article. For example, by not being content to accept or refuse articles, but by accompanying those that are accepted by a brief commentary by the evaluators. For example, by allowing all readers (or all the readers belonging to an ad-hoc network) to contribute to a collective evaluation of the articles initially accepted by a much smaller committee, a collective evaluation which might evolve in time (often, innovative articles have trouble getting through the first cut, but see their value progressively recognized when a community broadens.)

Evaluation according to other criteria. Roberto Casati envisioned replacing a pure and simple editorial evaluation by an automatic count of links, indexation, etc. Between current criteria of evaluation and automatic evaluation, there are many possible compromises and combinations. I would like to know not only that such and such an article was accepted by a particular editorial committee, but also by how many positive and negative votes (or the distribution of readers' ratings on a scale of 0 to 10), perhaps according to several criteria – that it is often cited by researchers of such and such a sub-discipline or tendency, that it is often cited in course syllabi, etc.

In short, the very function of evaluation can evolve and become diversified. It can do this through individual and institutional initiatives of varying sorts. There is thus no good reason – but what does Stevan think of this? – for evaluation to remain for long as the exclusive reserve of journals, even if they go from paper to network.

Dan Sperber

Do not confuse the reform of the system of access with the reform of the system of evaluation

Dan Sperber writes: 'If we agree with Stevan Harnad's propositions, which I am willing to do enthusiastically, the only essential role which will remain to scientific journals will be the evaluation of articles.' That is so. A scientific journal is merely a service-provider (and so, we might add, it only provides the administration of an evaluation service by peers, since the service of peers, like the service of authors, is a free service.) It is the 20,000 existent journals which have the established reputation, the prestige, the expertise and the relevant experience. The journals with their peer committees have never been anything but providers of peer review service. Qualified specialists in each field will always remain the same regardless of who the publisher is. (This is why I have so little confidence in the movement that seeks to boycott journals that do not want to give away their contents and, if meeting refusal, to create new journals: 20,000 journals! And they are not even necessary since self-archiving by authors yields the same result – to liberate the contents of all journals – and the continuity is preserved while avoiding 20,000 headaches!) For the moment, institutions continue to pay the costs of evaluation and certification by paying institutional subscription prices, but perhaps one day, by paying the costs of evaluation (for each paper submitted) financed by a little part of the windfalls that come from terminated subscriptions!

My principal goal is to liberate peer-reviewed literature from the useless access costs that now block the impact and productivity of our research.

The system of peer-review certainly has its imperfections, which merit research to better them. But that is a completely different programme, independent from the question of liberation. I do not see the advantage of linking the destiny of an objective whose path is already certain to the that of an objective that is still in its early stages and thus less sure. Moreover, it is more prudent and instructive to manipulate one variable at a time. It would be such a shame further to delay a destiny already sadly retarded, ideal and ineluctable as it may be, to wait for the achievement of a destiny which is much more vague.

Stevan Harnad

More thoughts on subversion

I have read and, indeed heard, Stevan's post-Gutenberg anomaly with its selfsame nine steps to frustration and its 'subversive proposal' on several occasions. We have even had a small e-mail discussion on the latter to do with authority and version control (and how the poor researcher – or his mother! – is supposed to decide which version is the article of record, the definitive version to cite), although I do not think my points were ever really answered by Stevan. But, be that as it may, there is clearly an anomaly surrounding journal charging that publishers, libraries and, to a lesser extent, authors have to face and address.

Maybe I am too timid or stick-in-the-mud to attempt the self-archiving route or maybe I just cannot believe that there is any point. Will such a recourse really stop publishers in their tracks? I doubt it – there is too much invested in the print publishing model. Certainly, I agree, universities are finding that they can afford fewer and fewer journal subscriptions (and I suppose this might suggest insufficient funds to begin and maintain an e-print archive) – this is beyond question – but, as I have said elsewhere in these discussions, work needs to be done at the library – publisher interface.

The gradual move to electronic journals offers a unique opportunity that is so far being largely squandered. There were in 1999, according to one source, over 10,000 e-journals available – over 1.2 million issues or 21 million articles but 66 per cent of publishers then offered free electronic access with print subscriptions and only 47 per cent of publishers sold the electronic version on its own – 53 per cent were still only bundling it with print.

We – meaning publishers and librarians, both – seem largely unable to move beyond the paper-based model despite waxing lyrical over added value, access and reduced shelf-storage and vandalism. Why do journals still have volumes and issues? Why has some enterprising publisher not taken the electronic bull by its virtual horns and developed a just-for-you journal that lands on my electronic desktop replete with only and all the day's articles that will interest me? The answer I suspect is the one that might ultimately be responsible for Stevan's subversive proposal – they cannot come up with a pricing model that will satisfy all parties.

Let me offer, not a subversive but a surprising, proposal. Journal aggregators such as Ingenta could, instead of bundling journals in a way that frequently means university libraries have to subscribe to journals they neither need or want in order to acquire those that they do (a license that, incidentally, removes collection development decisions from the librarians best able to take them), offer just-for-you, personalised e-journals to academics. The SDI model is not new, after all! The scholarly, peer-review process remains in the hands of the journal publishers who would still be able to sell subscriptions but an alternative revenue stream is provided for publishers while readers are better served.

The model could largely free university libraries from their huge journal budgets, leave in place the basis of scholarly publishing, and provide a better, faster, more targeted service to readers. It is radically different in approach and will exercise publishers' minds in developing an acceptable costing and profit model. There are also other issues to be dealt with – such as the anomalous position (in the UK, at least) of value-added tax which is levied on electronic but not print publications, causing the bundling of print and electronic versions as a way to avoid it. Some sort of parameters would need to be set up to prevent a library from creating a profile so broad in scope that it would, for one license fee, capture every article printed!

So let's not get locked into the e-print archive as being the only solution. Publishers and libraries are two links in the same information chain; surely it is not beyond the wit of man to come up with an economically-viable and -acceptable delivery model?

Chris Armstrong

New subversion or old wine in new bottles?

The anomaly, in my view, is that journals are charging readers and their institutions anything at all for access to the author's give-away work. It is not that journal publishers cannot and should not sell products that add value to the author's research, be they on-paper texts or on-line texts. But as the author does not seek or get royalties or fees for his text – unlike book-authors or journalists – and instead seeks as many readers/users as possible, so as to maximize the uptake and hence the impact of the research, there is no longer any need or justification to hold the on-line refereed research reports themselves hostage to those add-ons and their access tolls. They can and should be sold as options (and I for one am not particularly interested in the price charged – as long as the no-frills on-line draft is available free for everyone).

The only non-optional element of added value provided by a refereed journal publisher is the implementation of peer review (the peers themselves review for free too). The true cost of only this essential *service* (to the author's institution) as opposed to the full cost of the optional *product* (to the reader's institution) can be amply covered out of institutional savings on their expenditures for the product (if and when demand for that drops to the point that it no longer covers the costs of the essential service of peer review) for the simple reason that the author-institutions and the reader-institutions are the same institutions.

Stevan Harnad

Harnad's distinction between give-away and non-give-away literature

Harnad is absolutely right that this distinction is valid, that it is fundamental, and that it is frequently overlooked. Authors of scholarly journals articles give them away. They don't write for money but for impact. The fact that the same scholars might write books and hope to make money from them, and the fact that most intellectual property of all kinds is produced for revenue, obscure the distinctive reality of scholarly journal literature. Authors give it away in order to advance research in their fields and to advance their careers.

Before the Internet, we needed publishers to package this give-away literature and bring it to readers. The Internet allows give-away authors to reach readers directly, making publishers unnecessary. (Publishers are unnecessary for give-away literature, even if they are still necessary for most kinds of revenue-producing literature.) Worse, publishers who stand between give-away authors and their readers, and charge money for access, do serious harm. They limit the access of authors to readers and of readers to literature, thereby obstructing both research and education. The good news is that publishers can be cut from the loop at the author's initiative through the method that Harnad calls self-archiving.

Harnad is also right that free on-line research articles can and should be peer reviewed, and that self-archiving can be implemented at every university at trivial cost and without waiting for any change of policy from legislatures or publishers.

Harnad has said all of this very well and has said it for years. I have nothing to add except that the same argument applies to give-away literature which doesn't happen to fall into the category of scholarly research literature. For example, the statutes and judicial opinions of every legal system are written and disseminated for their role in public life, not for profit. They constitute a very important type of give-away literature. The public can and should have free on-line access to them, although often it does not. The set of non-scholarly give-away literature includes corporate reports and other forms of grey literature.

In every discipline, free on-line access to journal literature is growing, though at uneven rates. Harnad was not the first to see the opportunity to make this happen, but without his clarity in analysing the issues and his energy in advocating that we seize this opportunity we would be many years further behind.

Peter Suber

Quality control and copyright, more about costs and...

After watching the phenomena that Dr Harnad describes for the last three decades, I agree with his assessment of the situation. I believe that now we have appropriate technology in place. However, I believe that most of the change must take place in the traditions of quality control and copyright.

With regard to his section on Quality-control and certification: peer review, (p. 50), would ask: What about the role of editors and scholarly societies in enforcing (a) appropriate copyright agreements and (b) refereeing and distribution services? In my opinion, editors might exert considerable influence in regard to the role of publishers. It is also my opinion that scholarly societies that contract with publishers may exert even more influence by scrutinizing contracts or composing contracts that enforce more appropriate policies.

It is also important for senior scholars to show the way, and to encourage mentees by introducing and encouraging new ways of quality control. It is senior scholars who must begin to recognize and reward publication through new and changing venues. It is senior scholars who must understand and advise junior scholars concerning appropriate publication. It is senior schoars who can afford to take the risks of publishing in the new venues so that new venues achieve elite status.

I think Dr Harnad is right to begin to attack the various issues with pragmatic responses. Another group of scholars have formed the Public Library of Science. However, I do think that Dr Harnad has neglected to consider carefully the full costs of self-archiving and insitutional costs for electronic archives. These facilities are not inexpensive. Building and maintaining appropriate interfaces and search engines are not cost free. While it is true that institutions will be free of subscription costs in the hundreds and thousands of dollars, those dollars may go quickly to information systems that will provide access to archives. The considerable shift in institutional responsibility will not happen in the wink of an eye.

Lorre Smith

A few analogies between digital scientific publishing and the new economy

These reflections are part of the debate over quality control and copyright. The debate raises essential questions about such things as organization, managing change, investments, investment returns, quality and reliability, for the project described and defended by Harnad in his article and in his subsequent clarifications.

These questions bring us to current concerns with the digital economy (or 'new economy') after the euphoria of the years 1999–2000. Harnad's position recalls, in fact, with its enthusiasm and radicalism, the arguments that fed the digital revolution and mobilized a formidable energy around projects of radical technical and social innovation, extending from the social sphere (communitarian initiatives) to the purely commercial sphere (the dot-com initiatives).

Yet why have there been so many abandoned projects? What lessons can we draw from these failures in order to improve the chances of success for the digital initiatives which are being pursued or started today? The subject is vast, and I shall concentrate on just a few points which seem essential to me.

What of the logic of substitution, where digital scientific publishing replaces paper scientific publishing? The digital initiatives which continue to develop in spite of the crisis are, for the most part, one of the conduits for communication and distribution amid a larger network with multiple contact points. With the exception of Yahoo!, Google, Amazon, and eBay, on-line brands do not exist, whereas off-line, well-known brands such as Tesco, SNCF or Nokia exist. By analogy, one might expect that a scientific journal would continue to play the essential role of confederation, dialogue, and reference and that innovation would occur thanks to the co-existence and complementarity between media, paper and digital, in multiple forms – a hypothesis already presented by Roberto Casati in his article. And what of the attitude toward technological innovation, where not all of us wish to realize the totality of the cycle of production by ourselves? *Empowerment* was one of the fundamental values of the digital economy. But in practice, in the digital world, to render something autonomous means to expect that one can appropriate complex techniques which, for the most part, are in full evolution and are unstable. This appropriation requires a great deal of personal investment and strong motivation. These values are not shared by the vast majority of the population which has a very pragmatic and conservative attitude vis-à-vis the new technologies. Another reason for the failure of the first wave of digital services and tools was precisely the fact that they were conceived by technologists for conservative pragmatists. Here, I would like to recall that the right level of autonomy cannot a priori be defined in only one way without running the risk of alienating an important proportion of its potential users from the innovative project.

Finally, in today's Internet industry the law of Return on Investment applies. Projects may be less ambitious, but their chances of success are so much greater. As for costs, the debates cited above have allowed us to push the analysis of required investments further, at least as concerns editorial and archival work. As for benefits, it is important to be equipped with more precise measures to justify the project to a third party: not only in terms of the volume of scientific information exchanged, but also the impact on communication and scientific research along the model of measures of performance of electronic business sites.

Francesco Cara

4
Transmitting, Reacting, Remembering: Journalism on the Internet

Bruno Patino

The stock market crash of the new economy in April 2000 silenced all those people who had proclaimed the Internet as the future of all things good and cleared the way for the detractors of the network. As far as the latter are concerned, the global network promotes a world without intermediaries and therefore without mediators. A mere mouse click is all that separates information and its final destination. Furthermore, the deluge of contents of all kinds being published in electronic media favours short texts and even breeds illiteracy. Finally, digital technology represents a mix of genres, the end of barriers separating information from commerce, communication, advertising or rumour. According to these analyses, multimedia journalists are accomplices and victims of a system which is leading them into a state of disorientation, and to the collapse of their profession.

Journalism schools, on the other hand, at first adopted a self-referential definition: a multimedia journalist is a journalist who has mastered the technical tools of multimedia. This tautology has the advantage of being simple (the schools are required only to teach a little about network computer use as a specialization in the final year), but it is far from satisfactory: the whole of society masters the tools in question. It is not so difficult to put a well-presented and fairly well written personal page on line.

The fact that the media have been present on the Internet for several years requires that we take a closer look at these critical analyses and that we go beyond simple technical definitions. Yes, there is a form of journalism which is specific to the Internet. This is because firstly, the Web, having started off as a pipeline, has become a part of the media. It is a medium with its own dynamics and issues. Secondly, it is because in order to assert itself, Internet journalism has to conquer a temporal order under threat from the very logic of the network, while a spatial order never before known to journalism is opening up before it – a space whose limits will be defined by journalism itself.

Internet: from pipeline to medium

The Internet is probably unique in that, for the first time, a new medium was created without generating a new language. It is true that the global network has been built on specific computing protocols. However, for the user, these protocols are unseen and the available content appears in a format which is already familiar; it is mostly in written, at times in audiovisual form. This has no doubt facilitated the spread of the Internet: while the global network became a reality, multimedia language remained at best an aspiration.

The network as a broadcasting tool

The use of an already known language encouraged all the traditional media to try their luck on the Web. At first many newspapers considered the Internet as a supplementary means of circulation. Or rather, as an unexpected economic boost: thanks to the decentralized multiplication of phone lines, the traditional production process of 'manufacture first, then distribute', with its heavy industrial constraints, came to be replaced by a lighter post-industrial order where distribution came first and local-ized manufacture followed, on small digital machines. The Internet was a source of savings for the press groups and promised to be a goldmine for journalists: newspapers had to negotiate royalty agreements with their editorial staff. This confirmed, once again, the nature of the World Wide Web as a distribution tool, or legally speaking, as an instrument for the secondary use of contents.

Moreover, the type of file initially used on the Web was pdf, a format which accurately reproduced the image of the page, and the articles which compose it on the screen. Thus pdf preserves both the editorial fiction of the newspaper as a unitary collection of digital files, and the legal notion of collective work. Everything changed, but everything remained the same: at a time when the tools of distribution were increasing, digitalization would guarantee the permanence of the content. The Internet would be the spearhead of an army of digital media to come: second-, then third-generation telephony, personal organizers, mobile Internet, interactive television, and so on. It was all in the name of convergence, the promised land of twenty-first century publishers. But this promised land turned out to be, for the most part, a source of income for industry. In fact one axiom has emerged out of the practices of the last few years: the convergence of media leads to the divergence of contents.

The Internet as a medium

Little by little the Internet has generated its own logic, its own relationship with time and space. The Web remains a means of distributing information, but it has now become a medium *per se*. This shift has come about thanks to the establishment of a mode of consumption on the Internet, which differs from that of the medium of origin. In France, the average reading time for a daily newspaper is somewhere between 25 and 35 minutes. The time spent on a newspaper website is four times less: 6 to 9 minutes on average. Leafing through a newspaper allows one to have an overall view of its content. Reading follows. On a newspaper website, the gastronomical tour is replaced by the day's menu. Articles have to be 'one or two clicks away' from the home page in order to be read; the surfer only 'passes' through five or six pages on average when consulting the site, which allows for the reading of three articles at best – often related to one another. In short, one does not consult a newspaper website in the same way as one reads a paper. The consumption of information on a website is quick and fragmentary, and most of the time sedentary. With a newspaper it is slower; it yields an overall picture and is often nomadic. Older people have stuck with newspapers while the younger generation seems naturally attracted towards websites.

This renders the whole debate about the 'cannibalization' of newspapers by the Internet obsolete. Or at least pointless. Strictly speaking, there is no such thing as the automatic substitution of a newspaper by its website. Rather, there is one mode of consumption which, for younger generations, is more natural than the other. To put it more bluntly, one can be quite certain that if the French daily *Le Monde* were to close its Internet site it would not significantly increase the sales of its printed newspaper. On the contrary, it would prompt some surfers to shift to the website of another daily. However, it seems that there is reason to hope that the presence of *Le Monde* on the Internet makes it easier for surfers to get used to the idea of reading a daily newspaper.

Media dynamics: flow and index

A newspaper is consumed differently on the Internet, by different people, and so has to find its own dynamic. The World Wide Web does not yet merge the world's languages, but it has created a merged mode for the organization of contents. As a permanently changing medium, it forces information to maintain an uninterrupted flow, on the model of press agency wires. As it is constructed in database form, structured by hypertext links and presented in a visual form, it allows for infinite indexation. As a result, each existing medium has to adopt a new form of organization. The climactic rush of all media to the novelty element illustrates this in a paradoxical way: television and radio, two flow medias, fell into the trap of excessive indexation in the first versions of their websites, with a proliferation of links. Conversely, the written press, well versed in the practice of presenting contents menus, tended to opt for first generation sites which resembled agency wires. Today, sites mix both approaches and the journalists working on them are discovering a way of thinking specific to multimedia, which has given birth to a specific journalistic know-how. The medium has created its own brand of journalism. And, in a circular way, it is the journalism that is constructing the medium.

Journalism as a defining element of the medium

Over the past few months, criticism of the media has grown forceful. Critics close to Pierre Bourdieu have resurrected the theories of Karl Kraus. Kraus founded *Le Flambeau* at the beginning of the last century, with the intention of attacking all newspapers of the time. The modernized version goes roughly as follows: 'honest and respectable' journalism is under threat from a double phenomenon: one, the ongoing process of media concentration within an increasingly small number of media groups (the phenomenon of limited choice); and second, the standardization of the emerging message as a result both of advertising requirements and the development of marketing techniques (the phenomenon of profitability). On this view, concentration and standardization are two elements of a self-repeating matrix whose dynamic is ensured by the market and by its economic necessities. After a while, demand – in other words, the reading public – becomes standardized, the media caters for the masses and thereby makes way for increased concentration, which in turn leads to increased standardization, and so on and so forth. Supply becomes more and more powerful. The resurgence of Karl Kraus's theories while the network is expanding in all directions is paradoxical, to say the least. Indeed, the Internet seems to have inverted the problem of access to the medium. Where concentration was once the locus of fears, the phenomenon of proliferation on the Web is now the cause of puzzlement.

Concentration, that is to say limited choice, results from a physical barrier. In the case of the press, the barrier is the industrial nature of production; for analog television, it is the limitations of terrestrial frequencies. By dividing the cost of television broadcasting by six, through satellites, or by enabling the reversal of the relationship between manufacture and distribution for the press, digital technology may certainly have made the barriers less insurmountable. But the Internet has literally made them explode. Creating and distributing are now within everyone's reach. Admittedly not in the same conditions: the ability to manufacture and distribute in bulk is only a real possibility for a limited number of players (depending on management systems and bandwidth), but, generally speaking, anyone who wishes to have a personal Web page, accessible from any point on the planet that is connected, can do so. The URL address and the referencing technology have a formidable ability to equalize powerful and individual players.

Given all this, how is it possible to differentiate an Internet media from another type of site? One might perhaps be forced to admit, in the end, that the Internet really constitutes a parallel world in which all kinds of things coexist: supermarkets, databases, slanderous tracts, rumours as well as information media bearing the work of editorial teams made up of journalists. The fact that all manifestations of this world are accessible in the same way is certainly cause for concern: we all require reference points to reassure ourselves about the nature of the messages we receive and therefore about the medium we are consuming. Such reassurance is perhaps provided by the printed nature of the press, by the presence of this printed press at specific outlets, by the access to a frequency resulting from a state decision, by the link between an object and a form of technology: a television set, for instance, is used to receive only television programmes. The computer is an instrument, which has no fixed identity. It is illusory to believe that messages alone are capable of asserting their nature on the Web.

On the other hand, identities cannot be enforced: the idea of an imprimatur, a hallmark establishing a typology of websites, is vain, because it profoundly contradicts the originally decentralized nature of the network. The mission that certain portals have undertaken, consisting in orienting surfers towards sites which they have already classified, as in a 'marshalling yard', resembles the creation of reference points. But their ambiguity, and the commercial orientation of some of the links proposed, mean that they are imperfect tools and indeed are perceived as such by their clients. In the end, the reference points are more often than not brands already familiar to surfers, known for their original activities. The more credible the original media, the more credible their website will be – the more credible it *has* to be, one might even say. Yet these brands are the product of a slow construction process which, for the newspapers, is linked to years of work by constantly renewed editorial teams.

As for the greatly feared phenomenon of standardization, said to result from the capacity of suppliers to impose what customers must read, hear and see, today it seems likely to disappear. The inward spiral has given way to an outward spiral and power has shifted from supply to a part of demand. For the media, the challenge no longer lies in the ability to respond to demand: across all media, technical instruments of personalization select the elements that correspond to the expectations of surfers. Little by little, surfers 'manufacture' their own media content, focusing either on single themes ('I only want sports articles') or on a selection from several sites ('give me all the front page titles of the following media'). The challenge therefore lies in the ability to develop an offer which stands out, in quality and in depth, from others. To take an example, the dispatches from Agence France-Presse (the French Press Agency) are now present on several French websites. The consequence is that these dispatches have become what economists call a commodity, a basic product without any great value. Audience dynamics illustrate this, as they did notably on September 11, 2001: it is in-depth analysis and quality which make a site stand out and make it succeed. For news sites, this comes down to the work done by journalists and an editorial team capable of standing out from the rest. Since sites are all equally accessible through their website addresses, the resulting state of profusion requires the surfer to distinguish between journalists and to appreciate added value. Just as journalism has made it necessary to avoid mixing genres, it is again journalism which is the solution to the news sites' quests to establish their own identities.

The conquest of time

Where does it come from then, this fear that one can feel lurking in the background? It stems from a vague feeling, a mixture of disbelief and anxiety: the fear of seeing the medium establishing itself at the expense of the mediator, and the digital leviathan devouring the people who feed it every day and make it grow – it is the fear of a 'cannibal universe'.

Now that the economic bubble has burst, now that the digital revolution has been accepted and the media adopted, theories flourishing in the dusk of the new economy limit the Internet to 'a simple process of information acceleration'. Quite. But even if it were only that, are people aware of the scope of implications generated by 'a simple process of information acceleration'? Speaking of the subject we are concerned with here alone, the consequences are immense: the acceleration has compressed the time which journalists can make use of. These memorialists of the ephemeral now fear becoming mere purveyors of the instantaneous.

To do their jobs, journalists start from a more or less raw body of data (dispatches, interviews, reading material, etc.) to which they bring the added value of their knowledge and their talent for manipulating language. From the 'groundwork' of the dispatch – lightweight creation – to the report – heavyweight creation – being a journalist also means fitting into a production process whose endpoint is the transformation of various data into information – all of which takes place within a mechanism of organized collective intelligence. Thus, a newspaper is designed – during editorial meetings – and is 'put to bed' – when the editorial team meets again – within one whole unit of time and space. The 'putting to bed' highlights two aspects that are an integral part of the identity of a newspaper: production by batch and the inviolability of the written word. This, in part, defines the job of the print journalist.

All the important news at the time of publication: such is, in a simplified form, the mission of a printed newspaper. The consequence that follows from this is quite clear: it matters little when the daily paper is in fact read, what counts is when it is made available to buyers, notably in the newsstands. And so, for the journalists who create it, what counts is the moment when the clock is stopped and when the items, like train passengers, wait for the one and only departure time. The train passengers who have gotten on early (the so-called 'cold' pages, that is to say the items written and prepared first) will arrive at the same time as those that got on the train at the last moment (the 'hot' pages of the last hours).

The mission of a news website, as taken on by the site of *Le Monde*, is to give 'all the important news at the moment of connection'. Putting the paper to bed, as such, does not exist; or else it is a permanent process, which is the same thing. The impetus has changed sides. Ideally the media have to have some new relevance at every 'request' (that is the technical term) made by the surfer, and update its information every second. Therefore it is the surfer who determines the moment at which the medium has to be relevant. One can easily understand the dizziness that this induces in many people. How is it possible to organize a time which no longer exists? How can one work when there is no longer an answer to the question: 'When does that have to be ready?' How can one organize a flow of information when one cannot control the person who sets it in motion?

If the flow takes everything in its path, 'multimedia' journalists will, for their part, be paralysed by this excess of movement. They will be glued to their chairs, in front of their computer screens, permanently editing a site without having the leisure to think about its organization, in a race against time which, little by little, will put his very mission in danger. It is a danger familiar to television channels broadcasting non-stop news, such as CNN. They are well versed in this activity, but the race for up-to-the minute news is a new pitfall for daily newspapers who only experience it, at worst, once a day. To succumb to this race entails admitting the disappearance of journalists' usable time; it is to accept that their role as monitoring authorities has been abandoned and, in the long term, it is to jeopardize the credibility of the media in which they exercise their profession. Not paying any attention to it amounts to denying the specificity of the Internet as a medium, and therefore to stifling the development of a journalism which is close to its medium. It is a strange paradox. Today, so it seems to me, we only manage this paradox through hit and miss.

Managing permanent flow without being overwhelmed

The Web provides journalists with a medium in which to exercise their profession. It remains for them to conquer a time for their activity, through publishing methods. The idea of elaborating a 'programme schedule', setting up appointments, such as is the case in radio and television, comes up against the problem of geographical limits and the condensed nature of the consultation time. Regardless of what one thinks of a programme schedule, it corresponds to mass behaviour patterns and therefore to a time zone. Given its planetary nature, the Web does not address a single body of people doing the same thing at the same time. Over 40 per cent of connections to a site such as *Le Monde* are from abroad. The rate is close to 60 per cent for *El Pais*. Simply creating a programme schedule is not a solution. At best it is just an approximation: a necessary one, for it artificially recreates a 'publishing' time, which is alone capable of generating the process of collective intelligence required for the identity of a medium. Yet it is not sufficient, for it cannot omit the principle of permanent updating. The solution chosen by *Le Monde* was to create several daily editions (at least three) in order to give the editorial team the chance to think about the general organization of the website and the ordering of information and to constantly update these editions without necessarily changing the organization. It is one solution among many; but it does not reestablish the journalistic signposts dispersed by the Internet. For the impact of time directly affects the raw material that press journalists work with.

The end of the inviolability of the written word

By putting an end to the correlation between writing and the printed word, a correlation which participated in conferring its sacred status on the book, the Web has shattered the inviolability of the written text which from now on can, and perhaps must, constantly evolve. This might transform our civilization. On an infinitely more anecdotal but also more immediate level, the working methods of journalists have already been utterly changed.

A text written by a journalist for a daily newspaper is transformed into an article after having gone through a process which combines correction, re-reading and validation. Once the pass for press is given the text is no longer touched: it is sent to publication and then to the printing press. The presence of a signature clearly shows that there is an author, for evermore, of a piece of writing whose life span will be that of the medium it is hosted by. In a daily newspaper, articles are like bricks stacked together.

The Internet transforms these bricks into modeling clay. The paradox of a website stemming from the written press is that it often contains finished products (articles which have already been granted pass for press) and can in theory thrust them into a process of infinite modification. Some American sites illustrate this well: the written articles appearing on them are constantly updated, even in the body of the text itself, provided the modifications are highlighted by a particular graphic code (parentheses, italics or bold). Two, three or even four people can make changes to the one text, updating, modifying and cutting it as time passes, depending on the incoming news. The text becomes magma-like, no longer meant to ever solidify. Little by little, the notion of the single author fades away.

This trend is no doubt inevitable. It is, moreover, already taken for granted within the dreams of multi-platform editorial teams imagining a central editorial team that 'dispatches' a single content to numerous media. It is XML that makes such organization technically possible and not the nature of journalistic work, which is not limited to publishing activities, even if, in the digital world, the task of adapting is becoming increasingly important. Today, to divide work between information 'producers' (independent from any medium) and information 'adaptors' (who modify the matrix in order to make it fit with the intended medium) is a journalistic nightmare sustained by a technological utopia. Multimedia journalists probably have to be pragmatic and combine the two functions, as needs dictate: creating, editing or adapting in order to synthesize.

Instant and memory

To limit journalism to the temporal constraint of updating information, however, would be to neglect the immense spatial scope available to journalistic work. The Internet is not just the medium of the instantaneous, it is also that of memory. Increasingly, people consult sites in order to 'catch up' with news when they have missed out on a juncture in the unfolding of events. The emergence of special reports, summaries and reference material (chronologies, related documents, biographies, bibliographies and contextual information), made possible by the infinite space available on the Web, and so the absence of physical constraints (such as pagination in the case of the written press, or time slots in the case of radio and television), no doubt highlight another characteristic of the Internet as a medium: the development of all subjects according to a double temporality, the instantaneous and the recapitulatory (we return to the flow and the index). The events of September 11, 2001 illustrated the extent to which synthesis was necessary on the Internet. *The New York Times* and CNN produced special reports, which were astounding for their quality, their wealth of information and their synthetic grasp. In this activity it is important to avoid piling up items on a single subject, and to put the subject in perspective instead, by readapting all the items. This is where multimedia comes into its own: it makes it possible to combine different languages (writing, animation and audiovisual) in such a way that they are mutually complementary.

Disseminating, reacting, remembering

This is a difficult and onerous exercise, which must be carried out by editorial teams that are often small in size and still at a learning stage. But the point here is that, now that the Internet has become part of the media, it requires journalists who are trained in the exercise of constantly switching between permanently updating information and putting the past in perspective, in a global approach to their medium. Internet journalists could be allocated to the areas they originally came from. However, grouping according to theme, although it has a certain logic, in the long run risks limiting the website to the role of a secondary tool for the circulation of information. On the other hand, to organize the groupings according to a temporal logic would, certainly, separate editorial teams, but it would also bring to the fore both the possibilities of the new medium and, paradoxically, the interactions between the original medium and its digital progeny. The editorial team of a newspaper's website has to exist according to three different rhythms: that of its original medium (a daily newspaper for example, with the construction that is so particular to it); that of permanent updating; and that of the time of synthesis or of memory. This requires specific and innovative types of organization, which cannot take shape without the assistance of the original medium and the awareness of the difference in working methods. In this sense, the creation of interface services seems a fruitful one. Disseminating, reacting, and remembering: this sums up the daily task faced by journalists on the Internet and the original nature of their work.

Discussion

The role of today's newspapers in the future Web 'press'

The question I would like to pose to Bruno Patino is similar to the one I addressed to Stevan Harnad: From the moment when certain functions of information and analysis that fill the newspapers can be carried out by the Web without the investments, logistical problems, etc. linked to the printing and distribution of paper, from the moment when there is a public for these new sorts of publications, do you think that traditional newspapers will remain the principal entrepreneurs of the Web 'press' for long? It is clear that they are in the best position from the start because of their know-how, reputations and staffs. But does this not imply a risk of conflict of interests, of the bridling of innovation by the primary concern to preserve the interests of the paper newspaper? Is not the most likely scenario that we begin – we are in the thick of this – with newspaper websites that move away from the paper model, but not to the extent that the interests of the paper newspaper are not longer served; and then – this is beginning – an increasing number of purely Web newspapers and magazines (like *Salon.com*) appear which can move as far away as they like from the initial models. And beyond this, the need or desire for information, first-hand accounts, analyses, and debates could give rise to innovative projects which, for the most part, we have yet to imagine, and which will be related to rather than resemble what we currently refer to as newspapers and magazines (and this being the case whether or not current forms survive.)

Dan Sperber

May the best man win

My response to Dan Sperber is as follows. For the traditional press, the Net is indeed what is called 'disruptive', that is to say, it forces a modification of the criteria of its traditional activities. A number of newspapers have spent a long time improving the performance of their industrial equipment so as to maintain their competitiveness. The quality of printing, the shortening of the chain between 'putting to bed' and home delivery, the quality of distribution which is increasingly shouldered by the press itself, have been the key factors for success that appeared to be barriers to the entry of new competitors. The stronger one was in these domains, the more of a difference one could make editorially and the more solid one's competitive position appeared to be. In theory, the Internet could destroy these givens and thus provoke an internal over-cautiousness in the press, in terms of both analyses and investments. There is a sense of 'DYB' '(destroy your business)' which is always a difficult undertaking. Nowhere is it written that every newspaper will be able to make the transition. Nor is it any more certain, thank goodness, that they are bound to disappear: in the first place, because the Internet allows them to bypass two 'walls' that they have been up against for several decades: an inability to renew their readership, and the physical constraints of distribution, which has difficulty reaching a readership that is increasingly less unified geographically. The Internet did not create these problems, on the contrary, it has produced tools to resolve them; readership renewal has already occurred thanks to the Web: under-25s find it 'legitimate' to get their news this way. Moreover, the Internet allows for easy distribution: if we think about the experience of the *New York Times* in the 1990s, which launched the *New York Times* by fax in order to reach a distant readership that could, henceforth, watch CNN, and thus found it of little use to read a newspaper that arrived with several days' delay. The Internet thus brings solutions to these – essentially logistical – problems. By focusing the debate around this theme (internal conservatism/open possibilities), there is a risk that it will leave unexploited the theme of the novelty of the medium. But there again, each newspaper must explore this new frontier itself, faced with new arrivals confronted with the same set of problems... The past brings its know-how and conservatism, just as it fosters an intuitive presence among web users. The new actors will perhaps have the privilege of being better adapted to the new world... without being certain that they will all survive. Adaptation or birth, the debate is open for these two categories.

Bruno Patino

The best or the profitable?

In Bruno Patino's paper as well as in the response he just gave I am struck by the absence of references to financial profits. It seems to me that the successive on-line versions of *Le Monde* can also (and above all) be explained by the search, which remains unsuccessful today, for a return on investments. The case of this newspaper is all the more interesting since it was the first to commercialize its archives on the Internet. Should this not lead us to think that the truly new profession of on-line journalist will exist only when entrepreneurs and eventually, journalists, will have invented (if the day should come) a new world of financing for on-line newspapers (as was the case for the invention of advertising in its day)? For the moment, if I understand it correctly, the on-line version of *Le Monde* is there to sell the paper version. If this function endures, on-line journalists will be, first and foremost, the foils of their paper colleagues, no?

This does not mean that current attempts are not fascinating to watch and full of lessons to be drawn, and from this standpoint, Bruno Patino's paper is edifying. But they are due, in my opinion, to the natural experimentation of any media in search of itself.

Jean-Michel Salaün

The birth of a new genre?

Bruno Patino discusses what seem to be the teething problems of what is a recently born 'genre', Internet journalism. These teething problems, which he identifies in general as a tension between the need to conserve the identity of the journalistic profession and the need to maximize the potential of the Web, are related to a view of the Web as offering nothing but a logistical support for journalism. From the reader's point of view, it is true that it has become vital for many to be able to access the newspapers of any country at any time, at the click of a button, to search them by keyword or go straight to the wanted theme. In this sense, the reader might not really perceive in what way Internet has changed the nature, rather than just the ease of access, of newspapers and magazines.

Patino argues persuasively that the profession must wake up to its new role and to the speeding-up of communication. Both Dan Sperber and Jean-Michel Salaün wonder how this wake-up call can proceed in a situation where internet editions are, in financial terms, supported by the print version and used as showcases for it. It is also the case, I think, that many people still prefer the materiality, the crispness of a print newspaper, as well as the ability to turn pages, browse, have an overview of a number of articles spread out on one page. Yet, readers' habits are also changing, faster in the younger generations, but also quite surely in the overall population. Could it be that the teething problems of this new genre also have something to do with the contradictory needs of readers who want, on the one hand, up-to-the-minute information along with traditional format and editorial quality, and on the other, magazine-style in-depth analysis now accessible in new formats and in multimedia? This might be a question for Bruno Patino as well as for any other journalist who has had to wonder about the role to give the website of their paper or magazine.

Noga Arikha

Babbling?

Bruno Patino's paper has the great merit of presenting an analysis of Internet journalism starting from a practical knowledge of the current situation and of certain questions which are particularly for the journalist. He recognizes from the start that what we have here is new medium with its own dynamic and problems.

Does not one of the questions he brings up concern precisely the evolution not only of the journalist of the written newspaper, but also that of information itself?

We have managed to link information to events with an increasingly rapid temporal rhythm, appropriated from the media (daily for newspapers, hourly for radio, etc.) The Internet submits these rhythms to the pressure of instantaneousness with the possibility of continual and immediate access to what is happening on the planet.

Patino indeed underscores the fact that the constant proliferation of information only reinforces the need for analysis and synthesis required to understand it. One could thus imagine an evolution of the functions of the media in terms of information.

But above all, won't the Internet raise the fundamental question as to the very nature of information? Until now, information was conceived as a product manufactured by experts and distributed to consumer-clients according to the classic pyramid model. And the traditional media have difficulty delivering any other type of information (letters from readers, questionnaires with binary responses, or open lines on radio programmes do not really alter this reality).

Won't the new question raised by the Internet and its multiple networks lead to a radically different concept of information, based on interactivity?

Patino is correct in underscoring that the Internet has already altered journalistic practices. The forums proposed by certain newspapers remain in their infancy but are forging a new path.

Couldn't we imagine that one of the potential avenues opened by the Internet is precisely the opening up the possibility of real interactive debates on subjects that could be initiated by the newspapers? We could thus come up with scenarios where the journalist would open the debates based on an article that would serve as 'modeling clay' and give rise to a form of subsequent, open, accessible synthesis very different from a printed article. He would become one expert among many in the 'elaboration of information'.

Interactivity will notably allow us to raise certain questions that the media – for diverse reasons of limitation – could leave in the shadows or which are obscured by the diversity of view-points: whether it be, for example, the crash of an Airbus in New York left curiously unexplained, or the stakes of the war in Irak or the situation in the Middle East . . .

There are still very few newspapers open to foreign journalists on a regular basis. Is it not conceivable that on the Internet, a journalist, a professor, or an expert might hold a forum at specified times, leading thus to a new type of information . . . interactive information?

Are we still talking about a medium maintained or attached to a written newspaper? According to what economic logic?

Jean Tardif

Slow food for thought

According to Patino, on-line newspapers develop a dual approach to content: quick coverage of what's news (with a risk of inaccuracies), and in-depth analyses in the form of 'dossiers' (with a risk of loss of attention span). This duality reflects the two-speed nature of printed content: daily newspapers and weekly magazines. We always felt that that newspapers may be a bit too quick, and magazines a bit too slow. I wonder if there is room for an intermediate product: the day-after-the-day-after on-line journal. It covers the facts of the day before the day before. It reports about those facts and about some of the comments made upon them on the day before. It has much more accurate coverage – one day can make all the difference of the world – and a wider perspective. Is there room for such a product? I think there is. People quite often use the information they find in journals as conversational prompts. They inscribe bits and pieces of know-ledge gathered from reading a newspaper into their conversations with friends. Now, it does not happen often that one meets and discusses on a daily basis. If one is not compelled to keep a constant update of one's knowledge of what's news, one may have a 'competitive edge' in conversation if the information at one's disposal is framed in a wider context.

Roberto Casati

Virtuality and notoriety

Roberto's idea that an 'intermediate product' half-way between daily and weekly would be appropriate and useful on the Internet seems a good one. *Slate* is a good example of a virtual publication that gets noticed and quoted. And indeed, the key to the success of any site of that kind is exactly this: it has to be noticed. It is still very hard for most people to think of Internet publications as noticeable objects, as effective things, endowed with any weight or consequence. Patino mentions in his text exactly this difficulty of knowing how to approach and handle information that is encoded within one unique, undifferentiated machine. Somehow the sense of importance, of something mattering, gets lost. There is still more edge in saying 'Did you see that piece by so-and-so in *The New Yorker?*' than in saying, 'Did you see that piece in *Slate?*', which for the moment is striking only because, in the end, rather unusual. Authors have affiliations with magazines; an author's fame bounces off the magazine's fame, and vice versa. This is the kind of editorial home one has to create on-line if people are to feel as glad to 'go to' an on-line magazine website as they are to receive or buy printed publications. It takes time to build a reputable editorial home. If the on-line magazine eventually finds its role – and Roberto's description of what this putative role could be is a convincing one – then it will coexist with print ones, perhaps on an equal footing. Meanwhile, the websites of print magazines can be places of contacts, exchange and storage; the indexed archiving of all *New York Review of Books* articles on their website is the best example of how useful this technology is to the diffusion and conservation of good writing and strong, noticeable ideas.

Noga Arikha

5
The Future of the Internet: A Conversation

Theodore Zeldin (interviewed by Gloria Origgi)

Theodore Zeldin: I prefer to have a conversation, rather than write a learned article. I am glad you have agreed, even though most of the contributors to your project have chosen to perpetuate the tradition of the academic paper and the enunciation of opinions to a seminar, except that the audience is invisible. How would that fit in with what you personally wish to achieve by your experiment?

Gloria Origgi: The idea is to throw a new light on the transformation of texts by the Internet, by developing at once an object of study and a means for the study of this change – a kind of self-referential object. My aim was not to invite Internet experts to give their opinions, but rather to have a brainstorm with an heterogeneous group of people in order to try to create this new object.

TZ: I agree. Many people have a purpose that goes beyond the search for knowledge. They are searching for new kinds of contact. In the past, it was common for people to believe that their ambition should be either to obtain power, or to accumulate knowledge. But I believe that most humans are searching for lovers, searching for friends, searching for gurus, searching for colleagues who are not bores, people with whom they really wish to work. The Internet may at first sight appear to be an ideal instrument to enable one to make contact with people to whom one has not been able to find paths in the past; but there are many obstacles. If I had merely conversed with you on the Internet – if you sent me questions, and I sent you answers – the result could quite easily be little different from a conventional scholastic exercise.

GO: In one way this is true, but we would also have had alternatives on the Internet, which makes possible a synchronic communication we do

87

not have with other means of written communication – like chat-rooms, for instance. It happens that we are not using chat-room facilities in this symposium; when we were conceiving the project, we did think of using synchronic communication, but then we opted for a more, let us say, academic format that preserves distances. But the point is that we have the possibility of synchronicity, and that is new.

TZ: Yes but we must be aware of the obstacles, as well as of the new opportunities. If you accept that our first purpose is to discover and make satisfying contacts with other people, it is true that the Internet, through the anonymity which it offers, does create the possibility of getting over the stereotypes which cloud our perceptions when we see people face to face. When I look at you, I may form ideas about who you are simply from your appearance. When I get e-mails on the Internet, they do not necessarily tell me who the senders are, what successes or failures they have endured, what country they inhabit, what gender or colour they are, who their fathers are. To that extent the Internet is a great destroyer of prejudice. We can start a different kind of conversation on that basis.

But there are limitations. The fact that I cannot see you means that I cannot communicate with you as I might if I could see you. I cannot get the hints which you give by nodding or looking or smiling. I therefore cannot get an encouragement to continue in a particular line of thought; I cannot see when my ideas are meeting a warm acceptance, or a mild agreement, or a cold rejection. Discussions on the Internet, even in chat-rooms, are not so simple. A physical presence both adds and substracts. We are inventing a new kind of contact with limitations we must be aware of. It is valuable, in the sense that on the Internet, you have more choice as to whether to reveal the fears or handicaps that trouble you and that might be more obvious in face to face meetings. Since we are all in some way handicapped, the Internet encourages us to talk without being held back by at least some of our inhibitions. This is a very important form of liberation.

GO: Yes, it is indeed an important form of liberation, and in a double sense, as you note: there are new limitations and new possibilities. It is true that e-mail communication frees us, in some way, from prejudice; but can it create other ones? Is it possible that it will recreate codes or implicit conventions that can tell us something about the person who wrote the e-mail and who remains invisible to the recipient? We already do read some information into e-mail addresses – one can see whether it is a professional or a private address, a free one or not.

TZ: There are two questions there. How can we discover as much as possible about a person? And how can that person tell us what he or she wants us to know about them? The technology we have does not provide the answer. Many people need a bit of help, and sometimes a lot of encouragement, to reveal themselves. They may be shy, or not particularly articulate or fluent. When you ask them, 'Who are you?' or 'What are you?' they may have difficulty in speaking about themselves. The Internet allows people to introduce themselves without being introduced, and that can work well in some cases, but in others the absence of an intermediary or the physical presence of a reassuring third party may be felt. You know that in e-commerce, consumers have been reacting against the idea that every kind of commercial transaction can be successfully achieved solely on the Internet, and they are demanding, for example, that banks should also have physical offices to which customers may go personally in order to have the reassurance that they are dealing with a real banker who can recognize their special needs and circumstances. The Internet is only one instrument among several, and we cannot completely eliminate human, physical, face to face contact. We must not think of the Internet as a self-sufficient world, and business has now realized this.

GO: But do you think that the possibility of eliminating the human, physical dimension of transactions is specific to the Internet? You mention banks: money has become so immaterial that it can be problematic. It seems to consist mainly of figures on screens, but many people retain the sense that somehow money must have a material existence for it to be real.

TZ: Yes, many people want as complete a meeting as possible. The smell of a person, the aura of a person, the look in their eyes make possible a more complete meeting; I can get hints from the way you dress, make assumpions, which may be right or wrong.

GO: Yes. And I can cheat, go to the bank and introduce myself as a heiress without having a penny, or adopt a fictive personality in conversation, a different one for each occasion. So while it is possible to cheat in virtual communication, it is also possible to cheat or breed misunderstandings in face-to-face encounters.

TZ: The Internet has increased the possibility for lying. People have for example deliberately pretended to be of a different sex on the Internet and otherwise to be what they're not. You can look at this positively and say that they are trying on different identities and experimenting and so on. On the other hand, they are also using it for purposes they have not revealed to those with whom they have contact. Again, it is a double-sided instrument; and as with all technology, there are always disadvantages. When we invented the motor car, we did not imagine we were also inventing traffic jams.

So I suggest that the purpose of our discussion should not be the analysis of what the Internet is and what e-mails are; but rather that we should ask, what is it that we want from the Internet, how can we adapt this technology to suit our purposes today, and how can we say to the technical people: please invent this and that, because that is what we need? At the moment, they are taking the initiative in inventing new software, new possibilities. Sometimes we become the slaves of these new possibilities. So what is it that I want from the Internet?

We all get a lot of unsolicited e-mails. Readers of my books send me messages, which add to my knowledge, but answering them is enormously time-consuming. I have only twenty-four hours in a day. The question of how we select the people with whom we wish to converse is one for which we have not found a solution. The search engines invented so far, the best of which are based on a popularity scale – that is to say, the more something happens, the more it is considered to be worthy of attention – cannot help me in my search for the kind of person whose questions will be most useful to me. This is a challenge to the technical experts; they may never be able to make such searches possible, and it may be that they will have to introduce human intervention, because the Internet is in some ways like a host or hostess who introduces you into a room. Whereas a skilled hostess will say, this is a person who I am sure you would like to meet, the Internet is still chaotic. Chaos can be useful, but it is also a lottery in which one frequently does not win.

Secondly, there is the question of whom is it desirable that I should meet. From my point of view, I wish to expand my curiosity and my talents, I am not satisfied with being who I am. I have had a certain kind of education, training and experience, and that is too limited for me. So how can I add qualities which I do not have? How can new technologies be used to satisfy the need I have to change? At the moment, education and careers are usually based on the idea that you have certain talents, and that these should be developed. You will be told that you are very good at road sweeping, so you should spend your life as a road sweeper. That does not accord with the new vision that some of us are beginning to have of what a human being is. We are now in the process of creating a new kind of human being. For the first time women are in the process of obtaining full and equal status as human beings and are incorporating new elements into what it means to be human. We have educated people, arousing their curiosity and imagination in ways that cannot easily be controlled, so they cannot be satisfied with having just one identity. Rapid communication enables people to be constantly on the move, or talking to another part of the world, so they want to know about civilizations other than their own and sometimes to participate in the culture of others. This is completely different from the human being who existed in the past, who was expected to do a particular job all his life in a particular village, to obey those who were superior to him, and to be content with his lot.

Therefore, the new generation does not resemble the past one. The ideal man for women today, according to a public opinion poll, is one who does not resemble their father. This is something which has never happened before. Likewise, more and more young men say they do not wish to follow in the same job as their father. There is a growing rejection of the existing models.

So we have to create a new model. That involves much more than the acquisition of more information, which is what the Internet is at the moment focusing on. The Internet is still in the age of Bouvard and Pécuchet, whose ambition was to copy all knowledge. Now we have this vast mass of miscellaneous information made available to us, and it is very valuable; it is wonderful to be able to access it, but the question is, how can we transform this information into knowledge and wisdom for our own purposes? How can we develop our own wisdom? The Internet offers no wisdom. Wisdom should give us the capacity to create a meaning for ourself which is useful for others, which allows one to feel that our life is not purely selfish exploitation but has a value beyond that.

GO: What about the phenomenon of personal homepages? There are plenty of ordinary people who build such homepages, just to tell their story, which can be a very ordinary story: 'We have three children and today Michael went to school...' and so on. There may be a use of homepages by people in large countries like the United States or Canada, whose parents might live hundreds or even thousands of miles away from them. But in general this search for meaning through the telling of one's particular story, and the fact of finding one's own story interesting enough to tell it in the first place, is definitely a new, rather strange phenomenon.

TZ: The personal webpage is saying: I am not what I appear to be. I have individual characteristics which distinguish me from everybody else.

But the webpage is still little more than a traffic sign, an idea still in its infancy. Most people in the world are now seeking not so much money and power as respect. The webpage is a search for respect, which means it is saying: Listen to what I have to say, please recognize me as being worthy of attention. There is a vast demand for attention, and not just attention, but interest and recognition and appreciation of who I am, so that I get a justification of my existence, and in addition a feeling that I am assisting you by putting my webpage up, that you are learning something from me and your life is in some way made better by it.

I have been developing methods by which people can go beyond what they do on the Web. Personal and commercial websites are very primitive. They give very elementary details, and most people are not artists able to produce brilliant autobiographies. I am in the process of experimenting with methods by which people can produce what I call a Life Picture. They need the help of artists and writers to express all that is in them – and also to discover what is not in them and what they would like to have. Their dreams need to be included in their picture. I hope to produce examples in the near future of how this can be done, visually and in text form – taking perfectly ordinary people. I'd begun doing this, of course, in my previous writings. Now I'm systematizing it and seeing whether it can become something more general.

GO: What is your aim in doing this?

TZ: My aim is to change the world, it is very simple! That is to say, there are six billion people in the world, and they have never met. Now that we have all this technology, we each of us ought to have the chance to choose more easily who and what in this world we would like to know. We need to be given at least the menu of the feast that living should be. In every civilization so far, most people have not participated fully in what their civilization offered its most privileged members, let alone known what other civilizations have to offer. We now have new methods which enable us to do what our ancestors were not able to do. We have to give people a chance to live more fully, or at least to have a small taste of all the variety that life offers.

GO: You seem to imply that this change in how people feel able to represent themselves is a top-down process, where people still need to be helped – whereas one of the hopes of new technologies such as Internet is that a bottom-up process will now be possible. Why are you sceptical of this possibility?

TZ: I do not believe that the world is changed very fundamentally by governments or by laws which cannot easily change mentalities. Nor do I believe that the world is changed by individuals on their own. Instead of collective and individualistic explanations of change, I believe in change taking place through the encounter of two people. I think that the stimulus for the creativity which can result from the meeting of two people is coming above all from men and women talking to each other, in a way in which they have never talked before. They are revolutionizing conversation by deepening its intimacy and so producing interactions which can transform both partners. When two people have a conversation of this new kind, they create equality – not an economic equality, but an equality of respect, because they listen to each other, and in the past men and women have on the whole not listened to each other. It is in the privacy of intimate conversations that we are already beginning to change the world. Every time two people meet and establish equality of respect, they change the world. Likewise the big changes in thinking come from encounters between two people, or a succession of such encounters, from different disciplines. New physical materials are created by the meeting of molecules which never combined before.

GO: But the meeting must be a real meeting, not a virtual meeting.

TZ: Well, one has to begin in some way. A meeting, a conversation, is not just two people bumping into each other. A lot of effort, of preparation, of thought is needed, and there are further obstacles we have not yet mentioned. We have talked about the obstacles of nationality, language, gender, and so on. There is also the obstacle of profession. One of the factors which struck me very much in looking at some of these texts that you put on the Web is that they are the work of specialists. They are mainly written in the style of the learned article; that immediately limits the audience. I've been looking at the way the professions – not just academics – have been evolving in the last hundred years. The profession began as a form of liberation. You came out of your family and you found a new family in a profession. It allowed you to do things which your father did not do. But in the course of recent years, professions have entered a period of crisis, because very often you cannot any longer practise your profession as well as you would like to do.

For example, many architects spend their time working in an office of a thousand people, doing a small drawing – very few have the chance to build the dream building that would express their genius. Engineers working in aeroplane factories make pieces of machinery without knowing what their purpose is in the overall construction of the plane.

Doctors are frustrated because they can only see their patients for ten minutes and have to limit their remedies for financial reasons, and they have little influence on the social conditions which produce so much illness, they cannot do all they would like to do for the patient. Lawyers are frustrated because they feel they used to be respected as the privileged confidant of their client, and now they have become experts in tax law – or rather in one small branch of that – or experts in certain kinds of commercial negotiation. Even those in the very large, American-based organizations who have increased their incomes astronomically feel they have lost their role as 'statesmen-lawyers'. I have spoken to people at the very top of every profession, and they all say the same thing: we are not sufficiently understood, people do not know what we are, the decisions are made by someone else. In other words, professions imprison you in closed worlds.

On the Internet, one sees this being repeated. When most people go on to the Internet, they normally go to branches of it with which they feel familiar. You do not usually explore the astrophysics sites if you are not an astrophysicist and you do not go frequently to law sites if you are not a lawyer. And so, although, in some ways, the Internet offers us the opportunity to explore the whole world, in practice it focuses our attention on those areas with which we are already familiar. When I questioned school children on their browsing habits; they said they looked at sport and finance – these were the only two things they had made a habit of looking at on the Internet.

One of the great challenges of the twenty-first century is to reinvent work and the professions. Too often they narrow our outlook and use up much of our energy in frustration. We have to find ways of making work contribute to the enhancement of our being, instead of being an intellectually or morally damaging, a servitude we have to endure. Most people are part-time slaves. They do jobs which do not make them better people or the people they could be. Changing that will not create a perfect world, but it is a liberation we cannot avoid desiring. We have to ask technology to assist us. Websites which simply sell more products are not enough.

GO: Don't you think that the economic potential of the technological revolution of Internet has been overvalued, while its cultural potential has been underestimated? It was forecast as a great economic revolution, but that does not seem to have happened in a clearly defined way. If it is a revolution, it is much more clearly a cultural and social one. Is technology the cause or the effect of the social changes you are talking about?

TZ: I do not think technology changes mentalities. That is a much harder process. If you look at what previous technologies have done in the past, they have very frequently reinforced habits. For example, did the train change the way in which people related to each other? No, it encouraged them to separate themselves into first, second and third class. In first class, you did not speak to your neighbours, in third class you still maintained the popular practice of being friendly with anybody because you were not afraid of losing your status; and so the train, which was invented at a period when the bourgeoisie was concerned with distinguishing itself from others, adopted, or reinforced, the social conventions of that time. I think the business world as it is organized today is using the Internet to reinforce its corporate structure. Technology can diminish humanity. This is why I am saying that we must have clearer questions to put to the technical experts. How should they know what we need? On our computers, they are creating all sorts of tools for functions we never end up using. There is no real conversation between us the consumers and the inventors of the software. There are opportunities which we have not thought about, because we do not have a clear vision of the future. And the Internet does not produce a *vision* of the future. This is what it is important to construct.

That is why, when I say that my purpose is to change the world, I mean that it is to create my vision of the kind of world that I desire, and that I think many others might find desirable also, and at the same time to create the conditions in which other visions of the future can be invented. I am not a utopian. I know failure is part of any new endeavour. I am not searching for predictable results. But I believe that a new sort of collaboration between occupations and professions which have hitherto been self-absorbed and exclusive could open up interesting opportunities for more satisfying kinds of work.

Within each occupation, we have to ask, what do we want from it? What is it doing to us as human beings? It is not enough to learn the techniques of the job. What are the human consequences? To answer such questions, you have to have a general view of the kind of society and relationships you wish to encourage. The trouble with professional knowledge is that it does not normally focus your attention on the ultimate purpose of life.

GO: What you are saying, then, is that technology does not create a vision of society: it can be adapted to respond to our needs and wishes to change it. But you also said earlier that changes are happening: people are no longer looking for money and power but for respect and new forms of communication. So where does this change come from? Is it not a by-product of new information technologies?

TZ: I think the most important source of change is the new presence of women – this is absolutely fundamental, this is the first time it has happened in the whole of history. Secondly the new possibilities of communication and travel have opened our eyes to the existence of other kinds of people. And thirdly, we are beginning to use education not to make people compliant but the very opposite, to encourage them to be original. This is revolutionary, that everyone should have their own ideas! None of these influences can lead anywhere certain. But our working lives are still organized as a search for certainty and predictability. From the economic point of view, we need to know that we will produce five hundred shirts at the end of the day; but that is only one side of it. Though many people accept and even like routine, many others are increasingly looking for surprises, for an escape from boredom. They want to see new faces. How to make that search constructive, as opposed to distractive, that is the challenge.

I am interested in combining these diverse pressures into an adventure that gives a more exalted purpose to life. At the moment most people are finding consolation for the monotony of work in entertainment after work is done. The leisure society represents a wrong turning, because it allows us to retain old ways of working on the ground that we can recover from the damage in our leisure activities. We have got to clarify what it is that we want more profoundly, and how we can get all the accidental meetings of our lives to contribute to our search for fulfilment.

With e-mail, you are able to accumulate relationships with a large number of people, but most remain superficial. These relationships are usually on subjects which concern you at present. How can all the sides of a person which are not appearing on e-mail be connected with the others? How can one have more lives? Our economy is so organized that we are often largely what our professions make us. We have one life until we get older and then we retire. One of the originalities which women have introduced is the idea that we can have several lives. We can be several people, although that can become overwhelming too. How does one bring all those different people together into a creative cohesion, so that something more worthwhile comes out of it, and not just a series of disparate experiences? How can we become people who are more useful to others?

An interview realized by Gloria Origgi.
Transcription by Noga Arikha.

Discussion

Teaching and learning on the Internet

As someone who has worked for many years in distance education I have come to believe that the key to distance education lies in establishing relationships of a distinctive intimacy between students and teachers. I found Theodore Zeldin's comments very helpful in thinking more about this. The key idea we need to grasp is the potential of the Internet for new forms of relationship and new kinds of community, not simply in making information available 'on line'.

Rob Walker

Reply to Rob Walker

I agree with you that there is need for the introduction of a more intimate relationship into distance learning. When I was an undergraduate, my world-famous tutor never revealed anything about himself personally to me, and never showed any interest in me as an individual. His comments on the subject we studied were brilliant, but basically he was like an opera singer, singing a magnificent song about his own ideas. By contrast, the tutor I felt I could go to for 'moral' advice about what I should do with myself after graduating was the one who was always late, out of breath, apologising with explanations of the complexities of his own life, and always showing sympathy for mine. As a teacher in distance learning, do you think these two tasks, of instruction and personal advice, should be separate, and how would you develop the latter? Perhaps you have, perhaps you can think about how you could?

Theodore Zeldin

On-line education: the problem of interactivity

Rob Walker points to the potential for the Internet to create 'new forms of relationship' between educators and students. Like him, I wonder if current technology can achieve this intimacy: until on-line education (as one facet of on-line interaction) achieves the immediacy, the subtlety, of interpersonal relationships, can we hope to replicate the real-time interchange of know-ledge between students and their teachers? As long as we're using listservs or e-mail, for instance, the ideal of intimate on-line relationships is unreal-ized – as Rob Walker points out. The problem is lag-time, so to speak: the interchange of ideas cannot be facilitated through technology with built-in delays between the correspondents. It's like trying to teach through voice-mail: the connection is always deferred, never direct. E-mail will seem, some day, quite rudimentary: it will be replaced by technology that enables a mutual and instantaneous exchange of sound and video. Only then will 'new forms of relationship', unbound by geography, be possible.

Michael Ullyot

Which one is distance education ?

I would like to bring into the discussion on distance education my personal experience. I had a long experience of teaching in undergraduate programmes in Italian universities. Classes are public events in Italy: everyone can come in, sit down and listen. When I enter the classroom I can't tell who my students are and who just dropped by for a personal interest. As it is common practice in Italy, I am not informed of who will be my students, how many will attend the classes, and have a very vague idea about their background knowledge. A deferential attitude is another common feature of Italian students. If I ask them whether they have understood what I have said, silence is the most exciting reaction that I have. I can easily imagine an on-line teaching class with much more intimacy than the one that class-room teaching allows, at least in a public university in Italy:

(1) In order to participate, students have to register, to fill a form about who they are, what is their background, what are their expectations…
(2) Also, a system of self-assessment allow them (and myself) to monitor their comprehension of the themes treated and to intervene in particular cases.
(3) A forum may be set up in order to make it easier for a shy student to share his or her ideas. Voice doesn't break on the Web and you have the time to think about what you want to say.

(4) In an on-line class I can answer to questions in a better informed way, not just 'defending' myself, using my rhetorical means to avoid a criticism.

In conclusion, my classroom teaching in Italy has been very often an experience of 'distance' education!

Gloria Origgi

Reply to Gloria Origgi

I like your idea that students should provide more information about themselves. I am indeed carrying out an experiment trying to help individuals to make their own personal passports (completely different from the kind a government issues) saying what they personally would like others to know about them. Instead of putting a photograph in it, I am getting artists to produce something more original and imaginative. Instead of their date of birth, I want to know the age of their different interests and thoughts. Above all, I want to know where they are travelling mentally and emotionally. But autobiography is not enough, they may need someone to help them to say what it would not occur to them to say about themselves. Would it be possible to do this in the Italian university context you work in?

Theodore Zeldin

Learned conversation, post-Gutenberg

Why was I left so disappointed by this virtual conversation about the virtues of conversation, almost wistful for a learned article? Yet I too believe that there's the wherewithal to 'change the world' in there, somewhere.

The devil's in the details. Yes, our Blind Watchmaker designed our species' brains specifically to make them congenial to conversation and vice-versa: on-line, real-time interactive discourse at the speed of thought (or interactive thought at the speed of discourse). But I doubt that He did it in the service of what has bound 'chatter' forever into a cliché with 'idle'. I cannot subscribe to the 'social grooming' theory of the adaptive value of langue.

If not just chatter, then what? Could it have had something to do instead with the adaptive value of that productive oral tradition that eventually gave birth to writing, reading and the learned article?

But then what role does the Internet now play? Writing took discourse off-line, slowed its interactivity to a tempo sadly below the real-time speed of thought – but in exchange for many other advantages that one hardly need adumbrate here. Could the role of the Internet be to restore the interactivity to a tempo closer to the speed of thought at last, while preserving what is best of both media, and at a scale incommensurably surpassing either?

Stevan Harnad

The role of conversation in the transmission of knowledge

Stevan writes: 'If not just chatter, then what? Could it have had something to do instead with the adaptive value of that productive oral tradition that eventually gave birth to writing, reading and the learned article?'

Arguments for the adaptive value of conversation for other purposes than communicating information and increasing knowledge, such as Dunbar's social grooming hypothesis, may be debatable.

Nevertheless, it seems to me that chatter is not synonymous with 'idle'. Even in a scientific conference one needs a 'coffee break' to have the chance to exchange ideas in a different style that may throw a new light on the very topic of a scientific paper.

Conversation has been a cultural tool, at least in the Western tradition, to make ideas circulate in another way. Take for example, the role of women in the 'salons parisiens' of the Enlightenment. In this case, a category of human beings that was excluded from the public discourse could influence the increase and the diffusion of knowledge, on the basis of a different set of social rules of discourse.

The term *conversatio* in Latin doesn't have anything to do with language: its meaning is much closer to 'good conduct', the etiquette that tells you how to behave appropriately in social situations. I think that this social role of conversation has been complementary to the 'official' discourses (either oral or written) in the transmission on knowledge.

Gloria Origgi

Reply to Gloria Origgi

Your reference to salons emphasizes how inadequate the learned community has been in disseminating its findings. The originality of the salons was that women of exceptional ability acted as a sort of midwife to enable people with different talents to speak to one another, and not to be afraid of opening their mouths on subjects on which they were not experts. Who are the potential midwives of Internet conversation?

Theodore Zeldin

Archaism or forms of social ties?

For Theodore Zeldin, the Internet provides a means of going beyond stereotypes in our perception of others: thanks to the Internet and its international dimension, we can henceforth avoid the burdens of social categories (professional, neighbourhood, etc.) But aren't all these archaic elements (norms, values, skills, blood-lines...) first and foremost the stuff of social ties? On what foundation will the communicational man announced by Theodore Zeldin build his relationships? Certainly, he could make his own website and there present his family in a very creative way and have a few exchanges on that basis, but how can one go beyond this without reintroducing stereotypes, bureaucratic pressure, critiques, crises...and other such elements that lend body, sense, interest – in the broad sense of the term – and reality to human exchanges?

Agnès Camus-Viguè

Reply to Agnès Camus

I agree that we cannot eliminate all our prejudices and all the institutional obstacles that diminish the value of our encounters, but we can escape at least partially. What else is art, but escape from seeing the world as everyone sees it? I share your desire for conversations which break through the barriers we place between ourselves. Have you ever thought of documenting the way this happens and studying how it can be made to happen more often?

Theodore Zeldin

Thank you for your comments

Thank you for your comments. I have found them all enlightening and stimulating for different reasons.

I have been struck first of all by the temperamental differences between the participants, suggesting that professional antecedents have placed quite a few in environments which do not suit them emotionally, or which satisfy only a small part of them. Those who enjoy the adroit deployment of erudition and the excitement of disputation seem happier exercising their talents here than those for whom human warmth matters more.

Some participants have been puzzled by the issues raised and have not responded. Some have asked questions and received no answer, which could not happen so easily in a face to face conversation. The Internet allows you to advertise your opinions, but it does not require you to listen carefully to others, let alone to put yourself in their shoes. That is not a weakness peculiar to the Internet, but it emphasizes that this new technology is doing little to put an end to 'the dialogue of the deaf' which plagues so many attempts at communication.

I feel I have only glimpsed shadows of individuals, wrapped up in their professional expertise, and sparks of light escaping through chinks in armour, mere hints that interesting emotions lie concealed behind the text.

How can the Internet be used for creative purposes? Bringing people together who might not otherwise have met is the preliminary to the possibility of creativity. But for such encounters to be productive, much more sympathetic exchange is necessary. In the past, we had teachers, librarians, booksellers whom we valued and relied on, because they shared their thoughts with us in a way that was personal to us, and who often by some brief suggestion have encouraged us to look where we might not have. The moderators of the Web take over where they leave off, they have an important new role to fulfil.

So I welcome Gloria Origgi's proposal that we should think more about the kind of intimacy we want in serious meetings on the Web. Her initial belief is that an academic symposium does not require more than a common intellectual aim and acceptance of the same conversational rules. It would be a pity if we defined the debates we have been having as an academic symposium. The originality of the Internet is that it allows anybody in the world to participate. And for that to happen, it is essential that they feel welcome, that they are not judged on their past formal qualifications, but on their ability to interest and stimulate at least some participants. Since there are still people who are frightened of going into a bookshop or a library, the Internet has many hurdles to overcome.

In a conversation you cannot talk like a learned article, you must pause to let the person you are speaking to react. That reaction should ideally help you to enrich and redirect your thought. Some talkers intimidate others by the weight and length of their interventions. On the Internet it is harder to be sensitive to reactions one cannot see. We have to develop new sensitivities or we shall become even more rebarbative than we are in real life.

If you think academics (and others) should go on treating one another as they do at present, then let the Internet perpetuate their existing habits. But if you think we could do better, let us use the opportunity offered by the Internet to help us develop the kind of relationships we desire. There is no reason to be satisfied with less.

Theodore Zeldin

6
Reading: The Digital Future

Jason Epstein

If only there lived a mighty wizard with literary inclinations, readers today could use existing technology to download and read, either on an electronic screen or in a paperbound volume, any book or other text ever written. Scholars could instantly find their sources within a vast, multilingual virtual library, while even now some college students are reading textbooks on line, with audio-visual enhancements, interactively with their professors if they choose.

Today it is widely assumed that digitized books and other texts will be read mainly on computer screens or on hand-held reading devices such as Palm Pilots or Gemstar readers. But a significant market for books read on screens has not yet emerged, and in my opinion this may never become the major mode of distribution for books on line. The more likely prospect, I believe, is that most digital files will be printed and bound on demand at point of sale by machines – now in prototype – which within minutes will inexpensively make single copies that are indistinguishable from books made in factories.

These neighbourhood machines for making paperbound books can, like ATMs, be placed wherever electricity and supplies of paper exist – whether in Kinko's, Starbucks, or high school and university libraries and residence halls, to name only a few possible sites. With them, readers nearly everywhere with access to a computer screen may eventually search a practically limitless digital catalogue linked to innumerable databases where digital files are stored; retrieve and browse the titles that interest them; and transmit the files they select to a nearby printing machine, which will notify them when their books are ready to be picked up or delivered. From the time the reader makes a selection, the entire transaction can be completed within minutes. Given the durability and convenience of books printed on paper as well as the sacred status granted them by most cultures, readers may prefer – especially for books of permanent value – a volume printed and bound on these machines to transient images on an electronic screen. The exception will be dictionaries, atlases, encyclopaedias, directories, and so on, which must be continuously updated. Their current data will probably be read on screens as needed.

The convergence of the Internet with the instantaneous transmission and retrieval of digital text is an epochal event, comparable to the impact of movable type on European civilization half a millennium ago, but with worldwide implications. In the digital future groups of writers, editors, publicists, and website managers anywhere in the world will combine to form their own Web-based publishing companies and sell their books directly to readers. Some may contract with specialist firms to manufacture and distribute physical books to traditional retailers, which will coexist with their digital competitors, as theatres, cinemas, videotapes and DVDs all coexist today, and as today's physical bookstores coexist with on-line competitition. Though factory-made paperbacks sold in bookstores at retail markups will be at a competitive disadvantage compared with paperbacks printed on demand and sold directly to readers, not everyone will prefer to order books on line. The stock in trade of bookstores in the digital future is hard to foresee, but it is likely that shops offering carefully chosen inventories of new and used titles, especially books in hard covers, art books, and many kinds of childrens' books which cannot economically be printed on demand will become neighbourhood meeting places, while outlets that specialize in hardcover commercial bestsellers will continue to do so. But many readers who may not have access to a well-stocked bookstore will depend on digital catalogues and neighbourhood book machines for books they cannot otherwise find, as such readers now turn to Amazon and other on-line retailers. Point-of-sale book machines will be especially useful in developing countries where bookstores are scarce and shipping costs for single copies are high. Even in today's rudimentary digital marketplace some authors have linked their websites to sites of related interest, hoping to create their own expanding communities of loyal readers with each new book they write. Minor technological modifications will soon enable writers to sell their books to readers throughout the world directly from these Web networks, bypassing publishers who may have rejected their work, while established writers may choose to forego the security of a publisher's royalty guarantee in exchange for keeping the entire revenue from the sale of their books. In today's tightly structured publishing environment, manuscript submissions are largely winnowed first by agents and then by publishers and booksellers before readers make the final decision. For readers accustomed to an orderly literary marketplace the much less disciplined digital future may seem as threatening as widespread literacy seemed to the priests of the fifteenth century. But the human capacity to discriminate what is readable from what is not, and over time to discriminate what is truly valuable from what is merely readable, is no more likely to be overwhelmed in a marketplace where anyone can claim to be a writer than the critical faculty was defeated by the torrential energies released when the secularization of literacy swept across Europe five hundred years ago.

Since digitized books occupy no shelf space they can remain in print and in stock as long as digital storage devices survive. And because digital texts can be transmitted directly to consumers, they can be sold for much less than books that are shipped physically from printers in Illinois or China to publishers' warehouses in Maryland or Ohio and from there to regional chain store depots or wholesalers' warehouses and finally to thousands of retail bookstores from which, after a few months, unsold copies are returned to their publishers and destroyed. Because books published digitally involve no physical inventory and will cost their publishers virtually nothing per unit to produce and deliver, authors will contribute relatively more value to the final product than publishers and can claim a larger share of proceeds than from books sold in today's overconcentrated and inefficient literary marketplace dominated by book chains rooted in the five-hundred-year-old Gutenberg system of centralized manufacture and physical distribution.

To the extent that unmediated electronic distribution of books printed on demand at point of sale with its greater efficiency and low costs replaces this archaic system, today's book publishers will either devolve over time into decentralized teams of writers, editors, publicists, and website managers or be replaced by such groups. Thus book publishing may revert to the cottage industry that it was before today's homogenized retail marketplace, dependent on a steady supply of promotional titles, imposed a corresponding obligation on the publishing industry.

But there is no wizard to create with a wave of the hand this digital future. There are only mortals finding their way, by the slow, indirect, and uncertain means by which human beings have exploited previous paradigm shifts. To expect a practical business plan for unmediated electronic publishing to arise full blown from the existing industry would be to disregard the waywardness of human endeavour, the complexity of the emerging digital future, and the understandable, if quixotic, wish of today's publishers to enter the digital future in approximately their present form. But to assume on the other hand that a reasonable business plan may not sooner or later emerge would be to ignore the persistence and ingenuity with which human beings have invented their world so far.

This is not to say that every powerful new technology necessarily becomes a viable business. The SST and high-speed rail travel in the United States may never overcome competition from cheaper or more convenient choices, while genetically altered and irradiated food are shunned by many consumers. No such obstacles confront the unmediated transmission of digital files whose cost per unit is minimal compared with the cost of distributing physical inventory, while the convenience of transmitting words electronically is evident to anyone who downloads e-mail attachments or receives faxes or has already bought a digital book. From the consumer's point of view the experience of ordering a digital book selected from an on-screen catalogue and printed at a nearby site will differ from buying a factory-made copy of the same book from an Internet retailer only in being nearly instantaneous, less likely to result in frustration if the physical book is out of print, and at a price that includes only a fraction of the retailer's markup.

Because the obstacles to an unmediated digital future are not technological but institutional and emotional, the inevitable transformation will be contentious as new forms of production challenge old assumptions and practices. For example, the relatively greater value contributed by authors to digitized texts has already been noted by literary agents, who will expect authors' future earnings from digital editions to be adjusted accordingly. But to increase the author's share of revenues in keeping with the publisher's minimized cost of digital production and distribution will, as digital publishing supersedes the conventional model, diminish publishers' revenues, though not necessarily their net profits. To sustain profits, however, publishers must reduce or liquidate redundant facilities related to previous technologies, especially in the areas of marketing, sales, warehousing, and production. Book publishers, especially those dominated by their sales and marketing operations, will react defensively to such challenges to their boundaries. Meanwhile agents are coiled and waiting to strike.

Authors' royalties traditionally represent between 10 and 15 per cent of retail prices, or between 20 and 30 per cent of publishers' net revenues. Another 40 per cent or so of revenue is absorbed by executive and other administrative costs and by the costs of printing, selling, and distributing physical books, costs which are irrelevant to digital publication. Therefore agents demanding 70 per cent or more of digital revenues for their authors will open the bidding for new titles to upstart firms with no embedded customs or infrastructure to maintain. Under this competitive pressure traditional publishers will reduce their redundant functions in order to accommodate higher royalty payments or they will lose their authors, who, in today's aggressive literary marketplace, are no more loyal to their publishers than their publishers are to them. Such adjustments are typical of the interregnum between a departing economic model and its successor and may help explain why today's publishing conglomerates have approached the digital future with caution.

The revolutionary function of the Internet as a commercial medium is the revival by electronic means of face-to-face commerce as it existed before today's obsolescent middleman's marketplace evolved from the replacement of primitive trading by centralized manufacture and distribution. Had publishers taken advantage of the Internet a decade ago by forming a consortium, open to all publishers on equal terms, to create a universal catalogue and a combined warehouse from which to sell books directly to readers, they would have taken a crucial first step toward the future face-to-face digital marketplace. But with imperfect vision, the press of day-to-day business, and deference to the book chains, and perhaps also solicitude for the remaining independent retailers – the last survivors of publishing's glorious past – publishers missed this opportunity. Similar inertia deters these firms today from exploiting the infant electronic marketplace by creating in digital form the joint catalogue which they failed to create in conventional form ten years ago.

Dell, the upstart firm that pioneered the direct selling of personal computers, bypassing traditional retailers, provides the model for the unmediated sale of digital books which, like Dell's computers, exist only *in utero* until customers order them. For electronic publishing, however, the obstacles to entry will be harder to overcome than they had been for Dell, whose customers need only an electrical outlet to enjoy their purchases. The marketplace for digital books printed on demand requires that thousands of book machines be maintained at remote locations. This will not happen on the desired scale until a critical mass of salable digital content has been assembled.

Since the mid-1990s nearly all books published in nearly all countries have been typeset from digital files which, with minor technical adjustments, can be transmitted worldwide and downloaded in readable form on screens or as books printed on demand. Moreover, many older titles, some of them long out of print and with expired copyrights, as well as scholarly and scientific journals, conference papers, economic reports, and so on have now been digitized. If publishers of general fiction and nonfiction were now to digitize their proprietary backlists as well and offer them along with their current digital titles directly to consumers on line, a rudimentary but adequate multilingual digital catalogue could be assembled today from these components. It would be large enough to justify the external infrastructure without which the digital marketplace cannot function. That infrastructure would include both innumerable databases of individual publishers linked to a comprehensive catalogue and many hand-held readers and point-of-sale bookmaking machines. But publishers have been slow to digitize their backlists, and the reasons why are worth examining closely.

With the advent of books in digital form, publishers have demanded, and authors have generally granted them, the right to publish digital editions under contracts signed since the mid-1990s. Thus publishers tacitly admit that the right to publish a digital edition, like the right to publish a paperback, foreign, or audio edition, constitutes a so-called subsidiary right for which appropriate royalty terms must be negotiated separately. But publishers have not yet attempted to acquire digital rights and negotiate separate royalties for backlist titles published before the mid-1990s. Instead Random House has simply offered a royalty of 50 per cent of net proceeds for all digital titles whether new or old, as if its right to impose a non negotiated royalty as well as its ownership of digital rights to its backlist are self-evident, unlike the case of titles published since the mid-'90s. This anomaly might be explained by the daunting cost of acquiring digital rights to tens of thousands of backlist titles, which publishers have always considered their own property, and then digitizing them at further expense, before a market for them exists.

Reasoning from this inertia that digital rights to backlist titles are therefore at the disposal of their authors, an upstart digital distributor calling itself Rosetta Books has recently bought from important authors, including William Styron and Kurt Vonnegut, exclusive digital rights to one hundred titles published before 1995 and plans to buy as many as two thousand more. The standard language included in all publishers' contracts, from which Rosetta's strategy derives, is that rights not granted the publisher are retained by the author. Claiming therefore that the publishers' basic right to print, publish, and sell in book form does not include the right to publish a digital edition to be read on line, Rosetta is now open for business.

Random House, three of whose authors are on Rosetta's list and which has recently announced its own plans to begin digitizing its backlist, feels that Rosetta has taken its property and the issue is now in federal court. Meanwhile Rosetta dismisses as irrelevant other standard contractual language which prevents authors from publishing or permitting to be published editions of their work that compete with the publishers' edition, language which on its face seems to prevent authors from selling their digital rights to anyone but their own publishers. To add to the confusion, Rosetta has disabled the printing function on its e-book software, limiting its customers to reading books on screens, an apparent admission that books transmitted digitally but printed on demand are indisputably the property of the publisher. Though the issues in *Random v. Rosetta* are being litigated, they might, as several observers have suggested, be debated instead by philosophers arguing whether the weightlessness of books read on line makes them contractually different from books printed on demand.

Though there is no telling how the courts will rule, to the extent that books transmitted digitally and printed on demand prove more popular than books read on screens, the issues in *Random v. Rosetta* may be moot, for even Rosetta agrees that the publisher has the exclusive right to sell printed copies. A more urgent question is the appropriate authors' share of revenues from digital books, no matter in what form they are read or whether they were published before or after 1995, an issue that will be decided over time in the competitive market for literary property. It is on the outcome of these negotiations that the future configuration of the book publishing industry depends.

Whatever the outcome of the Rosetta litigation, the digital marketplace will sooner or later emerge, even without a wizard's help or the cooperation of publishers. Many scholarly, technical, and scientific books as well as scientific papers, journals, corporate documents, publications of non-governmental organizations, and government documents can now be delivered electronically and printed on site as needed. The advantage of distributing such texts digitally, to be printed locally on demand rather than printing them centrally and shipping small quantities to distant regions, is obvious and will justify investment in book machines at numerous regional sites. Once these machines are in place and worldwide databases are linked to form a catalogue, a rudimentary digital network will exist, awaiting only publishers' lists of general fiction and nonfiction to complete the transformation. (I am involved in efforts to achieve such a network.)

In the meantime writers and readers might as well be patient as they await the birth struggle of what promises to be a historic paradigm shift, one which will not erase the past but will exploit some of its unrealized possibilities. Nor will this transformation be an unmixed good but only a reflection of what people make of it. Therefore a caveat: Sumerian clay tablets can still be read but the long-term survival of digital texts cannot be taken for granted. Libraries and other depositories must not think of digital storage, as they once thought of microfilm, as an answer to the problem of shelf-space but as an adjunct to their traditional activities. The transition to digital books will be unsettling enough. It should not be a pretext for pruning the legacy of the Gutenberg era.

Discussion

V-book reading: the virtual future (volumes will go the way of videos)

Jason Epstein's essay unfortunately shows some failure of imagination regarding the future of reading. The view seems to be locked in the eye/hand-unfriendly cross-hairs of today's paleolithic screens and screen resolutions. But let's fast-forward our imaginations instead to the inevitable virtual books (v-books rather than mere e-books): these are virtual-world objects that mimic the look, touch, feel, smell, taste and manipulability (for those who like to leaf with moistened fingers) of books as closely as we like, right down to the last sensorimotor 'just-noticeable-difference' if need be. (Our senses are at bottom digital too: we just have to approach the limits of their resolving capacity.)

This should not be hard to imagine, for all you have to do is to think of a real physical book (p-book), your favourite, and of being able to do and feel with it every last one of the things you want to be able to keep on doing and feeling: leafing through it in bed, on the beach, in the loo, even defacing it, if you like, with scribbles and turned-down page corners. Virtual reality can duplicate all this for your senses as faithfully as you like. The only difference will be that instead of owning many books like this, you will own only one, your generic v-book, into which the digital contents of your library will be downloaded on demand, onto microthin generic v-pages, carrying an update of your own personal graffiti, if that's what your papyrocentric nostalgia cleaves to.

But I rather doubt that we will not cleave to much of it for long. Some things about the Gutenberg way approached the optimal, but many did not, and were merely the decorative, incidental (and sometimes dysfunctional) byproducts of paper-specific functionality and habit. I suspect that we will want to relinquish some of the look/feel we have gotten used to when better possibilities present themselves, and get tried out. I'm not sure how hand-held manipulation will compete with being able to see the text, in any size and grain of resolution, on whatever wall surface we may find ourselves squirming toward as we readjust our bones periodically, our gaze direction faithfully tracked by an automatic 'reading assistant'. I'm not sure that we will want to stick with moistened-digital navigation when a head-nod will do the trick, voice can be even more specific ('Go back to the part where...') and the possibility of affixing our graffiti is augmented into full-multimedia interactive capability. But for present purposes, let us stick to the v-book conceived simply as a vr-simulation of everything we are fond of in our p-books.

It is in this light that we need to reconsider Jason Epstein's predictions: 'It is widely assumed that digitized books and other texts will be read mainly on computer screens...More likely...most digital files will be printed... within minutes...' What if they will be read neither way, but instead down-loaded instantly into our personal, generic v-book template? He writes then: 'readers nearly everywhere with access to a computer screen may eventually search a practically limitless digital catalogue linked to innumerable databases...' This will still be true. Except that the downloaded text itself, and the v-book in which it is displayed, will continue to be linked to the global databases, with some rather remarkable bonus capabilities as a conse-quence, including the possibility of hypertext-hopping from text to text, instant searches within or between texts, triggered by voice or digit, parallel texts, annotations, animations, etc. But, as a special case, it will also permit the emulation of classical, Gutenberg-style eulexia.

By way of an exercise for those who are convinced this goes against nature, and cannot, will not, and should not be so, ask yourselves why we don't have the same specific-object fetish for personal copies of movies that we have for personal copies of books. We are quite happy with videos; but when they are replaced by downloads, no one will shed a tear. Why? Because there was no interim Gutenberg phase of becoming imprinted on the incidental accoutrements of movie-viewing: a movie never needed to go through the phase of being a decorative personalized object that we had become accustomed to hand-turning for ourselves, magic-lantern-style.

I am not, by the way, belittling the sensitivities of bibliophiles. A fondness for the look and feel of books and libraries betokens and accompanies a far far finer and deeper aesthetic and cultural profile than today's video, CD, DVD, and computer-game culture. It is merely the kind of inadvertent brake on the optimal and inevitable that an obsessive attachment to, say, illuminated manuscripts in the face of the philistine Gutenberg technology would obviously have been (had it happened – fortunately it did not) that we also need to avoid today.

Stevan Harnad

Resistance of materiality

The comparison with videos made by Stevan Harnad to contest the superiority of the bound book over the digital defended by Jason Epstein is interesting because it can be turned around. In fact, and thank goodness for the movie market, there has always been a market for pre-recorded videos which today has shifted by exploding with the DVD. Obviously, one can say that this is a defence of manufacturers, but a market is made of the meeting of supply and demand and manufacturers cannot sell their products if they cannot find clients (which is what happened for a long time with the different versions of the videodisk.) There is thus a real demand for material objects permanently engraved with films that does not only concern movie buffs and fetishists and which is also not merely a residue of old habits since the support is new. In other words, there is indeed, as Roberto Casati suggested, a dual market, one for goods and the other for on-line services.

Without pretending to exhaust the subject (all the more so since I am not a specialist in this area), I would like to suggest two complementary interpretations:

1. These objects, as in the domain of book writing, act for each of us as sort of transitional objects toward a more vast, rich but disquieting domain of human culture, or at least, of that part of culture that is relevant in our community. Thus a private library of books (or a video library, or a recordings library) is a step towards this world. It must be material and manageable in order to be reassuring and open, just as childrens' toys are first steps towards the adult world.
2. The notion of finished work, already stressed by Roger Chartier, presupposes a finished, easily identifiable material representation. For the moment, we haven't come up with anything better than a material object or a performance limited in time. It doesn't seem very realistic to think that we have seen the last of them.

Jean-Michel Salaün

Buy or rent?

But are we not discussing something more profound here than the relative virtues of buying versus renting? Is the genetic or cultural attribute that determines whether an individual prefers to keep a concrete object in a private drawer a very important variable for the future of reading? Especially given that the virtual book that I write will already satisfy all of our decorative and functional needs during an entire sensory-motor encounter in real-time (downloading on-line) and that what will remain will be just our vague instincts of off-line possessiveness.

Stevan Harnad

The concrete and the mental, the stable and ephemeral

Stevan Harnad asks 'But are we not discussing something more profound here than the relative virtues of buying versus renting?'

I have no firm answer to that question but I tend to think so. No doubt, someone more qualified in this area than me would have a clearer point of view. But here are the arguments:

Who does not reel before the abundance of knowledge that the Internet makes immediately available and thus even more terrifying?

Who is not overwhelmed by the rapidity with which knowledge is changing, even more accelerated by being put on line?

Moreover, who does not cringe before the more present than ever 'dark side' of the Internet: pornography, paedophilia, fascism, scams, sects, rumours (barely touched upon during this colloquium which, in spite of their existence on the net, has favoured the legitimate), or its flip-side which is just as scary: Big Brother?

Faced with these very classically human anxieties, technological responses have little efficacy. That is why one of the hypotheses I proposed was the security represented by a stable object (or indelible symbols), finite, limited, easily accessible without technical intervention and nonetheless symbolically bearers of openness towards the world of knowledge, just as paper books were profoundly useful to the humans we are, as the real toys of children have not been replaced by all the playstations or gameboys of the world. Thus to possess objects would not be frivolous, but quite useful for our mental structuring. This is not contradictory, but complementary to the development of the digital, which allows access to the infinite, the ephemeral, the forbidden.

I would add that these reflections (to the extent that they are not completely delirious) are not contradictory with advances in artificial intelligence which now incorporate emotions. I have not doubt that Stevan will figure out how to incorporate these dimensions, but is it really indispensable?

Jean-Michel Salaün

The book as totem, icon, memory object and spiritual channel

Professor Salaün redirects the discussion to a set of interesting and significant functions of the book as object. In addition to the book as a structural paradigm in learning and cognition, there are at least three elements in the set:

1. The Book as totemic and iconographic object. 2. The book as physical storehouse of the memory of the experience of reading. 3. The book as metaphysical connection to the spirits of its readers.

The above are uses of the physical book object that are not within the function of electronic texts. The first set has become the foundation of the growing field of Book Art. As texts become dematerialized, there is an increasing interest in finely printed and bound books, sculptural book objects, and bookworks which are tactile and structural explorations of the relationship of text to material, areas I call 'Book Artchitecture' and 'Material as Metaphor'.

The second set is predicated on the observation that no two books in an edition are identical once they leave the bookstore. People have an intimate relationship with their books. They generally know where every book is in their home, and can pick out their favourites from across the room without reading the titles. Just seeing the book reminds one of the time spent with it. Opening its pages brings back memories of that time – the coffee stain on page 57, or the crease on the corner of the board, all the marks of use have associated memories. In my incarnation as a bookbinder I have had many books brought to me that were of value primarily for this non-textual meaning. For example, a dietician brought in a tattered cookbook full of food stains. She could have obtained another copy of the book for a fraction of the cost of the repair. But it was the food stains that gave this copy of the book unique meaning. Each stain was a memory.

The third element is the one that interests me the most. It may sound odd, but at one time I collected books, primarily incunabula and early printed books, solely on the basis of the vibes I got while holding them. It all started when I was a graduate student in Economics at Brown University in 1968. One day, sitting in a carrel in the Rockefeller Library, reading *The Wealth of Nations*, a strange thing happened. I had read several printings of

Adam Smith's classic work, including a mid-60s trade paperback and a 3-volume set from 1904. The edition in my hands was the first (1776), and the particular copy had been the property, when new, of the Minister of Finance of France. Holding this pristine leatherbound volume, with its handmade paper pages letterpress-printed from handset type, I was translated to eighteenth-century France. The hands of one of the world's most powerful economic decision-makers had held this book and turned these pages. I began to feel his presence seeping into me through my hands. The text took on an entirely new meaning, and I began to understand it from the perspective of the original owner. I went to the card catalogue and found the French precursors, works by the physiocrats Walras and Quesnay. There were no English translations, so I waded through the originals with Cassell's at my side. Were it not for this unique copy of Smith I would never have thought to read them. My entire understanding of the history of economic thought changed that day.

A new interest in books as objects was also instilled by that experience. Once one becomes receptive to the 'vibes' in books, they are often as or more interesting than the texts. With the advent of the e-book all of this changes. The magic of the individual book is gone, along with its associations with one's reading experience, and the ability to communicate spiritually with past and future readers.

Richard Minsky

Buying or renting bis

Jeremy Rifkin has made a fetish of this distinction in his *The Age of Access* (2001), in which he suggests that a whole new world of 'renting' is replacing our older one of 'owning' – in real estate, job security, automobiles, many things…also with regard to books and our general access to information…

That this change will occur more gradually than Harnad thinks I believe is a point made by Epstein, that it will change more rapidly than Epstein thinks is to some extent Harnad's point. Will those v-book texts be purchased and 'owned'? As for 'print to digital': I do not know that anyone can predict the exact rate of The Shift, but that some such shift is coming seems to be commonly agreed.

I am not so interested, myself, in parsing endlessly the question of how much will be left over of the older media. There are scriveners and farriers around, still. Here in downtown San Francisco, just in back of The Gap's new building, there is one famous lone blacksmith still plying his trade, open fire kiln and anvil and all. I expect there to be elegantly-ticking pocket watches, and fountain pens, and horses, all around for a long time as well. Fine press books will survive too – this is the town of The Grabhorn Press – printed books of various kinds will be on my grandchildren's shelves, I am convinced.

But Epstein's economics interests me a great deal. He is an industry veteran – knows 'the biz'. Authors always have been naive about the real work involved, and the real costs, of book editing and formatting and producing and warehousing and marketing and distributing and administering – and the extraordinary costs of anything involving 'the customer', such as billing, and bill-collecting, and 'handling returns'. All of this does involve money: perhaps not the 85–90 per cent charged by so many print publishers now – only 100 per cent markup? Some say it's more like 150 or 200 per cent... but a lot more money is involved, at least, than authors ever imagine. Digitization cuts vast swathes out of inventory warehousing and other overhead costs, and competition – where that is permitted – should take advantage of that.

I do not share the view that it will be all that easy for authors to 'sell directly the books to the readers', on-line. One recent and important e-publishing contribution has been the forcible educating of a lot of authors in the harsher realities of these economics. Among the failed dotcoms of last year were a great number which had tried simply to throw 'content' up on the Net and then watch it sell itself, giving little or no thought to follow-up or follow-through or any sort of real business plan. They found out the hard way that there is a 'business' side to e-commerce – things don't sell themselves.

To me the most interesting question, going forward, is not the medium removed from the 'business' side of 'e-publishing' – Harnad's proposals tend a little in that direction, as refereed journal publication is a somewhat unique animal, and v-books either conflate or do not address these issues. I want to know what the new economics of the new commercial e-publishing industry are going to be. Already I buy my 'e-books' – many of them – from Amazon.com for one tenth the cost of the p-book...Rifkin says that I am not even 'buying' them, only 'renting' their texts...

The economics justified in buying a text – p-book, e-book, v-book – will lose that justification once we no longer are buying and owning the thing but only renting it. The psychology is different. I will be willing to pay only a lot less per 'rental' unit, than I will be willing to pay for something which I 'own'. I may, though, be willing to pay for a whole lot more units – and I may even dump them and later go back to see them again – if the e-publishing industry succeeds in redefining and protecting its new distribution structure, as the e-movie industry now so busily is doing, Epstein makes this point.

An economy of scale, then – one allowing the publishing industry to 'move' many more units, many more times, to many more customers, slashing its per-unit pricing in the process – 'pay-per-view reading', perhaps known as such by the reader, perhaps not. It's the book retailer's dream: beyond the wildest distribution fantasies of W.H. Smith and Pierre Larousse.

'Libraries' have been doing this for centuries. I mean, do I really want to have my own personal library of p-book texts? of v-book texts? Will I pay unconscionable margins to obtain them? I don't share Epstein's view that all of this will involve more paper: Xerox and Hewlett-Packard fortunes would be soaring – and they're not, any more – but that is another topic.

So Salaün is correct, I think, to suggest that there is some role going forward for 'the book as a thing', an 'objet stable', and for 'ownership' of same. Harnad joins him by extolling the creature comforts of his v-book idea: not something I would want to take to bed with me perhaps, or out under the apple tree, but yes even things digital can exhibit 'look, touch, feel, smell, taste' and, I suppose, 'manipulability' – hopefully Steve Jobs will design it. Epstein does not disagree with this: he even thinks bookstores have a future – as 'lieux de rencontre de proximité' – 'The Shop on the Corner' lives on, in spite of the big chains, and now it's 'got email'. . . All the media old and new may persevere, in various parts of the market – even on-demand printing. I'm for keeping 'physical' libraries around too, myself – I like them.

But to me the most interesting new economics underlying e-publishing is 'pay-per-view reading' – for pennies, versus the many dollars sunk one-time-only into current text 'ownership' – multiple mass e-text distribution, by all these various means, at low unit costs…importantly of anything, even of an academic text with a printrun of only 2000 copies…Perhaps this will allow e-publishers to up that author's percentage a bit, as well.

Of course some people may insist at some point on getting back to ownership: some lawyer somewhere will figure out how to sell a 'condominium text', eventually…better a 'Florida beachfront' short story which you 'own', than one stuck in traffic outside Chicago which you are only 'renting'. . .

Jack Kessler

Economics, technology, and the time line

The discussion so far has established several paths of inquiry that converge. Stevan Harnad begins by maligning Jason Epstein for addressing near-term technological development. The notion of interactive universally hyper-linked virtual books is reasonable. But one could as easily note that Professor Harnad's mid-term model still relies on physical entities, v-book objects.

If we begin on the 'fast-forward' path why stop midway? Researchers have already produced 'cyborgian' cells that combine biological and digital elements, have implanted and connected prosthetics that enable the blind to see and that control artificial limbs. DNA computing technology is developing rapidly with billions of dollars invested in research, along with molecular computing and nanotechnologies. It is no longer far-fetched to visualize our brains connected directly to the information network, where Professor Harnad's 'head-nod' is a relic of inefficiency identified with nostalgia for physical interaction.

The economic and business models for that era will be revolutionary. So perhaps we can return to the near-term model and examine developments one step at a time. The vending model has been played with since the videodisk-based kiosks of the 1970s. An earlier version of demand publishing used microfilm and Xerox CopyFlow technology. Currently the kiosk is used in music stores to make instant CDs with your own choice of songs.

The technology for making CDs is simpler than that for producing a paper book, and less prone to failure. Perhaps books could be produced in copy shops that already have staff trained to add ink or toner, clear paper jams, call the repair technician, and the other tasks required to make paper copies. The CD kiosks have already solved the issue of royalties. On the other hand, MP3 file-sharing opened another can of worms. Who needs a CD when you can download files to your player?

I doubt the paper book kiosk will be a successful model. The time to market is unlikely to beat technological developments, even within the limited world of e-books. I have seen many businesses fail recently because they could not develop their products fast enough to keep up with competing technologies. It may not be the v-book that closes the window of opportunity on paperbook kiosks. Before the virtual reality book happens, electronic paper, which now exists in a rudimentary form, will be able to replicate the physical book as a multipage object with pages that turn. Inexpensive flexible colour display technology is on the verge of mass marketing. You may have the opportunity to slide a disk into the cover, but a high-speed wireless modem will probably be built into it that will receive the encrypted file directly. This will be particularly relevant in countries without land lines that have recently become connected via cellular telephone systems, as in parts of Africa and South America. In the mountainous areas of Brazil, for example, balloons are used instead of towers for cellular antennas, each giving a large unobstructed radius through difficult terrain.

As a web publisher, one might maintain a chat room and a store as well as manage content to a niche audience. Even if the anarchistic model of self-publishing (is it 'vanity' or 'art'?) becomes dominant, there will still be reviewers that people look to for advice. They may have the advantage over traditional publishers in that they are independent of the products being reviewed. Even more likely, forums for review like the *Amazon.com* model or e-bay may dominate, where anyone can give their opinion and books get rated by the *vox populi*. Everyone expresses their opinion. Judge for yourself. You look at how many stars are posted by the title. Thumbs up and down. Ancient Greece or Rome? Pop culture flaunting in the face of quality? Did the Futurist manifestos get it right?

On the other hand, as digital society rose over the last twenty years, so did the Book Art movement. Thousands of book artists are producing limited editions both on the computer and by letterpress, and as unique objects. Perhaps we are seeing books go the way of other technologies – when they become obsolete commercially they become the tools of the artist.

The development of electronically disseminated information has often been compared in significance with Gutenberg's use of individually assembled letters to compose a page of text. Movable type led to immense changes in society. Gutenberg enabled the modern concepts of freedom and the French Revolution. It's ironic that the new electronic literacy may cause the loss of the personal freedoms Gutenberg generated. Carnivore and other government programs already examine every communication on the internet. Since the attack on September 11 people have come to accept this as normal. The Electronic Frontier Foundation and many others are trying to deal with these issues. How will this impact on the development of electronic publishing? Is a new form of censorship and control of information in the electronic future, or will the technology make it easier to maintain freedom of the press?

Richard Minsky

How does one become an e-publisher?

Two points come out clearly from Epstein's text and the debate: (1) New forms of publishing are developing and will soon predominate; (2) There is some uncertainty as to which technologies (print-on-demand, e-books, open formats) will prove successful, and for how long.

Imagine someone who, given her interest and competence in a certain field of literature or scholarship, wanted to start today a small e-publishing house. How should she go about it? Bet on one technology, and which? Avoid committing herself to one technology, and how? Forget it?

Dan Sperber

Reply to Dan Sperber

I agree with Dan Sperber that it is impossible to know which technologies will survive, but it seems to me safe to assume for the near term that books will be distributed electronically and read either in printed or electronic form. My own guess is that most reference material will be read on line and most traditional fiction and nonfiction will be printed on demand at point of sale. Commercial bestsellers, at least in the US, will be printed centrally, as they are now, and distributed physically.

Whatever new technologies may eventually prevail, human beings will reject information that is poorly composed and laden with stale jargon. We still read the psalms, Homer and Shakespeare because they make sense, and we reject language that doesn't make sense. This seems to be an aspect of the human design that persists as various technologies come and go.

Jason Epstein

7

Babel and the Vintage Selection: Libraries in the Digital Age: Bibliothèque publique d'information

*The Bpi team**

Let us for a moment imagine the hunched figure of Jorge Luis Borges as he walks through one of our modern libraries on the arm of his guide. What literary constructions might this patron saint of librarians, himself a librarian, be inspired to dream up before the sight of all these texts displayed, circulated and manipulated on computers? Our modern libraries would no doubt provide the author of *Fictions* and *The Book of Sand* with material for new ideas concerning the theme of the library of Babel.

Public libraries are places devoted to the conservation and communication of a heritage of culture and information, above all of the textual variety. Today, they are directly concerned by the most recent developments of computer technology. The use of computers in libraries is admittedly not so recent, whether for the computerization of collection catalogues (introduced in France in the 1970s), or direct public consultation (introduced in the 1980s). However, what is changing radically and what calls for serious reflection is the strong increase of electronic documents in collections – their acceptance in mentalities, in other words – and above all an opening up to the Internet. To a certain extent, these new resources have given rise to a new sort of library, an immaterial *virtual library*. The advantages of these new resources are quite concrete for users, however they neither duplicate nor replace real libraries.

This gives rise to a question which requires detailed and critical analysis: in what way could the traditional functions of public reading establishments – i.e. selecting, acquiring and processing documents, making them available to the public, conserving them or withdrawing them from collections – be transformed, and with what consequences?

---

* Authors listed on p. 136.

In an attempt to provide an answer to this question, we will draw on the specific example of the Pompidou Centre Public Information Library (Bpi) to address an issue which in fact extends well beyond the example taken here. 'Example', then, should be understood here in the sense of a simple illustration, and not as a 'model'. The question will effectively be addressed from the particular point of view of an open access encyclopædic library of national stature, but through general themes which concern all establishments, regardless of their size or location. The guiding principles for our considerations will be the chronology of different library operations and, above all, the circuit followed by electronic documents in the library. We will follow the course of these documents from their selection to the point at which they are made available to the public, leaving room, along the way, for a few remarks on the question of their modalities of appropriation by librarians and by the users themselves.

Between the illusion of completion and the quest for the elusive: managing digital collections

Unlike audiovisual technology, the appearance of writing on screens did not stir any debate in the library world at first, for the simple reason that fundamentally it was just text: closed, stable, finished text, presented in the form of material objects – most often as CD Roms – which were freely available. Librarians weren't too worried about these documents that they could take on board without great difficulty, though at the cost of losing certain landmarks.

Leafing through a work

As a librarian one doesn't read a work, one leafs through it, one recognizes the name of an author, a publisher or a collection, which is an assurance of quality. Every week, one leafs through book reviews and the press to locate points of interest, then through new publications to have an idea of their content. Acquiring a librarian's skill entails learning how to recognize the access routes to this content: the title

One cannot leaf through an electronic document or easily recognize its quality. When one wishes to analyse its content, identify the authors and publishers, one has to investigate it in detail. It reveals the secrets of its organization only after thorough consultation. The table of contents doesn't provide the key to a logical order and the indexes are not always known or presented. Making it available to the reader page or the cover, the publishing details, the summary, the index – everything that gives added value to browsing or a cursory read. The librarian measures the quality of a document through the sum of these criteria and notes these in the catalogue, but goes little further in the presentation of a document.

means decoding its subtleties and its immaterial form requires the library to provide instructions for use, a detailed description of the content, a guide, and so on, in the form of printed cards, as on-line aids tend not to be consulted very much.

The real rupture – the leap into the unknown, outside of the library – occurred with the advent of the Internet. With the Internet, the librarian no longer acquires, but provides access. A troubling dispossession indeed.

Consulting, accessing?

The collection of documentary objects is stable, identifiable, catalogued and finite. The library is the owner of the objects, books or CDs that it has acquired. All the librarian's work is based on these objects. At any given moment it is possible to know the state of the collection. Works are 'weeded' out of the collection according to publication dates, obsolescence of content and degree of wear, or added so that it remains up-to-date. On the other hand, when a documentary object available for consultation is no longer in its place, sometimes a lot of time can be spent looking for it. It can be torn, stolen or made inaccessible for many reasons. However, the feeling of having the object in one's hands remains.

The collection of electronic documents on Internet cannot be stolen or torn. However, its accessibility is sometimes problematic, and remains subject to the ups and downs of the technology in use. There can be various material problems, from an overburdening of the network to a simple electricity cut. Internet sites offer a multitude of links and openings towards the infinite, but they change their addresses, make information available then decide to withdraw it. The electronic document seems volatile and difficult to contain.

The Internet is by definition a world without limits, without beginning or end, like Borges' *The Book of Sand*. New resources are created every day, others disappear, migrate or undergo changes in content. The most serious work stands side by side with the bizarre, the irrational, the commercial, or even the despicable. The reliability of a piece of information is rarely established, nor is the order of importance of the results of a search query, and the relevance of the data gathered and classified by the search motors is also sometimes quite questionable.

This universe, unstable in both time and space, calls into question the traditional know-how of librarians. Indeed, the cause of difficulty for the profession is the *permanent information flow* which prevents – or at least complicates – the acquisition of the available information and above all its control. How is one supposed to monitor what is being made available to readers when they are being offered open access to Internet? How is it possible to exercise one's professional expertise, which starts with a motivated, qualified and coherent selection? How, above all, is one to prevent the user from being buried under an avalanche of information, far from the safe paths so carefully kept by the librarian? One can draw a possible parallel between television and Internet, both of which librarians sometimes tend to consider as places in which the reader is lost.

Between the library of Babel and the connoisseur's choice

What is at stake, in reality, is the traditional notion of a public collection considered as a contained, coherent and permanent whole, a preconstructed cultural proposition. It is clear that in the Internet era professionals remain attached to this ideal, which they maintain, for example, in carrying out selections of sites that are explicitly conceived as collections, indexed, classified and sometimes integrated into the catalogue. This does not fundamentally alter the role of the librarian: he or she still has to make a choice, to propose evaluated and validated resources to a public, whether close or distant. One might effectively think – and of course this is what librarians think – that faced with this excess of information, professional advice will become more and more indispensable, not only in order to locate relevant information, but also, and above all, to establish defined and lively collections. National libraries themselves are little by little renouncing the pursuit of impossible exhaustiveness. As for the Bpi, although it is often compared to a culture supermarket, it does not see itself that way: it may be encyclopaedic, but above all it gives a *choice*.

'When it was proclaimed that the Library contained all books, the first reaction was that of extravagant happiness...' This reader's dream, 'all books, right away' can quickly turn into a nightmare. The library of Babel may evoke the infinite, the multiplicity of human languages and desires, but it makes harmony impossible and leads to an impossible harmony and to terrible disorder. On the other hand, choice, selection, informed advice would be the sought after qualities of the wine connoisseur (if we can admit this farfetched comparison). Like the latter, capable of telling the difference between the value of a great wine and an average one, the librarian has at least to know the good vintages, the premier choices and the hallmarks of quality.

However, librarians must still convince (and firstly convince themselves perhaps?) of the validity of such a selection process. One can easily understand that every document or every access to paid information should be analysed and that, budgets being limited, there is an obligation to make choices. But what happens when the immaterial is also free, as it is with a great number of sites selected by the Bpi, duly catalogued but offered in controlled access so as to prevent the user from 'going out' freely on the Internet? What policy can convince the reader that the selection carried out by the librarian is not an infringement on his or her freedom? How can he or she be made to admit that, here, 'small is beautiful', that here boundaries are productive?

Between fixed menu and à la carte: Bpi services

At the Pompidou Center Public Information Library, two types of electronic resources are now available: the first is a selection of CD-roms and websites, accessible in the establishment and indexed by the catalogue in the same way as the other documents physically present on the shelves; the second is a whole set of links which are organized thematically, commented and regularly updated, available on the library website. Moreover, fifty terminals providing open access to the Internet (although with certain restrictions) are also available to the public.

The selections of electronic resources proposed, whether *intra muros* or on the library site are the outcome of choices made within an overall collecting policy. They are not juxtaposed with the existing resources but considered in terms of their complementary nature. For example, a selection will be made of a site giving the table of contents of a printed paper journal conserved in the library collection, and an insufficiently developed section of the Bpi will be complemented by a whole host of links, opening further doors. The Internet's wealth of images will allow for the art section to be enriched, as the use of multimedia CD Roms will provide virtual visits of museums, portrait galleries and crossover looks at works and eras. In the same way, giving access to the on-line press has the advantage of expanding the selection of titles on offer and geographic and linguistic horizons, as well as providing a more resistant medium for daily use.

The introduction of this volontarist policy is mobilizing a great deal of labour and material resources, without prejudice to questions about reactions from users, who, as can be expected, immediately rush towards the terminals which allow open access to the Internet. One might very well question the logic of this parallel offer, as indeed do the librarians of the Bpi. Is there not a contradiction with the mission of the library, such as it is defined in the decree that marked its creation ('to offer everyone... *a choice* of French and foreign collections which is constantly updated')? Is it merely giving into public pressure to increase the number of these terminals (30 at the reopening in 2000, 50 currently)? Should we return to the old dialectic of supply and demand and resolutely favour demand?

Before going any further, one should note that this 'open' access Internet is not entirely free, and that the library has set up some safeguards, as much from the point of view of access conditions (free, but limited to 45 minutes) as from the point of view of content. While one can easily understand the consultation of pornographic sites being banned, refusing access to e-mail services is less well understood by users. Yet this restriction, motivated in part by practical imperatives – to avoid being overwhelmed by demand – first and foremost relates to a policy decision expressing a certain idea of the library: a public service, which the users are free to appropriate for their private use, but only up to a certain point. The limit in fact marks the frontier between a public space whose vocation is to offer everyone open and democratic access to information, and the private – and commercial – sphere which the library, for right or for wrong, associates with e-mail. The library is not a cyber café, or a post office!

The librarian is undergoing a transformation from manager of a collection to provider of a service, at best as someone who encourages and facilitates research. Why then propose the Internet in more or less open access in addition to a qualified but limited offer? There is no shortage of reasons: to respond to the strong demand of the public for access to the entire Web (which is in the logic of Internet); to offer users 'fresh' information, and thus to conform with the Bpi's mission of keeping up to date; to make innovative technology available to the public, accompanied by introductory sessions, in accordance with its pedagogical role, and so on and so forth. However, above all, librarians are aware of the formidable mass of information which the Internet represents and that nobody can seriously try to contain it, even by calling on intelligent search engines or agents. Do they have the right, while claiming they present their public with the best part of the Internet cake, of depriving them of the rest? Because choice means restriction. In a world as vast and as fast-moving, how can we be sure of not penalizing the users by preventing them from having access to whole areas of information?

Confronted with this dilemma, most public libraries make the same choice as the Bpi. They let people have their cake and eat it, they provide the connoisseur's choice *and* the library of Babel, restricting Babel somewhat as needs dictate (by limiting the number of terminals or the connection time, imposing a booking, recuperating part of the costs from the users and so on). These measures serve to regulate demand as much as possible. In a library like the Bpi, which registers 7000 visits per day on average, it is more or less a question of survival.

Memory and actuality: a different relationship with time

Another strong value of the library is called into question by the advent of Internet: its memory function, its relationship with time. The missions of public libraries are numerous and sometimes contradictory: while they have to respond to users' requests today, they also have to preserve the interests of the reader of tomorrow. They are – in the sphere of the imagination as well as in reality – the memory of the community, and their responsibility in relation to written heritage is indisputable.

The advent of the Internet destabilized this relationship with time and at least partially called the principle of the collection's permanence into question. Admittedly, the professionals of public reading no longer only consider the collection as an intangible heritage slowly constituted through accumulation, but also as a living whole in perpetual construction and reconstruction and subject to regular revisions and 'weeding' (withdrawal of documents). However, the principle of coherence which remains at the heart of the notion of a collection implies a certain stability which is difficult to guarantee when it comes to electronic resources. For example, it is necessary to constantly verify the validity of links on the website collection. As for the conservation of collections in digital format, it turns out to be extremely complicated and in fact offers a lot less security than microfilm, or than paper for that matter.

Yet, a growing part of library collections is migrating towards digital technology. This is notably the case of periodicals. As long as the different media coexist, a library with adequate means such as the Bpi, can still enjoy the luxury of presenting them side by side. The French daily *Le Monde* is, for example, made available to readers in various forms (on paper, microfilm, CD Rom, and on line), each medium having its advantages and disadvantages, and showing itself more or less suitable for a particular type of use. However, even at the Bpi, this costly policy cannot be generalized. This is all the more true since libraries will soon not have any choice in the matter as already certain titles are available only in a digital format.

The use of digital technology has, of course, numerous advantages, as much for the library – if only in terms of space savings – as for the user who, at least in theory, is provided with many facilities, such as access from a distance and full text searches. But subscribing to an on-line periodical means paying access rights which can be terminated with the end of the subscription or the disappearance of the title or even that of the publisher. In the past, when confronted with such a situation, the library remained owner of the collections it had accumulated throughout its subscription. What is the current state of affairs? As the library has often not made any formal act of acquisition, is it still capable of carrying out its mission to conserve written heritage? Does the responsibility of conservation return *de facto* to the publisher? If such were the case, then conservation would be out of the hands of the public service and be taken up by a commercial structure, which conforms to a different logic.

On the other hand, digital technology is opening up wonderful perspectives in the heritage area to libraries, and not only to the most prestigious of them. The examples of the French National Library, the BnF and the Gallica Library immediately come to mind; that of the Lisieux municipal library is probably less obvious. It proves that a library of average size can build up a digital heritage by digitalizing its local collection or by republishing forgotten texts whose rare copies lie dormant in storerooms. Many libraries now make the treasures of their collections available to the community at large without affecting the integrity of the fragile original: it is in this way that the people of Valenciennes – and all interested sections of the public – can consult a virtual copy of the manuscript of the oldest conserved poem in French, *La Cantilène de sainte Eulalie*, on the website of the Valenciennes municipal library. Better still, these new techniques enable collections to be built up from documents that in the past were destined to quickly disappear because of their fragile condition, making them unsuitable for conservation and/or considered to be ephemeral and without heritage value: grey literature, various brochures, newspapers and press cuttings, or documents of mixed forms, combining texts, images and sounds. Thanks to digital technology, nothing stands in the way of such documents being conserved now, and above all, one-off events organized by libraries can be permanently maintained in circulation: exhibitions which remain on library websites well after the end of the event, live performances, conferences and debates which the Bpi has systematically recorded since it began, but without yet putting to use this new form of heritage accumulated over the years. The possibility of offering an anthology on the library site and broadcasting oral events live is currently under discussion. The Bpi is a library devoted to current events but the notion of what is current changes, and the frontier between memory and the present is constantly displaced. Digital technology requires that we consider the dialectic of the 'perishable' and the 'conservable' in different terms. It allows us, perhaps, to create and to transmit a 'heritage of the temporary'.

The material nature and the visibility of electronic documents

Making a reasoned selection among the different modes of access and electronic documents currently available, and creating relevant collections in this area, is one only step. The collections still have to be made available to the public in the best possible conditions. But how can we make visible that which, by its very essence, has little or no material form, no well-defined contours, nor even a place of its own? How can we make what is both present and absent appear clearly? How, above all, can we try to provide easy access for everyone? A new signposting system has to be invented, whether for the general presentation of the services and material on offer, the guides or even the catalogue. We are in effect confronted with technical objects which call for other practices, other strategies of appropriation and use and other ways of thinking, among users of multimedia libraries as much as among librarians themselves.

Touching...

Paper, printing, binding, cardboard, stacks of books on the desk. Who said that librarians had an intellectual profession? Do they work on content when they use a Stanley knife, lift kilos of

There is no need for a trolley to deliver a CD Rom, it comes in the post, a thin packet of undulated cardboard wrapped in plastic, or in its ultra light full-size box, as empty as a cereal box. Be careful, handle the disk with precaution, books, and tick off hundreds of newspaper and journal issues every day? Yet, what a feeling there is of a mission being accomplished at the Bpi when everyone is breaking their backs, ruining their hands and clogging up their lungs in putting more than 350,000 volumes back on thousands of miles worth of shelves so that the readers can find what they are looking for.

and quickly transfer it to the correct department. There is no need to reclassify CD Roms a specific server gives open access to their content, but without the reader having direct access to the physical object. The last step in the dematerialization process is the website: one orders a keyboard and mouse at the tips of one's fingers, in a few clicks. For others, access to information is at their fingertips.

Seeing...

With books, CDs, video cassettes, music scores, cards and journals, the accumulated collections are presented to the gaze of visitors as they walk into the open access library. Well stocked shelves hold the promise of fruitful research and dense holdings. They arouse the admiration of the reader for the librarian and a touch of jealousy towards the person who has power over this mass.

The choice of not displaying the books in the open, but first showing the means of access to electronic documents in the new layout of the Bpi means that what one sees is screens, a lot of screens. However, there are questions about the visibility of this particular system. How can these screens give the reader an idea of the wealth of the digital collection? And yet the work of selecting and guiding was carried out with just as much care by the librarian.

The precise place attributed to each type of medium in a library, as well as its number, in itself reveals the value that the institution grants to the particular medium. Thus, the person who walks through the spaces of the new Bpi only reaches the printed materials after having passed through or having stopped at one of the 400 or so computer terminals placed at the entrances of the consultation spaces. The message is clear, all the more so given that a good number of multimedia terminals are equipped with flat screens of the plasma type – the latest technology. The goal of trying to familiarize the greatest number with the new means of access to information and culture is in this way openly concretized at ground level.

Some problems arise as a result: is this ostentatious presence of electronic resources perceived as complementary to the presence of printed books? If a given bibliography, for example, is no longer bought in its paper version, it disappears from the shelves, leaving a gaping hole. How is it possible to show, in a library with total open access and without any storage space – and which practised, moreover, an active 'weeding' policy – that this is not a deliberate act of intellectual vandalism, and that the item is still present but in an electronic version? One is tempted, as it is often the case, to turn to the tried and trusted system of using information cards on the shelves: 'In future to consult XXX, sit in front of a flat screen in such and such a sector, then look for the document you wish to consult in the catalogue or by clicking on *CD Roms and selected websites…*' However, in this case, can one still speak of total open access? Paradoxically, the immaterial nature of the collection on offer and the confrontation with the screen sound a little like a return to the indirect access library where people had to go to a counter and go to great trouble to obtain a work stored in a faraway and inaccessible storeroom.

However, the presentation of the Bpi's electronic resources isn't limited to the omnipresent screens. It is complemented by a classifying apparatus, the purpose of which is to localize in the different areas of the library precisely those things which do not have a set place or could easily do without one: websites of course, or CD Roms, which are loaded onto the hard drive of a central server located at a distance from the consultation spaces. In order to introduce the electronic resources, the usual guiding techniques and storing techniques for documents have been reproduced: what belongs to the area of botany has not only been selected and catalogued, but also 'shelved' with works of the same discipline. The consultation of specialized CD Roms and selected sites takes place close to the information offices for each area, and benefits from the proximity of experienced mediators, that is to say the librarians, whose assistance is often more efficient than on-line help for the new users. However, one can also see a strong will to hold down, or rather get a firmer hold on a means of access to information that one perhaps fears will escape from all control. In other words, the librarian's grip can be felt when he or she is confronted with objects which, by their nature, are beyond his or her traditional know-how: the spatialization of knowledge.

The spatialization of the Bpi's electronic resources, again, is not dictated by technical reasons but by a freely chosen policy. Thanks to a federating computer interface, it will be entirely possible to consult the general catalogue, to read a CD Rom or to access a website from any of the terminals in the entire network. This option of opening the system was, moreover, kept for the catalogue, given that it was unthinkable to limit access to this essential tool. The description given in the catalogue effectively constitutes the major link used by the librarian to ensure the connection between material or electronic documentary resources and the user. It is thus vital to facilitate both access and use. Unfortunately, although the use of computers is considerably widespread in the public, difficulties in locating documents continue, and the user must on occasion navigate between 'noise' and 'silence' among the responses provided by the computerized catalogues. At times confronted with such an enormous number of results that it is difficult to find really relevant information, and at other times with a somewhat disconcerting absence of responses, the inexperienced user is often disoriented. The organization structures of various documentary research systems introduce constraints which are difficult to overcome. Thus, despite the conviviality of the new on-line catalogues, their operational logic some-times remains unfamiliar to the public. Unlike the printed catalogue, their architecture is not apparent at first glance. The localization process is slow, taking place through the succession of increasingly precise screens. It is moreover legitimate to think that with time there will be new ways of capturing and locating information on screen (and will it still be possible to speak of reading in this case?). Finally, when the systems offer several modes of research, there is always one that imposes itself by default, and most users are unaware that they are only using a tiny part of the catalogue's potential. The under-use of available technical means is in fact one of the major problems of which librarians are becoming aware. Up to now it was masked by the material's apparent ease of use or by its relative ability to attract users: someone sees a flashing screen, they stop, they tap a few keys, without necessarily obtaining results, or else they carefully avoid the confrontation with these technical objects.

The person who manages to familiarize him or herself with the subtleties of the new computerized catalogue can nonetheless profit greatly from its expanded research and navigation possibilities. Each request by title, author, subject, and so on, in effect leads to a detailed notice which, in turn, thanks to hyperlinks, leads to other lists that can be explored: these are of other works written by the author or authors; of other titles contained in the Subject list, or, further still, of other titles in a collection or other documents printed by the same publisher. In this way the user can define his search to a precise subject of interest or enlarge it at will, 'surf' on the catalogue to a point where, whether intentionally not, the initial project has been left behind. With a little experience of computers, it is thus possible to enter into a form of computerized navigation in open seas unlike the coastal navigation where users only wander around the library shelves and remain subjected to its physical space. In consequence, we must tone down the criticism of indirect access evoked above, since for some people this possibility of meta-research maximizes the chances of finding an unknown or simply unexpected document.

It is possible, in sum, to suppose that the computerized catalogues of many libraries tend in some respects to resemble the search engines offered on the Internet. This is true, with the minor qualification that in the first case the librarians try as much as possible to avoid 'noise', whereas in the second the search engine designers seem to go to every possible length to avoid 'silence'. Nevertheless, at a basic level, the objective sought by each is the same: to provide the user with the greatest possible amount of relevant responses. But it is expressed and put into action through two different visions of the world. Clearly, the specificity of the librarian's profession encourages these professionals to aim for cultural excellence, or at least, a certain conception of excellence. This is no doubt what leads them to consider television, radio and Internet as 'noisy' sources of information, and books, CDs, videos and CD Roms as more 'silent' sources of information.

Conclusion: traces of use

To make a collection of electronic documents available, as we saw with the preceding examples, is one thing. To monitor the use the public makes – or does not make – of it is another thing, and it is just as important. In truth, most libraries have some difficulty precisely measuring the success of their digital resources. Quantitative tools turn out to be disappointing in assessing practices which are still only used by a minority. According to the last survey carried out at the Bpi, in total 11 per cent of visitors declared they had used the Internet in the library (in open or selective access) on that same day, and 4 per cent a CD Rom. This apparent under-use of the CD Rom collection is confirmed by the consultation statistics produced by the servers. Moreover, nothing in this quantitative data allows us to estimate the 'quality' of the uses which are made of these documents except perhaps for the duration of the consultation. We know effectively that a good number of CD Roms – notably the bibliographical tools – are difficult, if not to say complex, to handle and that it is not rare for a user to abandon them. As for the selection of catalogued sites at the Bpi, its performance is uneven. Next to the bestsellers – the on-line editions of foreign newspapers, for example – which have clearly found their regular users, certain resources seem to escape the attention of users. The terminals that allow users to navigate freely on the Internet, on the other hand, are taken by storm: only the number of available places limits the consultations.

On the ground, librarians are finding that these new tools generate surprisingly few questions. It seems that users are more willingly address their neighbours than the personnel to resolve their problems. It is difficult, therefore, to have a precise idea about this public – not to mention the virtual public of the library website, which by definition is at a distance. In fact, what the librarians notice above all is the abuse of the facilities! For example, various dealings around 'free' Internet and its reservation system, the use of the note-taker programme to write personal texts in order to overcome the absence of word processing tools, and so on.

Sociological studies show that usage is still being built and that most people who use these tools autonomously in a library have already been familiarized with them in their professional milieu or through family or friends. Public reading establishments tend to be places in which users can explore without any financial constraints. Faithful to their mission of democratizing culture, they also frequently offer introductory courses to this new technology. This is all the more important that, given the first results of a current study at the Bpi, the people who wish to learn how to use the Internet tend to do so for much wider purposes than those of documentation, and often for professional considerations. They must find a job, sit a state exam, locate class programmes or connect to a professor's website. It would seem that in our societies, a great number of institutions, companies or universities consider that knowledge of these tools is an established fact or in any case that it is up to each individual to learn how to use them.

We should not turn a blind eye to all those left on the shore because they are not ready to embark on computerized navigation, regardless of its form, or who, simply, refuse to do so on principle. The attraction of the new, the technological, the high-speed – in themselves quite understandable – must not distract public cultural establishments from their fundamental mission: addressing the greatest number without distinction of any kind. At the moment of writing, the technological evolution is continuing its high-speed race. New objects are appearing which will complement and perhaps even surpass existing computer facilities:

electronic books, multi-function personal organizers, and more. New types of users will probably emerge as a result, bringing new requests with them, new ways of doing and probably of thinking. Moreover, competition from the private sector is likely to start making itself felt: in the United States it is now possible to hire private research and information supply services. There is no doubt, therefore, that libraries will be facing new, fundamental questions in the near future. If we wish to keep up with this movement it will be necessary to invent new on-site or on-line services and the profession will have to develop new skills.

Article written by Angélique Bellec, Eliane Bernhart, Agnès Camus-Vigué, Danièle Chatel, Claire Dartois, Isabelle Dussert-Carbone, Christophe Evans, Françoise Gaudet, Gérald Grunberg, Philippe Guillerme, Bernard Huchet and Emmanuèle Payen.

Discussion

The role of the p-library and the e-library

If I have understood it correctly, the librarians of the Bpi are thinking of transferring to the world of electronic texts their role as selector of texts in the world of the paper book. It seems to me that this poses an important problem. In fact, the basis for the choice of the librarian is very different in each case.

The paper-books chosen by the librarian

The paper-book has already been evaluated on many levels upon which the librarian has relied at least partially when choosing titles to be acquired: by editorial committees of publishers, the press, etc.

How the library serves the paper-reader

The library pre-selects and classifies the books most relevant for the library's typical reader.

The library gives access to materials that the reader does not wish or hasn't the resources to buy.

The e-texts chosen by the librarian

What are the criteria used by librarians when selecting the sites they will make available to their readers? I have visited the sites chosen by the Bpi under the rubric 'literature' and I am a bit perplexed: in the poetry section, we find the site of an independent journal attached to the University of Chicoutumi, which would leave any specialist of rhyme and meter completely puzzled. I then put myself in the skin of a student (the typical Bpi reader) who would come to work at the library and who depends, confidently, on the *crus classés* of the Bpi when analysing his alexandrines.

I am lost once more. Then I come across the site reserved for 'African tales': is this really a representative image of African childrens' literature? Or is representativeness not the main criteria?

How the library serves the e-reader

Undoubtedly, the task of the pre-reader will become more and more complicated when he is confronted with the explosion of content available on line. State institutions could play a crucial role in this domain: we must furnish the possibility to all to learn how to find the information he or she seeks. This practical knowledge should not be confused with the ethical knowledge that consists of identifying the truest, the most beautiful or just contents. Faced with the e-text explosion, libraries must redefine how they serve the reader. There are several (not mutually exclusive) possibilities.

(1) We consider that libraries will continue to classify/inventory/make available to the public an ensemble of texts selected for their typical readers. We must then think about the criteria for these libraries when they select e-texts (cf. supra), given that the reference points provided by the paper-book are no longer applicable. In particular, one must beware of three things: (a) the ghost of the paternalistic library (why not e-Harlequin novels if they are to be found in the paper-collection?) (b) The library should not entirely take the place of paper-book selection committees (or should it do so, it should be in a responsible way and it should provide itself with the means of its policy, for example, by asking specialists to select sites in their specialities appropriate to the library's reader profile). (c) Lack of care in considering the complementarity of the e-library and the p-library. In particular, there is a ton of unpublished texts on the Internet which should be evaluated, classified, inventoried, labeled so as to orient the typical reader. Why not links from published p-texts to unpublished e-texts?

One should also enquire into the role of the selection committee of the e-library. The financial criteria of the p-library cannot be transposed to the e-library: 50 terminals for just a part of the Internet cost the same as 50 terminals for the entire Internet. One can orient the typical reader without censoring e-readers. Of course, there is the problem of the reader who uses the library like a free Internet café. But is there not a way to shut off the faucet of messenger service-only servers? (And since there is neither music, nor popcorn, nor the telephone, nor coffee, etc. the Internet café client will perhaps eventually prefer to pay rather than put himself in the skin of the e/p-library reader?)

(2) Libraries assume a new role: to teach the reader to look for and evaluate e-texts. The problem is that the specialization necessary correctly to fill this sort of function has not yet appeared. But librarians are well-placed to take

on this new role, since they are information specialists. Moreover, professors have neither the time, nor necessarily the competence to do this. Why not ask philosophers, historians, specialists of historiography, computer programmers to join librarians to work out a module, which would eventually be computerized?

(3) Aside from guiding the reader, librarians could establish structures that would help readers to find their own way together. A computer structure could thus aid the p/e-library user to guide any reader from content A to content B if he finds the pertinent link (and eventually give him the possibility to justify this link). And why not ask certain book authors to guide the reader toward e-texts (by the bias of library sites, for example, which could be updated by the authors whenever they wish?)

Fabienne Martin

The bookmarks of the cyber-wine collector

I have had occasion to observe how Internet workstations are used in public libraries and to see that the bookmark collections which are the choice of the cyber-wine collector, had little success in general. There are two principal reasons for this. Firstly, this field is in its infancy. The problem with the Web is the number of vintages and the fact that, within each vintage, new growers are born and die each day. The mutualizing of bookmarks is inevitable, just as was that of catalogues. But I am not sure that this occurs thanks to intelligent agents. The community directories, for example, that of the Open Directory Project: *http://dmoz.org/*) seems to me a more interesting as well as accessible alternative (artificial intelligence is particularly prodigal in un-kept promises…) The second reason why users reject collections of bookmarks that are not their own is the intoxication they wish to experience, live, without mediation, by plunging into the immensity of the Web. It is possible (and I would say probable) that this wish of Web users is infantile and will gradually disappear. Until then, it indicates to us that the personal and affective component is very strong in relation to the Web. There will undoubtedly be as much difference between a mutualized collection of bookmarks and a catalogue as there is today between a library and the Web.

Serge Pouts-Lajus

Replies to Fabienne Martin and Serge Pouts-Lajus

What the Internet represents to the Bpi is something even more diverse than certain commentaries would lead us to believe. Faced with a big population, varied in its expectations, our goal is to guarantee an equal distribution of access to different electronic resources. Four types of computer workstations have been defined to regulate this access. And it seems important to me to say that one of these profiles gives access to electronic documents on CD-rom and on the Internet (more than 200), acquired at a heavy price and representing a considerable budget. They are inescapable as sources of rapid reference, as textual sources with text-searching tools, as multimedia sources or simply because they do not exist in another form. It remains certain that today, if the 415 workstations of the Bpi gave access to the whole Internet, too many readers would be deprived *de facto* of resources essential to their studies, because someone is trying to find a job or resolve a problem in their personal life. The proportion of 50 Internet workstations thus seems right to us. A library cannot single-handedly resolve the problem of today's strong demand, which we think will continue, given the costs of equipment for certain persons. The increase in the number of establishments granting open and free access to the Web in communities and neighbourhoods, seems like a good solution. The recent setting up of 'multimedia cultural spaces' contribute to this evolution. As to the apparent arbitrariness represented by the selection of Internet resources proposed to readers, we are aware that there are imperfections and even lacks due, very certainly in part to an insufficient 'mutualization'. And, in spite of the increase in the volume of documents on the Web, and without pretending always to make the round of what Internet offers for free on all subjects, a directory of websites also reveals the difficulty of constituting a coherent ensemble of sources that treat the different aspects and levels of any question, quite simply because the Internet does not carry the entire intellectual production. By favouring French language resources, and without limiting ourselves to them, our goal is to offer guides to access to research information and to complete and enrich our general collection.

Ms Fabienne Martin expressed astonishment at two literature sites we selected. Let me clarify that the site on African tale does not fall under the rubric of children's literature but of tales and African oral traditions. This site, regularly updated, we found rich in information accessible to the public sought by the Bpi, because it gives all the events and activity throughout in this domain France, and it contains a rich bibliography of books and articles. As for the Quebec site, it is a university site of exclusively on-line journals, and it is one of our roles to familiarize people with these new documents. It is true that the selection is not very up-to-date and we will perhaps be obliged to erase it. A project to elaborate a base of links in collaboration with other public libraries needs to be established at the Bpi. We feel sure that a bigger group of professionals would reinforce expertise and produce a collection more likely to satisfy a diverse leadership. Serge Pouts-Lajus' remarks are very relevant and I would like to add that, for those of us who observe the Bpi, the majority of users who take no interest in selections of Internet links have not previously visited the library and come only in order to enjoy a rapid and free connection to the Internet. I do not pass judgement on this attitude which is, after all, legitimate. And I am among those who understand the 'intoxication' that one might feel on surfing freely on the net. During our orientation programmes for beginners, we are very much aware of this desire to deepen the functioning of messenger services or other means of using the Internet for private ends, aspects that we can only touch on. If we evoke all the facets of Internet, we would situate ourselves in the framework of a media library which favours the search for information or documentation. As to the Open Directory Project, I wonder what actual means are at the disposal of this enormous directory to verify the authority of the 'editors' who evaluate the selected sites when the committee of direction is small? But I recognize the value of such an undertaking, which, because it is founded upon a large community, may also be capable of reacting in the face of erroneous evaluations or selections.

Colette Bergeal

Rethinking 'collections' and selection in the post-Gutenberg age

Librarians, in virtue of their profession (ex officio, so to speak), are being propelled toward the digital future even faster than their users. Yet they are still not seeing far enough, hence not thinking radically enough. They are still thinking in terms of incoming 'collections', a Gutenberg, object-based view, updating only their notion of the medium of the collection (papers, CD-rom, on line). I think this is short-sighted. What is needed is a post-Gutenberg, bit-based view, of distributed access rather than local acquisitions.

There will still be some selection, but there will no longer be collection. Digital 'holdings' will be distributed worldwide, more like the current 'inter-library loan' model, but for all 'inventory' (which will only be virtual) and not just for those works that are not 'owned'! In other words, there will be site-licensing and/or pay-per-view for accessing the bits, which will not be held in a local 'collection', particularly (though sometimes it might be easier or faster to store some bits locally).

Yes, there will be some selection and taste exercised in designing the local license agreements, because no library will be able to afford limitless access to all bits for all its users (and, N.B.! we are only speaking of non-give-away bits now: I will return to the special case of give-away bits shortly). But these will only be default options, because, as is true with inter-library loan today, in principle, despite the limits of a library's specific, selected holdings, today's user can, by special dispensation and intervention, usually get a hold of unheld works too. (A digital library, by the way, is largely a consortium of users, giving the users greater access than if they had to pay for it individually.)

There will be only two exceptions to this. One will be the analog collection, which will be the digital library's counterpart of today's 'rare book collection'. (The Gutenberg book is merely the extension of the erstwhile rare book, into the post-Gutenberg age.)

The second exception will be a more dramatic departure from what libraries are used to doing, yet they are undoubtedly the best place and qualified to do it correctly. Research institutional libraries (e.g., most university libraries) will not only be *consumers* of the global distributed bits, they will also be *providers*, in the special case of the give-away literature: The refereed research output of their own researchers will be stored and made accessible as an *outgoing* collection, through interoperable institutional self-archiving.

In exchange for providing on-line access to this outgoing collection for free, libraries and their institutions will gain free incoming access to the full contents of all the refereed periodicals they currently have to pay for (dearly), because those will be the contents of all the other institutions' outgoing refereed research collections. And 70 to 90 per cent of the annual windfall savings on the former serials expenditures for this give-away refereed research will then be available to be spent on the licences for the much larger non-give-away corpus (while 10 to 30 per cent will need to be redirected to paying the journals for refereeing the instition's annual outgoing collection).

To a certain extent, this distributed self-archiving model will also apply to esoteric outgoing manuscripts that never sought nor would have found an access-fee-based market.

Stevan Harnad

The role of librarians

Librarians do engage in 'selecting, acquiring and processing documents, making them available to the public, conserving them ...'

But for me the interesting side of the work is in helping users find these documents, and, even more, in helping users figure out what documents they want to find. These are traditional functions too – they arose because the librarian knew better than the patron what available information there was.

This has normally implied person-to-person contact, but not necessarily. Providing subject and author access (otherwise known as metadata) is a way of doing it, and we have learned that it must be done in a very sophisticated way to do much good. Neither the libraries' traditional devices nor the current Web devices do well for this, except in the hands of a really experienced user, which in practice usually means a librarian. The 'embarras de richesses' is not just a catch phrase, but a real obstacle. Stevan, being an enlightened user, recognizes that 'navigational and classification help are always welcome'. But the digital medium by itself will not 'breed' the necessary means: intelligent analysts from a variety of backgrounds working together will invent the means – and I do not think this process will be either rapid or easy.

Whether libraries should be providers is uncertain. We are moving slowly in that direction, but we are moving primarily not through the distribution of the current output of our scholars but through the distribution of our rare materials and manuscript archives. That we might be the most appropriate campus agency for institutional self-archiving of current work sounds logical, but may not be the best fit in terms of university funding and politics. I am one librarian who thinks we should take it on, but that's only my personal opinion.

David Goodman

8
Reading without Writing

Dan Sperber

If you are reading this text, chances are that you use spoken and written language with the same ease. You and I live in environments where language is omnipresent in the form of either acoustic or visual stimuli, and every day we are likely to be processing more written text than spoken text. We tend to value the ability to read and write as much we value our more basic perceptual and motor abilities. We see literacy as essential to self-realization. We easily forget that writing is a recent invention in the history of Homo Sapiens, that universal literacy became a goal only a few generations ago, and that this goal is far from being achieved. Even when we do remember that writing is recent and that widespread literacy is new, we take it for granted that they are here to stay. Well, are they?

The most controversial thesis I will defend here is that the revolution in information and communication technology may soon turn writing into a relic of the past: it will be replaced by the automatic transcription of speech – whereas reading is here to stay. My aim, however, is not to prophesize, but to reflect on the future with the help of tools developed within the cognitive and social sciences.

However controversial this view, I should point out that an even more radical claim has been made elsewhere: it is that both writing *and* reading will soon be things of the past, a cumbersome pair of prosthetic practices that, in retrospect, will come to be regarded as a mere parenthesis in human history. This has been argued in particular by William Crossman: 'By enabling us to access stored information orally–aurally, talking computers will finally make it possible for us to replace all written language with spoken language. We will be able to store and retrieve information simply by talking, listening, and looking at graphics, not at text. With this giant step forward into the past, we're about to recreate oral culture on a more efficient and reliable technological foundation' ('The Coming Age of Talking Computers', *The Futurist*, December 1999). I argue, however, that there the is a relevant asymmetry between writing and reading that should ensure the survival of the latter.

The past and the present

Before taking a peek into the future, let us look at the past and present. In most of the human societies that have ever existed, children became competent adult without the help of any formal teaching. They acquired language, knowledge of their natural and social environment, techniques, rules of etiquette, tales, songs, and other cultural competencies without any formal training or schooling. They may have been helped by advices and corrections of adults and other children, but such pedagogical assist-ance comes in support of a spontaneous process of acquisition, and is very different from institutional teaching. Institutional teaching typically serves to transmit knowledge and competencies that would hardly ever be acquired spontaneously, and that therefore, if they were not systematically taught, would be unlikely to emerge and stabilize as elements of culture.

Particularly striking is the contrast between the acquisition of language and that of writing. In ordinary conditions, language acquisition occurs spontaneously in every child at a very early age. Pedagogical assistance (which is virtually absent in some societies) plays at most a marginal role. By contrast, writing and reading are acquired, if at all, through a lengthy and intensive process of deliberate training in interaction with a teacher. Is it that writing systems are more complex than languages? Quite the opposite. A language such as English, Amharic, or Chinese is a much more complex object than an alphabetic, syllabic or even a logographic writing system. In fact, linguists have not yet succeeded in providing a fully explicit grammar of any language, whereas writing systems are based on fully explicit rules. The remarkable difference in the patterns of acquisition of language on the one hand and writing on the other hand has to do with psychological predispositions: humans are predisposed to spontaneously acquire the language of their community. They have no such predisposition for the acquisition of writing. It is writing systems, rather, that had to adapt to human perceptual and motor predispositions that had emerged well before the invention of writing. How is it, given these conditions, that writing systems have emerged, spread, and stabilized at all?

Writing did not emerge as the commonly shared ingredient of culture that it has now become in modern societies, but as a specialized skill, practised by professional scribes in the service of the state. Specialized skills emerge because the demand for the products of these skills is sufficient to cause (either through economic motivation or through coercion by the end-users) a minority of people to become specialists. The cognitive difficulty involved in the acquisition of such professional skills is overcome, within the small group of specialists, by a heavy investment in training apprentices. Teaching the skill typically becomes the subject-matter of a second-order, didactic skill.

The development of writing resulted in the accumulation and diversification of written texts. This, together with correlated economic and political transformations, caused the costs involved in acquiring literacy to become lower than the benefits of literacy for an ever-increasing proportion of the population. In modern society the benefits are greater than the cost for the majority of the population, and illiteracy has become a stigma and therefore a cost in its own right.

There is another important factor that helps explain the generalization of literacy. Once the skill is properly acquired, writing becomes a kind of automatism: one can write without paying any conscious attention to the hand movements involved (and this is true of typing as well). Similarly, for the proficient reader, reading is just another form of automatic visual pattern recognition. Most earlier forms of writing, such as Sumerian cuneiform with its relatively cumbersome materials and tools, did not lend themselves to a similar kind of fluency.

Thus two facts explain the spread of literacy: the fact that the benefits became, for more and more people, greater than the costs; and the fact that, once the initial costs of acquisition of the skills are paid, the costs of using these skills are comparatively negligible. These two facts are linked. If the distribution of costs and benefits over the life span of individuals were more even, or, in other terms, if the marginal cost of writing and reading did not dramatically drop with proficiency, then people would read and write much less. (This incidentally, was the situation when writing had to be done in stone or in clay.) With a less frequent use of writing and reading, there would be fewer written texts to read, and fewer people disposed to read them. As a consequence, the benefits of writing and reading would be smaller, and might not compare favourably with the costs, except for a small group of professional scribes. Actually, once learnt, writing and reading are easy and generally profitable. The greater the number of people who read and write, the greater the benefits involved in being able to do so oneself, and the greater the motivation in having one's children acquire the skills. How then could the future of writing and reading be in doubt? The short answer is that writing is not the only way to produce written texts.

Until recently, many rich or powerful people would dictate to a secretary rather than write themselves. Some literary and historical works, such as Milton's *Paradise Lost* or Napoleon's and Las Cases' *Mémorial de Sainte-Hélène* were dictated. Dictating may be advantageous for reasons of speed, or it may be a matter of necessity as in the case of the elderly Milton, who had lost his sight. Still, if given the choice, most of us would rather write than dictate. The main reason, I presume, is that when you dictate you have much less control over your text than when you write. In any case, traditional dictation was a form of division of scriptural labour, not a way of rendering writing altogether obsolete. Now, however, the new information technologies are about to provide a novel form of dictation without the shortcomings of the old, and in such a way that the division of labour will not be between employer and employee but between people and machines.

Speech recognition software that provides speech-to-text conversion has been rapidly improving over the past few years, allowing one to talk in natural continuous speech at a conversational pace and see one's words appear on the screen. At present, the rate of error is still too high, the programme requires initial training, and many users who don't really need such a programme get discouraged. I take it for granted, however, that these shortcomings will be overcome and that, in a matter of years, it will be possible to speak normally, have the machine transcribe one's speech with very few errors while distinguishing, in the flow of speech, instructions (e.g. 'Underline!') to be obeyed from data to be transcribed. It will become easier to dictate to a machine than it ever was to dictate to a secretary. More generally, it will be easier to give instructions to the computer (and to all kinds of appliances, vehicles and other machines) orally than through keyboards, mice, and other manual devices. Machines will be able to provide information orally rather than through screens. Thanks to progress in text-to-speech technology, machines will be able to read aloud written texts, in a quite natural sounding voice. Natural language oral interactions with machines will become the norm rather than the exception.

However imperfect at present, these speech-to-text and text-to-speech technologies are already transforming the lives of people who, because of visual, hearing, or motor impairments, or because of dyslexia, have difficulties writing or reading. The obvious reason why millions of illiterate people around the world don't also take advantage of these technologies is just poverty – which explains why they are illiterate in the first place.

Soon, then, the costs and benefits of writing and reading will be compared not just with those of illiteracy but also with those of alternative ways of creating and accessing texts, provided by new technologies. How may this affect the future of writing and reading?

Individual choices

Whereas speech is an event unfolding in time, a written text is an object with a greater or lesser permanence in space (greater when engraved in stone, lesser when chalked on the blackboard). Because of this difference in their temporal and spatial mode of existence, speech and writing are suited for different uses. The development of writing has not resulted in the decline of speech. I know of no evidence showing that speech is less used, or less well used, in literate than in illiterate societies. If anything, the opposite seems to be the case. The development of writing has resulted rather in the emergence of new uses of language, in larger and denser social networks, and therefore, also, in new opportunities to use speech and greater sophistication in the art of speech.

What will happen if mechanical speech-to-text and text-to-speech conversions now become ordinary tools in the process of communication? Will they cause the emergence of additional uses of language, as was the case with writing, or will they displace writing as a tool, and, if so, with what consequences? It is important here to distinguish the activity of writing (handwriting or typing), the written text, and the activity of reading. If speech-to-text conversion were used systematically and text-to-speech conversion only occasionally (a plausible scenario), this would be the end, or at least the marginalization, of the activity of writing but neither of the written text nor of the activity of reading. If text-to-speech conversion were used systematically and speech-to-text conversion only occasionally (a much less plausible scenario), this would be the end, or at least the marginalization, of the activity of reading but neither of the written text nor of the activity of writing. If both speech-to-text and text-to-speech were used systematically (Crossman's prediction), this would be the end of both the activity of writing and that of reading and therefore of the written text: machines would use machine language to encode appropriate information for conversion from and into speech; these machine language encodings would not look like our written texts, and, anyhow, would not be seen, let alone read, by anyone.

Whether or not societies end up replacing writing and reading with conversion technologies will not directly result from a collective decision based on a vision of the societal consequences, but from the accumulation of individual decisions. To what extent, then, are individuals likely to adopt these new technologies?

Speech-to-text conversion

How well could individuals achieve, by means of speech-to-text conversion, the various goals they pursue in writing texts? At first blush and in general, what can be done with a written text does not depend on whether initially it has been handwritten, typed, dictated to a secretary, or transcribed by a machine. The few exceptions – holograph wills and scented love letters for instance – are no more obstacles to the generalization of speech-to-text conversion than they have been to the generalization of word-processing.

For an individual, choosing to produce a written text by means of speech-to-text conversion rather than by one or another form of writing is not going to be such a momentous decision and will be determined by considerations of practicality and taste. Speech-to-text conversion has one obvious and truly major practical advantage over writing: speech is several times faster than handwriting or even typing. It has one obvious practical disadvantage: speech is noisy and could not comfortably be used as a method for composing texts in most work, classroom, or even home environments of today. However, if speaking turned out to be a much more effective mode of producing written texts, working space could be reorganized (or maybe noise could be selectively controlled by means of yet other new technologies).

The main argument that may come to mind in favour of keeping up the activity of writing is not so much practical as it is intellectual. Writing allows one to express one's thought in a richer, subtler and more controlled way than speech. Writers can write, correct, rewrite and, in the end, produce a text free of the hesitations and repairs of oral utterances. The stylistic richness and specificity of the written text comes from the exploitation of these possibilities. Note however that these possibilities result not from the activity of writing per se, but from the fact that writers can read what they write as they write it. Imagine that, as you write, you could only see the words you were writing, and that once written they would become invisible and unerasable: then all the stylistic advantages of writing over speech would be lost (and worse: since writing is slower than speech, the amount of text that the writer could hold in short-term memory would be smaller, so that writing would produce shorter and simpler sentences than those produced in speech). Imagine on the other hand that what you dictated to a machine could immediately be read on the screen, and that, moreover, it could be easily corrected by means of oral commands (and maybe of some manual commands too): this essentially oral interaction with a machine would offer opportunities of stylistic elaboration identical to those of writing. The creative potential of writing does not come from the movements of the hand but from those of the eye. In other words what makes the process of writing uniquely valuable is the simultaneous reading of what you write.

There is an important aesthetic reason to prefer speech-to-text conversion to writing. However used we may be to moving a pen over paper or to pressing keys, speech is much more natural. At first it will seem awkward to dictate to a machine, but once the awkwardness is overcome, it may become an extraordinary relief to be free from the artificiality, the muscular tension, the fidgetiness of writing and to hear the sound of one's own voice as one expresses oneself through language. Once it will be possible to by-pass writing, many people may come to realize what a source of discomfort it always was to them.

If speech-to-text technology proves effective and congenial, people may end up giving up writing altogether without ever deciding to do so or even noticing that they have done so (just as many of us have, in fact, ceased to write by hand).The cumulative effect of such individual decisions at a cultural level is hard to predict, but it is likely to be considerable.

Text-to-speech conversion

Text-to-speech conversion is a way to have a written text read to one instead of reading it. Just as some wealthy or powerful people have used secretaries in order to dictate and not to write themselves, so they have had texts read to them by hired readers. What you get from a text read to you is different from what you get by reading it yourself. The tone of voice of the reader contributes to the way in which you interpret the text. In some cases – an actor reading a poem, a mother reading a story to her child – being read to may be wonderful. But in general, we would rather interpret what we read in our own silent voice. Moreover, we may never grow fond of the tone of voice of a computer and we may remain justly reticent to be influenced by it in our interpretation of a text.

Whereas it may be pleasurable and even illuminating to hear a narrative or a poem read aloud, there are other kinds of texts that are much better comprehended when read alone. Such texts are typically written to be silently read, and are hard or impossible to follow when they are listened to. Anybody who has been bored to death by a scholar reading aloud a written lecture knows what I am talking about. To understand why this is so, consider the role of short-term memory in comprehension. In the process of listening to speech (whether spontaneous speech or the reading aloud of a written text), the information given by every spoken sound must be attended to and retained in short-term memory long enough to allow linguistic decoding, or it is lost (although some of it can be reconstructed from the context). Not so with reading: the written text provides an effective external short-term memory store that can be scanned back and forth. This allows readers to follow the text at their own pace as opposed to listening at the pace of the speaker. Readers can first skim the text and then peruse it. They can choose to go back to some earlier passage if they retrospectively become aware of its relevance, or in order to check the consistency of the text. When you read, you loose the extra input provided by tone of voice and gestures, but you gain in the range and depth of what you are able to comprehend and extract from a text.

The fact that readers can see a whole page and readily access any other part of the text provides writers with opportunities not shared by speakers. Writers can use more complex sentences. They can highlight the organization of their text with paragraphs, titles, and subtitles. They can depart from a strict linear organization of the text by adding footnotes, cross-references, or appendixes. They can produce new kinds of objects that are at once linguistic and graphic, such as structured lists and tables. Even in oral presentations, most teachers and lecturers have found it useful or even necessary to provide written text and other graphic documents for the audience to read or examine, in the form of writing on the blackboard, handouts, or, by now, screen projections. Many of the current forms and functions of writing take advantage of the short-term memory effects of a visual presentation. Possibly, some of these functions could be fulfilled by talking machines, but not all of them. For instance, it might be easier just to ask the machine to read a short dictionary entry than to look it up using the alphabetic order. On the other hand, browsing is, and is likely to remain, more effective when done visually than acoustically.

From a practical point of view, listening to a text is much slower than reading. It is also noisier (but this can be easily corrected with headphones). Possibly the stronger obstacle to the abandonment of reading is the role it plays, not in accessing texts, but in producing them. As I pointed out, what we rightly value most in the activity of writing is not the hand movements (or else typing would not have replaced handwriting to this extent) but the fact that we can read what we write as we write it.

All this considered, it is quite implausible that the cumulative effect of individual decisions to use text-to-speech conversion will result in the replacement, at a societal level, of the activity of reading by the systematic use of text-to-speech technology.

Cultural implications

I have attempted so far to develop the following argument: practically all the benefits that seem to come with writing and to justify heavy investment of resources into teaching the skill are, in fact, benefits derived from reading. Even the apparent expressive advantages of writing over speech come from the fact that, as you write, you read what you are writing. Writing is essentially a cost paid in order to be able to profit from reading. This cost was unavoidable, and it still is – but not for very long now. As soon as technology will make it possible to see one's speech properly transcribed as it unfolds, and to modify the transcription by means of oral instructions (and also, probably, of pointing and highlighting hand movements), writing will present no advantage that is sufficient to justify its cost. In contrast, having a machine read aloud is in most cases less appealing than reading on one's own.

The cumulative effect of individual decisions to use these new technologies will soon bring about, at the societal level, the near disappearance of writing, whereas people will go on reading. The individual decisions I am talking about will be made by people who will already have paid the main cost involved in writing and reading, that is, not the cost of using these skills, but the cost of acquiring them. Even with this cost paid, it will become preferable to move to the oral production of written texts, just as the fact of having learnt to write by hand is not stopping most of us to write almost exclusively with a keyboard.

Once writing isn't practised anymore (except by calligraphists), what will happen to its teaching?

Whatever the tongue and the writing system, the teaching of writing always involves an overcost when compared to the teaching of reading. Reading can be taught on its own, whereas the teaching of writing presupposes that of reading. Since the teaching of writing and that of reading have been systematically linked, we have no controlled comparison that would allow us to estimate the overcost involved in the teaching of writing proper. Moreover, even a controlled comparison would not really allow us to estimate the economy of effort that would result from teaching children just to read, for all past and present pedagogies (with very few exceptions, such as cases of students with specific disabilities) aim at jointly teaching both skills. If reading were to be taught on its own, the pedagogy would have to be rethought, and particular attention would have to be paid to the role that computers could play in it. It is quite conceivable that, using the new technologies, reading could be taught on its own in a much more intuitive and easy way than the reading–writing pair.

Does all this mean that, once writing will have been replaced by transcription, only reading will be taught, and that the resources thus freed (children's, teachers', and parents time) can be used otherwise? Certainly not. Such a cultural transition is a complex process and meets various factors of inertia.

In developed countries, the people who might have the greatest interest in the demise of writing, that is children, are not in a position to judge, and anyhow won't be asked. The first generations of adults who will move to dictation after years of writing will already have paid the price of learning. The fact of having paid the price, the familiarity with the practice, the absence of distinction between the teaching of writing and that of reading, the contempt or the compassion for illiterate people, all these will converge and make these adults fervent defenders of the teaching of writing. Teachers trained to teach writing, and who often do it with outstanding dedication and patience, will be reluctant to admit that all this knowledge might be outdated. One easily anticipates passionate pleas and diatribes of defenders of writing, who, even though they won't anymore be practising writing themselves, will feel that they are defending culture itself against, worse than illiterates, henchmen of illiteracy. One may assume that the teaching of writing will long outlive its obsolescence.

This scenario, where writing remains among us as a compulsory scholastic activity, is not the only plausible one. It ignores various factors that could tilt things another way. Teaching in general is likely to undergo radical changes as a result of the development of the new technologies. The acquisition of reading skills might take place earlier and more spontaneously thanks to the interaction with machines, this resulting in a *de facto* dissociation between the teaching of reading and that of writing. Writing might end up playing a major role only in writing classes and being less and less used in the teaching of other subject-matters. In such conditions, the teaching of writing would rapidly loose much of its significance. New generations of adults could be tempted to grant it fewer resources and to render it optional.

Even this modified scenario does not take into account the diversity of situations across countries. In many countries, most of the resources for education are invested in the teaching of literacy, and the illiteracy, at least partial, of a great part of the population is a major obstacle to economic development. In such countries, the use of speech-to-text and also text-to-speech conversion technologies, if their cost were sufficiently lowered, might turn out to be an outstanding way of accelerating both the social promotion of individuals and collective economic development. If so, in these countries, education will have to be rethought on a new basis: while, at present, writing skills occupy centre-stage, they might in the future be made almost redundant.

Even if it resulted from the accumulation of modest and sensible individual decisions, the marginalization of writing and of its teaching might well have major cultural effects. These effects are hard to foresee at present. It is all too easy to speak of a return to orality. The most profound effect that writing has had on human civilizations has been to allow them to become truly cumulative instead of evolving forever within the limits of human long-term memory. Far from reversing these effects, the new technologies allow new forms of cultural accumulation as well as new ways of mining the accumulated information.

Still, the generalization of the oral production of written texts is likely to have significant effects on the texts themselves. These effects might be on the subtle rather than on the dramatic side, and be therefore comparable to the effects of the progressive replacement of handwriting by typing, and then of simple typing by word processing. This move has favoured the emergence or the development of new styles and new genres in a way that has not yet been systematically studied. The composition of written texts by means of the voice might have deeper effects. Various forms of writing have resulted in some degree of divergence (varying from tongue to tongue) between oral and written dialects. Will a return to the natural organ of linguistic expression put an end to this divergence, or will it cause the emergence of new dialects?

The very symbols used in the different writing systems result from a compromise between the needs of the hand and those of the eye. Printing, and now the computer, have made possible the development of new characters which, however, must still remain similar enough to handwritten ones. This constraint could altogether disappear; a new evolution of writing systems could emerge, exclusively guided by considerations of visual ergonomics and aesthetics.

One can imagine anything. On the other hand, to speculate in a manner that is both informed and reasoned is difficult. Difficult but not altogether impossible, I hope.

Discussion

Advantages of speech-to-text?

This article raises many interesting points, especially in the context of the transition from handwriting to typing on keyboards and then (hopefully) speech-to-text and voice recognition.

One group in society who would surely benefit from this would be people who suffer from RSI (repetitive stress injury) caused by typing – my opinion is that compared to writing, reading and speaking, typing would have to be one of the most unnatural and damaging activities brought about by the computer revolution.

The benefits for people who have not learnt to write are also obvious – perhaps speech-to-text could be viewed as the final leveller in humanity's progress from elitism (monks in abbeys) to dissemination (Gutenberg) and finally individual creation and autonomy (the internet). These are generalizations, doubtlessly, but the potential is there.

The only problem seems to me to be that we have been hearing about advances in voice recognition software for at least a decade now. Even if the technology does improve, in order for so-called 'illiterate' people (sorry, I find the term slightly offensive) to be able to make use of it, they must have access to that technology. People will still have to fill out forms issued by the state (e.g. welfare applications). They will still have to be able to read or comprehend street signs. Perhaps this view is inherently Western, yet I think the opposite view is too idealistic.

The critique of the traditional model of literacy (writing plus reading) offered here is instructive. Certainly a large gap exists between the teaching of literacy and the levels of literacy in the community (one survey published in Australia argues that up to 40 per cent of the adult population is 'functionally illiterate').

The question is: does speech-to-voice (and associated technologies) work to narrow or increase that gap?

David Prater

Sperber's response: the new technologies and the rich countries/poor countries gap

David Prater raises a very important question, which obviously cannot be fully answered today, but on which we may be able to reflect intelligently. Would effective speech-to-text and also text-to-speech conversion technology help bridge the gap between poorer societies where illiteracy is still massive, and more literate, richer societies?

This will depend on the cost of access to these technologies (appropriate machines and software). This cost must be compared to the cost of teaching writing and reading, which is high both for the societies that organize this teaching and for the individuals who have to invest much time in learning these skills. I don't have figures to offer (and they would be educated guesses at best since we are talking about future technologies and costs), but it does not seem implausible that, in a relatively near future, it would be more cost-effective for societies to provide the technological tools than to provide the teaching, and that it would be more cost-effective for an important proportion of individuals to invest in the technological tools and make them work to their benefit, rather than invest in learning the skills. If this is correct, then the new technologies might help bridge the economic gap between poorer and richer societies.

However, this might create a new kind of cultural gap, with two aspects. To begin with, in more developed societies it is likely that writing will continue to be taught even when it is not ordinarily used anymore (just as Latin is being taught even though it has been in near total disuse for centuries). The cognitive value of such teaching would be unclear (which is not to say it would be nil), but it would be a factor of differentiation between an 'elite' of people having learnt this now luxury skill, and others (just as having been taught Latin, whatever its uses otherwise, is a mark of belonging to a cultural elite in Western societies).

More importantly, poorer countries might resort not just to speech-to-text technology but also, and much more heavily than richer countries, to text-to-speech technology, by-passing not just writing, but also reading. This may prove cost-effective for many major aspects of economic development, but would establish not just a symbolic but also a genuine cultural inequality between those who had learnt the skills that allow elaborate text correction and composition, and others. Another, more general, way of making this last point, is that traditional literacy has combined long-term memory and short-term memory advantages. Replacing writing by speech-to-text conversion preserves both kinds of advantages. Replacing writing by speech-to-text conversion and reading by text-to-speech conversion preserves only the long-term memory advantages of literacy and forsakes the short-term memory advantages. This may be OK for business, but it obviously is not for many forms of cultural activity.

Dan Sperber

First reactions

Written transcription by the intermediary of the computer obviously presupposes that the transcribed word is itself a literate word. In other words, the dictated word must conform to a codified syntax and vocabulary as we know them today. It is, for example, improbable that a machine will ever be capable of transcribing a text such as Gildas Bourdet's *Le Saperleau*.

Under these conditions we are concerned with a 'simple' exchange of writing instruments. We would then give pride of place to oral expression. The form of writing would thus be altered, but one would still need a considerable mastery of the language to produce a text that wouldn't make the reader nauseous for lack of structure. Certain great professors know how to produce this sort of speech which could also be directly exploitable, but they are not legion.

The use of the word to replace writing while respecting the literate word has long been used in Jewish education. Over a hundred years ago children in the Yeshivas read the Talmud while listening to the commentaries of their teacher on the text without writing a line. What is more, this practice was bilingual. The Talmud was written in Hebrew (a written and not spoken language) and commented upon and translated into Yiddish (a spoken and not written – at least in very conservative circles – language). The students were thus obliged without taking a single note to understand the text of the Talmud in an unfamiliar language through the words of their mother-tongue while remembering by heart passages of the text in the original Hebrew. In this instance, it was the intellect of the students that served as a tool of transcription, since they ended up by knowing Hebrew and could cite it advisedly without reading it. This sort of mental gymnastics was probably not within reach of everyone, as we can see in the Yiddish author Scholem Aleichem's novel *Tevie the Milkman*. Tevie prides himself on being learned and studs his statements with citations from the Talmud or other erudite Hebrew texts but makes mistakes, misquotes, leaves out words, etc.

This is sort of the same process proposed by Dan Sperber when he assumes that machines will be more efficacious at transcribing and reconstituting without mistakes.

Patrick Altman

Literate and rhetorical words

Patrick Altman writes: 'Written transcription by the intermediary of the computer obviously presupposes that the transcribed word is itself a literate word. In other words, the dictated word must conform to a codified syntax and vocabulary as we know them today.' I would like to come back to this notion of the 'literate word'. It seems to me that in our cultural tradition we often use 'literate word' and 'written word' interchangeably.

The mastery of the literate word in our culture passes obligatorily by the acquisition of writing and the rules of grammar of the written language, with the exception of a few particular cases of transmission, such as the case of Talmud teaching cited by Patrick Altman. In learning to write, we also internalize the forms of literate speech of our culture.

But the new technologies render the contingent nature of the equivalence between 'literate' and 'written' even more explicit. For example, we are witnessing a progressive coming together of the forms of 'free' oral discourse and the written word, as in the case of e-mail.

If Dan Sperber is right in his predictions, one could witness the introduction into our culture and learning techniques of rhetoric and speech organization independent from writing. Moreover, the history of rhetoric in Antiquity shows well that the learning of the conventions of persuasive speech may be relatively independent of learning to write.

I would like to pose the following question to Dan Sperber. Would the learning of literate forms of speech that would facilitate a mastery of text dictated to a computer, be less costly and difficult than learning how to write, which has the advantage of already incorporating a majority of its conventions?

Gloria Origgi

On teaching writing

For Dan Sperber, the relative novelty of writing in the history of humanity, its steep cost in terms of learning and the imminent arrival on the market of an efficient technology to convert words into text incline one to think that writing will end up disappearing. Why not? It is true that the keyboard, in many cases, replaces the pen.

But for all this, must the teaching of writing disappear? For learning how to write is not just a matter of 'hand movements', of handwriting. It is also and above all the knowledge of different linguistic operations that come in when producing text: work on the grammar of texts and speeches, on the constraints of the writing style one has chosen, on operations of designation, characterization, textual cohesion, syntax...So many parameters that make necessary, when writing, incessant referrals back to the text. Dan Sperber recognizes this himself since he anticipates that what one dictates to the machine 'can be easily corrected by means of oral instructions (and perhaps also manual ones)' (p. 16). But it is these operations that actually constitute the act of writing.

Lastly, the current evolution of digital and communication technologies tends to contradict or at least to qualify Dan Sperber's remarks. Henceforth, in fact, as a direct consequence of the specificities of the new media (the virtual nature of on-line documents and structure) reading and writing have become two consubstantial activities (one speaks of 'écrilecture'): inserting and managing notes, searching for the frequency of words, putting hypertextual links into or between documents.

In other words, if it is conceivable that technology could one day replace handwriting with 'vocal writing', this does not alter the fact that it is still writing. The days of writing as a graphic activity are perhaps numbered, but not those of writing as an intellectual and cognitive activity. The teaching of writing thus is still relevant.

Thierry Soubrié

Dan Sperber: writing in the narrow sense and writing in the broad sense

When I hold that writing will soon be obsolete thanks to technologies that convert [spoken] words into text and that knowing how to write will cease to be indispensable for being a competent adult, and that the teaching of writing will no longer be a necessary condition for almost all other teaching, I am speaking – isn't it obvious? – of the manual activity that consists of drawing and linking together letters, or pushing the keys of a keyboard. I am speaking neither of spelling, nor of grammar, nor of style, nor of composition. It is true that, by a customary synecdoche, one designates all these aspects of the production of text by the name of writing. Nonetheless, neither primary and secondary school teachers, nor their student, have any illusions about this. In France, the teaching of writing strictly speaking is the business of the first years of primary school, whereas the teaching of the other aspects of 'writing' in the syncedochal sense is spread out over the rest of their school years. I did not question the obvious fact that the teaching of grammar, style and composition will remain essential as long as the textual quality of texts remains important.

To this extent, I am not basically in disagreement with Thierry Soubrié who writes: 'if it is conceivable that technology could one day replace handwriting with "vocal writing", this does not alter the fact that it is still writing. The days of writing as a graphic activity are perhaps numbered, but not those of writing as an intellectual and cognitive activity. The teaching of writing thus is still relevant.' This said, go ask a teacher whether or not it would make a difference to teach writing 'as a graphic activity' since in any case, writing in the broad sense will continue to be taught!

Patrick Altman supposes, like me, that if written texts were produced orally, 'the form of writing would thus be altered', and he adds, 'but one would still need a considerable mastery of the language to produce a text that wouldn't make the reader nauseous for lack of structure. Certain great professors know how to produce this sort of speech which could also be directly exploitable, but they are not legion.' One could very well be incapable of producing in the ordinary (or professorial) flood of words words that would be legible if one transcribed them as such, and nevertheless be completely capable of orally composing an excellent written text, which one could say at one's own rhythm, with all the pauses one likes, and which one could correct indefinitely. Dictation to a machine, from this point of view, seems to me to be less constraining than writing with a machine as it was done prior to word-processing, where correction resembled time-consuming tinkering, or re-typing.

Pursuing Patrick Altman's line of thought, Gloria Origgi wonders: 'would the learning of literate forms of speech that would facilitate a mastery of text dictated to a computer, be less costly and difficult than learning how to write, which has the advantage of already incorporating a majority of its conventions?' It seems unlikely to me that the teaching of the manual activity of writing 'incorporates' strictly speaking the more creative aspects of teaching 'writing' in the broad sense. To have learned at the beginning of primary school to draw letters is still today a prerequisite for being able to benefit from lessons (from the end of primary school and especially in secondary school) in grammar, style, and composition. What would be lost if one could skip this first stage? (This is not a rhetorical question; I am ready to believe that the learning of the graphic activity of writing brings cognitive and motor benefits beyond its use in written linguistic communication; this said, even if there are such benefits, it is hardly possible that this justifies the cost, that is, the time spent learning that particular thing, at the expense of other possible activities.)

Dan Sperber

9

New Architectures of Information

Stefana Broadbent and Francesco Cara

During the past four years, we have carried out hundreds of observations of people using the Web. In our usability labs across Europe, we have asked users to book tickets, buy books, find out opening times, read about koala bears, search for news, find information about cholesterol, write e-mails, download ringtones, etc. We have seen French students, Norwegian engineers, Italian software designers, American housewives, British barristers, old and young, kids and pensioners, pioneers and laggards, using every possible type of Website, wapsite, portal and digital product.

Having observed in detail how people use the Web and what they do on it, the downfall of the new economy has come as no real surprise. The first generation of websites has been built with a radical misunderstanding and misrepresentation of users' expectations and practices.

What do people do on the Web?

All Internet users can be divided into three main categories: expert, naïve and what we call 'light' users. Experts are the first comers to the net – the nerds, the ones who download software, who remember Mosaic, who can tell you the difference between Google Altavista and Yahoo!, who wouldn't be seen dead near AOL. Naïve users haven't moved into the Internet yet, they are still waiting for a good reason to log on; sometimes they are backseat drivers who ask their children to find them what they need. They still think that Internet is magic and that there is only one site for each topic.

Light users are regular Internet users. They use it one or two hours a week, doing a bit of e-mail, looking up practical content, such as train timetables and cinemas. This is a relatively new user population, which has emerged over the last couple of years as the Internet became accessible to a less pioneering style of consumer. On the classical curve of technology adoption (Innovators, Early Adopters, Early Majority Pragmatists, Late Majority Conservatives, Laggards), these users correspond to the pragmatists and conservatives, who don't rush to buy new technology but wait to see if it works, if it is really useful and if it is available at a cheaper price. The interest of this user group is that it represents the majority of new users on the net and the target of future expansion. If ever the Internet user population moves above the threshold of 25–30 per cent of the global European population, the newcomers will all be in this category.

Most light users have very stereotypical behaviours: after six months of usage of the Internet they stop even trying to do searches through a search engine and consult systematically the same six or seven sites. Search engines are too complex and deliver too many answers to weed through. These users usually give up searching because it is too costly for the results they obtain. The cost is both in trying to guess the correct combination of terms to search with and in assessing the results to find sources that are interesting and reliable. Their only way to discover new sites is to collect URL addresses in the press or other traditional media or from friends and family. In this case, new sites are visited by entering a URL in the navigation bar, and assessed in a couple of minutes for the value of their content, design and originality.

When left to their own resources these users tend to explore the websites of brands they are familiar with, which in general are well established offline brands. Brick and mortar brands are usually perceived as more reliable and solid than brands that only have an on-line virtual existence. Light users therefore will prefer to look for historical content about Mesopotamia on the British Museum website, rather than on the websites of obscure associations or colleges. It makes cognitive sense to transfer on-line what one knows of the off-line brand, and it is more reassuring.

Light users regularly visit only six or seven websites. Typically among these sites there is a portal (usually the one of their Internet provider), three or four very practical sites like the Yellow Pages or travel timetables, and a couple of sites related to their professional interests or hobbies. The only sites they actually identify as providing content are the ones related to their interests, the others are perceived and used as tools to achieve some practical task. Light users have been fast to recognize in the Web a reliable source of up-to-date practical information.

Navigation within sites is also very procedural and follows rigid routines: the same pages are visited, the same paths followed. If a path to some piece of useful information is successful it is always repeated even if it is not the most efficient. We see users following the most bizarre paths, getting to a site or a page from another site they are not interested in, just because this is how they found it the first time and, as they say, 'Well, it works'. Occasionally these users stray from their sites using the links on the pages of their favourite sites, but just like toddlers who never stray more than a few meters from their mothers, these users don't venture too far away from their familiar sites.

When new sites are explored the discovery strategy is one of 'tiny bites'. Users skim the content and plunge into three or four sections either looking for some precise type of information or assessing the new site by verifying the nature of the information provided in comparison with other supports they are familiar with. These users don't read full pages of text but skim through the pages and sections at great speed to get a general sense of the site's style, content and value.

In short, most Internet users don't use search engines, only visit a few sites – and always the same ones – prefer well-known off-line brands, don't read but skim through content looking for something specific. Proper reading starts only when they reach their target. They use the Internet in a very practical fashion to obtain specific information.

Internet penetration and usage are slowing down

Most analysts agree that, independently of the economic demise of many Internet-related companies, we are seeing a slowdown in the growth of the Internet traffic, user population and on-line time:

- In 1999, Internet traffic was growing at a rate of nearly 200 per cent. It is now growing at a slower rate of 88 per cent for the US and 106 per cent for Europe and it is forecast to continue at this rate until 2005.
- Last summer, data were published showing that in June in the US, the number of Internet users had fallen by 3 per cent as a combined effect of a lower number of new adopters and a decrease in the time students spend on line.
- In January 2001, the usage of the Web, as measured by on-line time, had increased by 46 per cent with respect to January 2000; six months later, in June, the increase with respect to the same month of the previous year was down to 14.7 per cent.

In short, the Internet has captured the early adopters, the enthusiasts and the curious but has not really moved into the households of the more pragmatic users, as has been the case, within a comparable time frame, with the mobile phone. The difficulty of attracting the more pragmatic type of user to new technologies is a well-known phenomenon described by Geoffrey A. Moore in his book *Crossing the Chasm* (see reviews at *www.epinions.com/book_mu-2801445*; and an interview with Moore on *The Home Automation Times*). In opposition to the standard high-tech marketing model that predicts the linear adoption of new high-tech products through a smooth penetration in increasingly large markets (from the relatively small market of Innovators and Early Adopters to the huge mainstream market of Early Majority Pragmatists and Late Majority Conservatives), Moore describes the gulf that exists between technically literate and mainstream users: a gulf of attitudes, motivations, expectations and practices; a chasm that can be overcome by offering high-tech products tailored to suit specific needs and segments of the population.

When one compares the practices of users and the first generation of websites, there is little reason to be surprised that the growth of the Internet population has not been as strong as was expected. The mismatch between what has been designed and offered and what users need is phenomenal.

First-generation websites

The slowdown in the use and adoption of the Internet and the reduction of the domain of usage by light users, are all symptomatic of a similar phenomenon: the difficulty of exploiting this new, powerful media at a reasonable cognitive cost. We all thought the Web to be an easy mass media from the onset, when actually it is a very complex technology: a unique mix of IT, networking, telecom and multimedia content. It requires learning, motivation, and especially proof of its value.

When we look closely at the behaviour of light users, we can see that most of their strategies are characterized by an effort to reduce their cognitive effort, in a search for efficiency and enjoyment. Most novice and pragmatic users feel that the effort needed to learn how to get around and to obtain anything significant is higher than what they are willing to invest, especially in a highly information-intensive society like ours. Most of the information people are looking for is available in other media and supports that can often be obtained at a far lower cognitive cost. If the time and effort to obtain some information on the Internet is greater than that of making a phone call or walking down to the library, pragmatic users will just not do it. Most users therefore simply give themselves a few days to learn how to obtain what is really unique to the Web, and then stick to well-established routines.

We will argue here that the main reasons for this complex behaviour lie in the structure of most 'first-generation', static websites.

In general, the common architecture of these websites consists of a large set of individual multimedia content pages organized according to a hierarchical tree structure (see Figure 9.1) that can vary in depth as a function of the nature and volume of the content published. Most of these first-generation sites are static: the content of the pages, mainly text and images, does not change from page load to page load, unless it is manually modified and updated.

On top of this hierarchical structure is a navigation system that typically allows users to browse the content from section to subsections and from page to page. A navigation system, consisting generally of one main general navigation bar for the sections and a second-level navigation for the subsections, enables users to move from one section to another, and from one page to other pages according to the underlying organization of content. It is the hierarchical structure that often forces us to move up to a site's home page or up to a section's entry page, to go from one content page belonging to one branch of the site to another, related page belonging to a different branch. Most of the time search engines provide 'shortcuts' through the structure to a list of pages related to the topic of interest. Naturally, the more numerous the subsections and sections, the more numerous also the intermediate pages; this increases the complexity of the site structure and navigation system, and lengthens the process of finding any significant content.

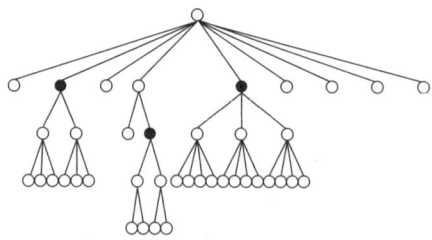

Figure 9.1   Representation of a hierarchical tree structure

As sites have become more ambitious, offering more and more content, the lack of transparency of this type of architecture and the limited range of actions that can be carried out have become apparent. Users spend all their time trying to guess under what section and subsection a relevant piece of information has been put, memorizing paths through the sections, using back buttons to walk back through their meanderings (according to some reports, 40 per cent of all clicks are on the back button), in their attempt to find the chunk of content that they are looking for. In this architecture the labelling of the sections as presented in the menus or other navigation devices becomes absolutely crucial, because it is the only clue users have with which to guess what lies below the layer in which find themselves at a given moment.

Hierarchical site structures are like a pyramid or an iceberg, where the vertex – the home page – is the main point of entry towards a huge amount of underlying information at the ground of the site. The deeper the site, the farther away is the piece of content that is relevant for the user. A lot of time is spent therefore on navigation activities that have little or no added value for the user, who just wants to get to what is relevant and interesting to him or her. This explains why users essentially skim the pages and don't read any text. Numerous studies on how users read Web pages report that three out of four users only skim text and one out of six actually reads text in full (see, for example, Nielsen and Morkes, 1997: 'How to write for the Web', on line at: *www.useit.com/papers/webwriting/writing.html*).

As we have observed over and over again in our labs, users' main activity is to rapidly analyse the page to judge where they are, if they are going in the right direction, if they have reached their target. We have observed that, when using information portals or newspaper sites, for instance, users either stay at the surface, just reading a couple of items that are 'advertised' on the home page, or follow the same well-known path every day to reach a section they are interested in and familiar with. In both cases the site is dramatically underused as the 'top layer skimmer' never drills down to anything deeper, and the 'familiar section' user never sees anything else than what he knows.

In the development of the site, a significant design effort goes in categorizing content so as to create a logical structure of sections and subsections that organizes all the content in significant groupings which are then reflected in the navigation systems. The organization of the sections can follow multiple conventions: topics can be categorized according to the conventions of libraries, of academic disciplines, of magazines or newspapers, they can mirror the internal organization of a company, lines of business, etc. Information architects who often have a background in library science and journalism have the responsibility of finding the most suitable categorization.

To take just one example, the site of the *French Public Administration* (*www.service-public.fr*) typically divides the information into sections and subsections leading each to static pages of information. The section on laws and regulations (*Vos Droits et Démarches*) is divided according to a classification of real life events such as Work, Children, Family, Health, etc. The same chunks could have been organized differently, had the information architects decided to group content by state departments, for instance, or by legal terminology.

The categorization process naturally creates a distance between the architecture of the content and the actual content, by introducing layers of descriptions of the content available, embodied in the 'directional' pages that only contain menus and submenus. This distance paves the way to mismatches between the representation of the content and the content itself (from the content categories, users create expectations about the richness and completeness of the content available on that category, an expectation which is hard to fulfil) as well as to misinterpretations, since labels are inevitably generic and the context is insufficient to support the intended meaning.

Alternative structures of information

Steps are being taken, knowingly or not, towards a reduction in the efforts demanded of users. The system can take over some of the work of finding relevant content. It is now rather common to encounter dynamic Websites whose content is constantly refreshed and renewed. The main building block in this type of site is not the page anymore, but content units or chunks (that can be pieces of text, images, video clips, audio clips, etc.) that are uploaded into a template to create a page. Content is separated from the display through the joint use of metadata (that is, data about data, used to aid the identification, description and location of units of digital content) to describe content, of templates to describe the placeholders for content (type, size, location, formatting) and of rules about what, where and how content is uploaded in the template.

The separation of content from form allows for modular site architectures combining, by means of rules, tagged pieces of content with placeholders for them within templates. These structures enable the dynamic grouping of related content to be presented on the same page, even when they belong to different sections or interact among themselves. Dynamic sites have dedicated areas, generally in a box on the right side of the page, for the display of content contextually related to the topic addressed in the main body of the page (see for example *http://www.lemonde.fr*). In other cases, we find on the same page the main body of content and the controls to modify its presentation, as with the *International Herald Tribune* site, where the layout of the article can be modified directly by clicking on an icon (representing the available formats for number of columns and size of fonts) beside the article itself.

What is particularly interesting with this architecture is that, once all content is 'tagged' and 'described' in keywords, indexed and sorted so as to become ready to be combined into rules, a new distribution of cognitive work between the site and the users can be achieved. The editors of the site are able to create richer pages around a topic that rely on all the information available, from other sections of the website, from the archives or from external partners. These contextual architectures open new possibilities for the linking of content and provide novel ways for users to discover and explore content. For instance, it is now more common to find areas of the page that enrich and develop the main topic: a list of related links, a set of spotlights, tools that are related to the content of the page, such as a mapping tool or a currency converter.

The possibility of showing contextually related content using the user's selection as a filter is a first step in the direction of reducing the cognitive load. Users are no longer doing all the work of searching and drilling to find bits of content in rigid hierarchies: instead the system itself is filtering the content and 'pushing it up' towards the user. The quality of the principles that rule the filtering process, and therefore the selection of content, determines how effective and relevant is the related information. If I click on a spotlight related to the death of Pierre Bourdieu and find next to it a section with a list of all his interviews, links to his papers and a full bibliography, I will be more satisfied than if I find a list of all those who died on the 24th of January, 2002.

Another step towards reducing users' cognitive load is a different form of filtering based on the identification of recurrent navigation paths: collaborative filtering. Contextual content is selected and brought up to the interface on the basis of the content that has been most frequently accessed, in statistical terms, with regard to a particular topic. The best known example of this is Amazon's feature 'Customers who bought this book also bought...'. Each user's interaction data is added into the system, thus constantly updating and refining the criteria that will select the related information to be displayed. This solution avoids the circularity of individual personalization, when a user's past behaviour cues selection, and augments the reliability of filtering because it works on the basis of big numbers: it is not the expert's opinion but a collective expertise. The collectivity that shares my interests shares the work with me of selecting interesting content. Isn't this what we call culture?

Other forms of information delivery

Text and images are not the only ways to display and present information. There are many interactive tools now available on the Web that allow users to compute and visualize extremely complex data in a very accessible way.

The Website of the *RATP* (the transport administration of the city of Paris) allows users to indicate their point of departure and destination and provides them with the shortest itinerary. This is a typical example of an interactive practical tool that users appreciate on the Web. Like other mapping and travel services that allow users to calculate routes (see, for example, *www.viamichelin.com*), it takes advantage of the computing power of the server it resides on, of the interactive nature of the users' workstation and of the distributed nature of the Internet; it provides very rapidly information that would be far more difficult to compute individually by composing information from a paper map and timetable. It also creates a hot spot around which related information can be pulled together in a very natural manner.

One of the best, classic examples in the literature on Interaction Design was the entry page of the *smartmoney* site, now available only in the subscribers' section of the site. The basis of the site, that is, financial information and services, is visualized in the form of a map of 1000 international stocks. Apart from the immediate dynamic representation of the stocks' performance and relative value, the map provides an entry point towards more specific data, analysis and tools on the stock market. Some of this data is directly superimposed on the map, so as to offer intermediate layers of information – for instance, about a company's identifiers and main performance indicators – between the overall map and a more in-depth page. With visualization-based solutions, the Website architecture is turned upside down: the available content is upfront, and can be zoomed in, producing a significant reduction in the cognitive load.

Another example of interactive tool comes again from the financial world: the numerous charting functions that can be found on financial sites like *www.bloomberg.com*. Users specify the timeframe and the stock they are interested in and the system charts the evolution of the stock within that timeframe and compares the evolution to global indices such as NASDAQ within the same timeframe.

All the examples above rely on real-time data of a complex nature, data that users could not have in books or traditional paper media, which is combined and computed using applications that reside distantly, and is visualized locally in a format that is comprehensible and accessible. In both cases users feel they are getting real value from the Web, obtaining information of a nature and at a speed that they could not obtain with a different media.

Conclusions

People do not read on the Web as they do on paper – but why should they? It would be like using a Ferrari to mow the lawn. The Internet is a powerful, still largely underused interactive media that can allow both editors and users to create new forms of access and new ways of sharing content. Its relational capacity, of which hypertext is a first instance, is what makes this media unique. But to this day, the relational potential of the Web has only been approximated. When deployed more fully, it will indeed change the way we relate to text and multimedia content.

Discussion

'Cool' and user-friendly?

In their report on what people do on the Web, what they want from it and how the Internet is evolving in relation to these needs and habits, Stefana and Francesco cross to the other side of the mirror and analyse ourselves as 'users'. Some of us might be 'Late Users', or 'Laggards', or even 'Conservatives'. What is notable here is that these practices are evidently changing, and that the technology is evolving to suit the needs of users. But how can sites evolve from here? What sort of 'user' will be the criterion for the definition of 'user-friendliness' in the next generation of websites? Will there be trends, will 'coolness' win, and who will define it in the near future?

Noga Arikha

Kids and robots

Noga Arikha wrote: 'What sort of "user" will be the criterion for the definition of "user-friendliness" in the next generation of Web-sites?'

The foundation paper of this discussion is about transitioning adults. The kids of today, growing up with computers and the Internet, will be among the 'users' Noga asks about. Today in the USA many 3- and 4-year-olds are using the Internet. Interactive sites like 'Playhouse Disney' direct content at young users. They will not recall a pre-net mode. Students in schools at all levels use the web for research. Teenagers use instant messaging to have instant parties at homes where the parents are away for a few hours.

The authors are right about the evolution of Web design. Technologies advance, high-speed computers and bandwidth get cheaper, programming languages develop, and interactive data-driven applications are written to satisfy or create demand. But the paper as presented is more a summary of the past than a vision of the future.

As cell phones and the Internet merge, remote cultures become participants, and the 4-year-olds become 34-year-olds, the taxonomy of information will change as well as its architecture. Nanotechnology, molecular computing, artificial intelligence, VR, robotics, cellular integrated chipsets (biological cells, DNA) will create new possibilities for interaction that are barely science fiction today.

The presentation has a decidedly human-centric view of the Internet and information. In less than thirty years we may find that there is an Internet being programmed by AI robots to communicate with each other for the purposes of their own evolution (if they are not already doing that!). That would be the expected development of today's AI survival robot experiments. The authors point out how this medium has evolved from static to real-time functionality. There are already non-human users that take advantage of streaming data, with remote sensors and wireless connections. Monitoring devices of all sorts are hooked up to centralized computers that control the flow of materials, send out service calls, track packages and inspect production lines that are operated by robot workers.

There can be a concern about how this all plays out with nationalism, barbarism, and other negative mindsets that cause wars, poverty, death and destruction. The fears of the humans, be they fundamentalist terrorists or RUR Luddites, may slow it down, and may even destroy civilization as we know it. Greed and the lust for political power have plagued Earth for millenia. These factors are central to the development of the www. It's no secret that military and governmental 'security' agencies have been involved in it since the beginning, or that the 'forces of evil' or 'forces of liberation' use it as freely as anyone else. Not to mention the hackers and cyberterrorists. These users are having a major impact on the development of the Web, and will continue to stimulate the Web security business.

The competitive nature of Web use and operating software development, with time to market being profit-critical, will continue to result in products being issued with security holes. As processor and connection speed increase, hackers will be able to spread viruses faster and reel in sensitive information before virus software updates are issued. I already download new antivirus updates two or three times a day. The Web is being used to spread today's worms using scripting languages that can automate the launch in the background of seemingly innocuous pages. Users have the option of turning off Java and Javascript, but then many applications won't work. One expects that hackers will develop malicious codes as fast as new scripting languages and applications develop. That may turn out to be a critical issue in the development of user confidence in the 'friendliness' of the web.

Richard Minsky

What are the criteria for a successful Web for the general public?

This paper appropriately brings up the question of how the general public uses the Web and whether its sites are adapted to it. I will thus concentrate on this aspect for a few remarks or questions.

(1) A medium does not possess a 'nature' that would lead to one particular type of use rather than another. Each medium is an aproximative construct that combines the imagination of engineers, the financial gamble of promoters and the appropriation by users. At the beginning of the nineteenth century, who could have imagined that radio would assume the form of stations broadcasting programmes to a mass public? This medium hesitated for a long time between an interactive version, of which there remain professional applications (marine, trucking, taxis...) or CB radios, and that with which we are familiar. In a field of possibilities, F. Cara and S. Broadbent indicate completely convincing paths that all share the common thread of the capacity for cognitive performance (how to provide information at the lowest cognitive cost to the user?) But, always from the user's perspective, are there not other dimensions to be identified? After all, if we follow their reasoning, we are talking about a cost-benefit relationship. What then are the costs to minimize for the user and what sorts of advantages can one maximize? In other words, what could serve as other criteria for the success of the domestic Web?

(2) The history of the Minitel in France also yields a few lessons. It was conceived at the outset to disseminate the press on line. It never really ever worked for this use. In fact, users rapidly brought out its two uses: message services (mainly telephone sex), and information-services (ticket reservations, schedules, weather reports, directories, etc.) Can we not consider that, as far as the general public is concerned, these are the two dominant services? In other words, once again for the general public, to consider the Web to be a news medium or even as a library of texts, beyond a basic encyclopaedia, would be in contradiction to the way it is used in the home.

(3) The authors do not talk about terminals. Wouldn't this be another important restriction for the general public? Rather than a Ferrari, I have the feeling that what is offered to the basic user is a big tractor equipped with a whole lot of agricultural implements to mow his lawn. Once the medium is more stabilized (should it one day locate its economy...) will we not witness the appearance of inexpensive terminals of which nomadic objects (e-books, Palm Pilots...) are but an imperfect forerunner? From this point of view, the French Minitel adventure also merits further meditation...

Jean-Michel Salaün

Reply to Jean-Michel Salaün

In our paper, we have tried to come up with two lines of argument. On the one hand, we have described what seems to be the first stabilization of uses of the Internet: the search for practical information, the existence of 'navigation' routines, the sharing and dialogue around specialized contents. We have not, however, touched upon the dimension of communication (messenger services, forums, discussion and chat rooms) which are practices also become considerably stabilized. As you do well to remind us, we have already seen all these practices of consultation and exchange develop and stabilize around the medium of Minitel.

On the other hand, we have juxtaposed the emergence of Web practices that are relatively meagre in comparison to the potential of the medium with the way that Web sites have been conceived and constructed up to now. The low degree of interactivity of these sites and their limited level of automation in the end produce an experience similar to that of the Minitel in terms of colour and image.

The few cases that we have presented correspond to so many attempts to make this medium evolve in a direction involving more visualization of information coupled with controls so that one can explore freely, more contextualization so as to make elements available to the user that are potentially relevant to the subject of interest, and more varied and layered reading levels so as to promote a deepening [of information] without losing sight of the whole context.

What we expect from innovations that move us toward increased multimedia and interactivity is a redistribution of cognitive work between the user and the system of information which offers a better basis for learning, discovery, and the sharing of knowledge.

Francesco Cara

The economics of Web architecture

Francesco Cara blames the written book model for stalling the widespread adoption of Web use.

It is reasonable to advocate the move away from heirarchical content navigation and toward dynamic interactive Web design, particularly for sites that deliver news, streaming data for decision-makers, and deep sites that require heavy mining to find what you need. I would not go so far as to assign historical attachment to a book model as the cause of a slowdown in the growth rate of Web usage.

There are several economic factors involved. These involve supply and demand, competition, the supply of trained labour and other issues. On the supply side the evolution of Web design depends not only on the theoretical development of information architecture, but on the creation of code languages and systems, their adoption as uniform standards, their implementation by website developers, and their incorporation into graphic design. Someone has to pay for all that, and in a declining economy there is less capital available for innovation. Even when Web capital was freely available there were implementation problems, which still exist.

The fight for browser dominance led to an oligopoly in which incompatible systems are being used by millions of people. When designing a website the cost is dramatically increased if you want to do fancy tricks and have them work in various versions of Netscape and MSIE on PC and Mac platforms. Each browser developer pushes the W3 Consortium to adopt its own rules by publishing new versions of their product that incorporate proprietary code. Designers were forced to begin Web page code with Javascripts that determine which browser a user has and direct the server to provide browser-specific content. Writing code for all this in Notepad is slow, and not many designers know how to do it. Developers of Web design programmes try to keep up with all this, or develop runaround systems that generate their own code in ever more complex methods of managing Web content. They rush their products to market replete with bugs to beat the competition. The software users often don't know enough code language to fix the bugs. Then the economy hits the fan and Web designers find themselves managing sites with products created by bankrupt companies. So they have no more upgrades or tech support to keep up with browser developments and are locked into heavy investment with obsolete proprietary Web management software.

At the same time, on the demand side, users are frustrated by data-driven Web pages that take too long to load (violating the 8-second and 30-second rules). Often the scripting on them is bad and users get useless or wrong data. Navigating through badly designed and coded data-driven sites can be more difficult than finding data in a heirarchy. Some pages cause browsers or systems to crash. Others require downloading plug-ins that users are afraid of because of all the virus scares.

There is also the demand issue of cost-of-entry. To enter the Internet world requires hardware, software, electricity, an Internet connection, literacy, and a perceived need. The global economic obstacles to each of these could be material for a book, or at least could provide a graduate student with a dissertation.

There are not many businesses that can afford the cost of keeping up with all this, either internally or through a Web design company. And the consumers are not out there to pay for it, particularly during a recession. One of the reasons Web architecture advanced so rapidly during the late 90s was the availability of cheap capital. Venture capitalists were jumping on every hare-brained idea with millions of dollars. IPOs were the game to play. Entrepreneurs spent all their time making executive summaries and business plans and none of it finding customers. Customer development was expensive. So a lot of money went into flashy websites to impress the investors. That meant millions of dollars for Web designers and architects. Then it all went bust and investors got less than a penny on the dollar. Capital stopped flowing into Web architecture. With no VC and no customers providing cash flow, Web architecture development slowed down.

Database software-makers are enabling reports to be generated as web pages and uploaded to the site. This allows small businesses to produce data-driven webs without hiring a designer or programmer. This development parallels the move from outsourced graphic design to in-house production. Laser and inkjet printers replaced typewriters, many fonts became available in every computer, word processing became design-enabled, and page definition (publishing) software was added to standard business packages. This had two opposite effects simultaneously, both raising and lowering the quality of printed matter. At the low end, things got better, as typewriter-produced documents, newsletters and announcements that had been mimeographed or photocopied got typeset and into some sort of basic template. Unfortunately for the typesetting business, and perhaps for design quality, the few fonts that were initially available were used for everything, by people with no design training. As time went on, automatic kerning and other typographic niceties became more sophisticated and could be overruled, even on common word processors. More design templates became available, and the casual users became more experienced.

Perhaps we will see the evolution of Web design follow this path, with outsourced Web construction being replaced in-house, more sophisticated Web architecture software produced for the business and consumer markets, and the casual Web designer who starts by putting up their home page on Yahoo using an automated system becoming more adept.

Part of what could make this happen is reducing the cost of Web architecture implementation. If the browser manufacturers would make their products compatible with the W3C standards so one page worked on all systems, websites would be able to do more with the available budgets. Products like *FrontPage* have enabled interactive database-driven sites for several years, but most designers find the bugs too annoying, as well as the need for MS proprietary servers. *ColdFusion* is preferred by many web architects, but it requires a skilled programmer, and even then usability problems occur. As businesses upgrade to newer versions of *Filemaker Pro, DB2* and other web-ready integrated relational databases we will see more of them on line. Faster processors and wideband connections make serving data-driven pages faster and cheaper. Soon we will have out-of-the-box AI database driven Web design software.

It's not that people are bound to the book model for Web design. It's just that it started there and is finding its own methodology. Investors are waiting for The Next Big Thing. If it includes Web architecture, we will see an upturn in the rate of development, and the additional usability it creates may add to the Web-using population.

When the economy cycles up, there will be more demand for Web content. Not just from on-line shopping, though *Amazon* did a great job in showing what consumer usability can be. A growing economy will develop markets not yet exploited (a word with several meanings), including those that are not yet literate, not yet connected, not able to afford today's technology. The technology will provide cheap wireless Internet gadgets. Wearable computers with wireless connections will add another demand segment. Countries that are just emerging into webdom will go through growth cycles. The number of languages on the web will increase, increasing participation. Providing good architectural building blocks for these new users is important, as they can now start from an evolved base that goes way beyond the heirarchy model.

Richard Minsky

10
Authors and Authority

Umberto Eco (interviewed by Gloria Origgi)

Gloria Origgi: When asked, in varying contexts, about the possibilities and risks of Internet, you have often evoked the problem of filtering information.

Umberto Eco: It is the fundamental problem of the Web. The whole of the history of culture has consisted in the establishment of filters. Culture transmits memory, but not all memory: it filters. It filters well, or badly, but if anything what has allowed us to interact socially is the fact that we have had all of these filters. Then of course the scientist or scholar can put in question these filters, but that is another matter. With the Web, everyone is in the situation of having to filter information that is so vast, and so unsustainable, that if it isn't filtered it cannot be absorbed. It is filtered unsystematically, so what is the primary metaphysical risk of this business? That we'll end up with a civilization in which every person has his own system of filters, in other words where every person creates his own encyclopaedia. Now a society with five billion concurrent encyclopaedias is a society in which there is no more communication. Moreover, the filters we resort to result from our having trusted what we call 'the community of learning' that, throughout the centuries, through debate and discussion, gives the guarantee, at the least that the filtering is reasonable; so imagine what would be an individual filtering performed by anyone, for example by a 14-year-old boy. We could end up with competing encyclopaedias, some of them completely wild.

GO: But today we have authoritative filtering systems that belong to this very means of communication, that is, search engines.

UE: That's not a filtering system. There are already polemics on the fact that search engines 'filter' only information that has been paid for.

I don't believe in the possibility of automating the filter's function. The only solution is that there appear authorities, external or internal to the Web, that constantly monitor what is found. Here's an example: I recently searched for 'Holy Grail' on the Internet. Thirty sites came up. I'm quite informed about the subject, so I could tell that one of these was philologically correct, two were correctly encyclopaedic and all the others were actually the work of delirious occultist crazies. I, so to speak, am an expert on the topic: but what about the poor sod who looks up the theme of the Grail for the first time? How does he manage to filter? He can be the victim of the first quack who built a site. But how can these monitoring groups take shape? How does one monitor the whole of the Web? Even if it had been monitored on Monday, it would be different already on Tuesday. There should be specialized monitoring groups, for example the *International Society for Philosophy* could continuously monitor all the philosophy sites, you know, a bit like the old lists of the Centro Cattolico Cinematografico in Italy that pronounced, outside the church, on whether a film was 'excluded to those under age', or 'for adults', or 'suitable for all'. Catholic parents who trusted the priest knew, at least, that that film contained dangerous scenes for a child: they had a filter. Now if I trust the International Society for Philosophy, which tells me: 'This site on Kant is rubbish', then I won't use that site. But I've already discussed how these filtering groups could emerge, and how they could manifest themselves: if they do so within the Web, how does the ingenuous visitor know that this site is the monitoring, expert one? If, on the other hand, they do so outside the Web, maybe on a special bulletin, or monthly and so on, it would be printed matter and would be available to a tiny percentage of surfers. We haven't resolved these problems. If I had the answer I'd probably become a billionaire, but I don't.

GO: How does one make the difference between the imposition of a filtering authority and something similar to a new form of 'censorship'?

UE: A filtering authority is not a 'censor' but a consultant. Excuse me but if I go to my economic consultant and I ask him to tell me which shares to buy and which ones not to buy, he's no censor, he's a consultant who tells me that it would be advantageous for me to buy these shares and not these other ones because they've caused a lot of trouble. So, what, the whole of culture is censorship because a teacher who instructs her pupils that two and two does not equal five is censoring the ignorant child – but this job of filtering is an aspect of education. To use censorship is to stop the circulation of information, while to use a filter is to judge the information that is circulating. Those are two very different things: I can criticize the primary school history book and be simply acting as a critic; or I can have it seized by the police, and act as a censor.

GO: We are here at the seat of the Master's in Publishing that you direct in Bologna. Is a publisher also a 'bottleneck' that filters information?

UE: A publisher is a filter, and I can be sure that Mondadori might also choose a bad novel, but not below a certain standard because it has a history behind it; this is all the more true if the publisher is Olschki, which prints only scholarly and philological books. The other problem with Internet is the spread of the *samizdat*. In the USSR, if one wanted to publish one distributed a *samizdat*, which circulated within a restricted group of people; now anyone who wants it can put his novel on line. This is a great act of freedom: at least it relieves publishing houses of a load of useless manuscripts, and it can allow an intelligent publisher to check what is on the Web and maybe even to discover a new talent. But in this case too, just put yourself in the shoes of a 14-year-old kid who goes on line and reads all these *samizdat* – the function of orientation provided by criticism is gone. When I was in high school, I used to buy *La Fiera Letteraria*, a cultural magazine that existed then, where there was a section for people who'd sent their poems to a critic who analysed them, saying 'This one is good', 'This one is bad', and so on. You can say what you will about this critic: but to me he transmitted the appreciation of discrimination. It could be that his taste is outmoded today, but he taught me that some verses were judged more beautiful for certain reasons, that some were junk, common old stuff – the point is, this filter, constructed by a magazine, gave me a taste for poetry.

GO: Who filters literary taste on the Web?

UE: That is a huge problem. It could revolutionize our literary taste. For example, it could establish an 'anything goes' of taste: it isn't true that Homer is better than John Smith. No: everyone takes whatever he likes. That could be such a revolution in taste that we can't even imagine its outcome. From the point of view of our cultural tradition it would be extremely dangerous. But there is another argument: taste filters in literature have only ever interested 0.5 per cent of the population. If today 70 per cent of the population surfs the Web and considers good any poem or story it encounters, we can say that these people had been excluded from the enjoyment of the literary product and that they have finally come in contact with some form of literary expression. Again, this will certainly be a revolution. A revolution that could be mitigated, in the sense that someone who educates himself on the Internet devours anything, but the minute he goes to university or gets a job, inevitably encounters parameters and evaluates his own previous excesses – but all this is pure prophecy.

GO: About this 'anything goes' you're talking about: the screen itself is a representation of it, it is a single means for everything, newspapers, publicity, texts that traditionally we call 'books'. What is it that still distinguishes a book from any other form of information?

UE: Above all, I think, the psychological mechanisms of attention. Our species has gotten used to a certain sort of attention, which involves turning pages, lingering with attention; the kind of reading effected on screen inevitably is different, faster, one scrolls with greater speed. Here's an example: there is still a huge difference between correcting proofs on a printed page and correcting the text on screen. There will always be more mistakes left on the screen than on the printed page, because there is a different way of fixing one's attention on a line. However, new generations are born with a mechanism for attention that is adapted to the screen. In the end, if we take a medieval manuscript we can't read it, while at the time of Gutenberg people were complaining that they couldn't read a printed page: they read the manuscript more easily! So mechanisms can change, but even while they do these various types of attention, I think, will continue to exist.

GO: So the fact that something is a newspaper, as opposed to a portal as opposed to a book, even if the means remains the same, depends on how much attention the user puts into it?

UE: Well, certainly if I want to know the weather in Amsterdam the computer screen gives me more than enough information, and it is even maybe more clear and convincing than what I get from the newspaper, where I have to look for it on the last page. If, on the other hand, I want to read the *Divine Comedy*...Here's an example (although I'm still a representative of the pre-computer generation): I have the whole of the *Divine Comedy* in the computer. If I have to write an essay in which I quote three tercets of the *Divine Comedy*, I get them from the computer and so avoid the trouble of copying them. If I have to consult the *Divine Comedy* it is easier for me to take down the volume, since I remember the page layout and so on, but I can't rule out that a next generation will find it more poetic to read the *Divine Comedy* on the screen. This is their business; for me it would be difficult: I use it on screen but I return to the book. But I would like to make this point: it has never happened in the history of humanity that the introduction of a technological means killed off all the practices of the previous means. Even the wheel did not entirely supplant the sledge; photography did not destroy painting, if anything it gave it a new direction; and all the statistics tell us that where people watch a lot of television there tends to be a higher rate of newspaper use: it isn't true that people who watch too much television don't read the papers. I believe that the increase in information, even if it is on screen, will not have an effect on the use of books; on the contrary it will increase it. The proof is that in the decade of the Internet there is a proliferation of mega-bookshops in all cities, visited mostly by youngsters. The e-book is another issue. For the moment it has not taken off and so we have to wait and see what happens. I am not at all opposed to the fact that an e-book could perfectly well replace the book, even though, by habit, I prefer the book – as far as reading mechanisms are concerned. Then there are the emotional, aesthetic, tactile dimensions – so you can leaf through the beautiful paper of a book, although here too it could be that in three generations things might well be different.

GO: If you had to describe to the students in your Master's in Publishing course how you envision a publishing house, let's say in ten years, what disappears? Does paper disappear physically? What does a publisher have on his desk? Can we imagine a scenario where authors negotiate directly with e-book manufacturers and stop using publishers?

UE: I understand the question but I refuse to give you an answer. Just some five or six years ago, when we began to make the CD-Rom of the *Encyclomedia*, I brought those who were involved (it was an Olivetti initiative) to an important Italian publisher. We showed them this project, asking whether they wanted to take part, and they said first that there was no future for CD-Roms, and second, that the winning formula would be not a CD but something or other that Philips had brought out and they wanted to bet on that. Nowadays this important publisher makes CD-Roms by the bucket. So if five years ago an important publisher, whose interests are, let us say, not cultural but at least commercial, was incapable of foreseeing the development of a new technology, imagine wether we're in a position to make exact predictions about the future. Of course we're teaching a Master's in print and multimedia publishing because publishing houses will increasingly become producers of printed matter as well as of multimedia. Which one of the two will prevail, I cannot tell.

GO: Now, about the problem of copyright. There are 'types of intellectual property' for which any paid access, given the quantity of information around, seems intolerable.

UE: Listen, the issue of copyright is, and I'm being generous, four centuries old. It began when the *privilège du Roi* started appearing in seventeenth-century books, which was a declaration that, in a sense, defended the rights of the individual book. That did not stop the publication during the whole of the seventeenth and eighteenth centuries of books that appeared maybe in *Adelphia* or under the names of non-existent cities, and which copied without any worries a book published in Paris or in Amsterdam – they would make another edition of it. Curse and delight for collectors, since at times it is very difficult to differentiate a real first edition from a pirated one: you have to look at the change in a bookmark. In sum: the defence of intellectual property is pretty recent. Just as it didn't exist in the past, it could well not exist in the future, or take on other forms. I am an author, I receive money from copyright, but when I learn that they made a pirate edition of my books in Cuba or even in Germany or China, while my publisher goes mad with rage, I'm not so unhappy, actually I'm very glad that my work circulates. There might be problems if I no longer receive even a cent for a book I've written. But as you see, such problems are easily overcome. For example, just as writers used to be sponsored by patrons, so today they could be sponsored by publicity. That would entail a great loss of freedom, because copyright has been a factor of freedom for the writer, who no longer had to give his due to the patron but to the general public, which bought him or did not buy him. So to lose copyright could bring about a dangerous loss of freedom, because if you're no longer paid in royalties you have to be paid by Berlusconi or by the Vatican or by the Social Democrats or by Coca-Cola, and this certainly is a big problem. Here too the solutions should be legal solutions of some sort. I just want to emphasize the point that, while the system could change, nevertheless the system of protection of intellectual property has signified an increase in democracy and freedom – to lose it might put us in real danger.

GO: Certainly the protection of intellectual freedom differs according to the type of text. In his paper for *Text-e*, Stevan Harnad argues that there is a fundamental difference between scientific publication, for which the author seeks maximal diffusion but no financial remuneration in terms of royalties, and other types of publication for which access remains and will remain paid for.

UE: A scholarly text should be financed either by the university or by research funds, so it should be public. Even the most successful scholarly book doesn't enrich the author. The problem is really one of so-called 'literary' property.

GO: The two kinds should thus be separate?

UE: Not only that. My opinion is that even if the latest Pulitzer prize novel were immediately to become free on the Internet, a part of the public, out of a desire to collect or to read on the train, would continue to favour the print format; so there would be a balancing out. That is to say, I might – well, personally I would never do it – or someone might read four hundred pages on screen, something that seems pretty difficult to me, because it would mean staying seated and damaging the spine for hours on end. Daniele Barbieri says that changes could occur in the form of large viewers in each room with which you could read a novel even while lying in the bathtub. But what would happen then? If I don't like the novel I delete it, and if I love it, what then? If I print it I end up with an object I can't use, which falls all over the floor and so I go out and buy a print copy. That might mean that authors with a large circulation would lose something in terms of royalties, but here too, what could happen is that the print copy will cost €20 instead of €10 and that what the author loses through on-line reading is recuperated through the public of enthusiasts. But you know, this is what is happening today anyway: the large American publisher produces a hardback and within two or three months it produces the trade version. Then within another two or three months the paperback appears, while all along the hardback continues to be published because while the young, or whoever wants to read the book and throw it away after, will buy the paperback, there is still a large part of the public that prefers a good, readable edition and is ready to pay more for it. Look, I am an author: when my book appears in paperback, I get very few royalties. They are all tied in with the hardback copy, and you only get some from the paperback if its circulation is very high. So today already the author is bound to a contract of the type: 'If you want millions to read you, you'll have to accept to get few royalties.'

GO: Another question about the variety of available supports: one technical possibility that was put forward at one point and that today is more controversial is that of print-on-demand machines. Jason Epstein argued in his contribution to text-e that this would be possible for certain kinds of books. What are your views about this prospect?

UE: I strongly believe in it. When Geoffrey Numberg, nearly ten years ago now, first told me about the Xerox project at Stanford, I immediately recognized the great possibilities of these machines. At the time it was only a question of money because a machine like that was very expensive and the possibility of receiving material on line did not exist yet. What, then, would happen? First, a book 'printed on demand' is a real book: the difference is that, instead of coming off the printer's press, it comes out of a computer. Second, it can be very 'friendly' because if, for instance, I have eye problems I can ask the machine to print the book in larger or smaller type. Third, it allows for the recovery of out-of-print book; today if one wants a book, even a very good book, which was published thirty years ago, you'll usually hear that it doesn't exist any more: the publisher hasn't reprinted it because he knows that only about five hundred copies would be sold and that doesn't suit him. Not only that, but there is a crazy law in many countries according to which the warehouse contents are taxed, so that if a publisher has a thousand books stocked there, each priced at, say, €1, he'll be taxed for €1000 even though in effect he'll have lost, not made this money! So: the print-on-demand machine would free publishers from the warehouse costs, it would give them the courage to take on new or avant-garde works, because they would not need to employ huge capitals to do so... There are many reasons for which print-on-demand could be very positive, culturally and economically. I've said that I don't prophesy, but if I had to make a science-fiction prophecy I would see a future bookshop that displays only the cover of the disk, just like in video stores, so you'd take that to the counter and request your printed copy. Maybe this is a little exaggerated, because the pleasure of the bookshop remains that of perusing the shelves, sniffing the book and so on. But a few pilot copies might suffice for the bookshop, even some printed-on-demand ones – so no printing press is required here either – and within five minutes the client would have the book. My prediction is that Stephen King's latest book would probably be printed because people would need to buy it in a hurry, like sandwiches, while if you wanted to read *Thérèse Desqueyroux* by François Mauriac, which might be out-of-print, then you'd need to have it printed.

GO: In his piece for *Text-e*, Dan Sperber predicts a literate society in which one no longer writes, that is, in which the corporeal capacity for writing has been replaced by the dictation to a machine.

UE: It is highly likely, because this is what is happening with multiplication tables: our generation still knows that eight times six is forty-eight, but the new generations that use calculators will lose this capacity. There's an excellent, fifty-year-old science fiction story by Isaac Asimov which tells how in an extremely tense cold war situation, following a black-out of all computers, the Pentagon finds in Oklahoma the only person who still knows multiplication tables and imprisons him because he is the only calculator they have. In the same way we might lose our capacity to write, which would be the preserve of artists. But in an era of mechanization, there are still many youngsters who learn manual skills. So writing would not be lost, it would just be practised by a small number of people. At this point, since writing is educational, schools could intervene and promote the taste for writing as 'sport': you no longer write because you need to take notes, you do so in order to win the calligraphy or rapid writing competition, just in the same way that one doesn't run to go from one place to another because we have cars, but one does so to exercise. That could be an important task for the schools of the future. A last point: the French annoy me sometimes with their attachment to this principle of good education – which was fundamental in my day – according to which a letter should be written by hand, so that I never understand what they're writing to me. But it could happen that lovers who get tired of text-messaging on their portable phones rediscover the taste for personal handwritten letters as gestures of affection – in the same way that we could end up in a society in which women conceive children through chemical means but where people don't lose the habit of making love because in the end it is quite a lot of fun.

GO: I would like to ask you to comment on the future of libraries, which has been discussed at length in *Text-e*. Is there still a need for libraries, of an archive for the memory of a culture?

UE: The problem of the future of libraries is twofold. The shift took place in the middle of the nineteenth century, when one stopped printing on cloth-based paper and began printing on wood-pulp-based paper. Wood-pulp paper has a seventy-year lifespan. But if you look at some fifty-year-old French books, they risk crumbling into pieces before you even open them. The first problem is that, since most of the work published after 1850 is destined to perish, one has to find ways of preventing this deterioration, and many international commissions are studying this. The other problem is the scanning of all this material for it to be transferred onto electronic supports, so that if you want to consult the *Figaro* of 5 May 1921, you'll probably find it on line soon. Some collectors of old papers might try to buy the original copy and put it under glass in order not to touch it too much, for it would probably crumble. There is of course the issue of how to make the electronic support eternal, while renewing it constantly. It is a huge problem but we'll have to get there. As far as old books are concerned, libraries are like art galleries: you do not replace the Uffizi with a good CD-Rom that shows you the Uffizi, however useful that CD-Rom may otherwise be; there persists the desire to go see the original, just as one wants to touch the old book, to look at the binding and so on. In this sense the great historical libraries must remain. On the other hand, what will happen to student libraries, where one can find text books, etc.? That, I do not know. Certainly new texts, once the problem of copyright is resolved, could be on line: that would solve the problems of theft, of books already on loan, and so on. It could also increase solitude, because libraries are also meeting places, although university libraries could also become large spaces with screens where people go to read and can talk with others as well. I think that, for now, there will remain the need for paper memory, so that along with libraries for everyday use you'd still have the Library of Congress with its printed books and journals. But there is also the problem of the physical space for archives, for example those of periodicals and journals, which at one time contained four pages and nowadays contain a hundred pages. It could really be the case that annual runs of journals become the preserve of collectors only, who also embody a form of memory and conservation. Two months ago, I bought for quite a lot of money the entire collection of *Lacerba*, the journal edited by Giovanni Papini, and it is very moving to have it before one's eyes: even if they put it on line one day, it is very nice for me to have the historical record. In this sense, I would also be a collaborator to the social conservation of memory.

GO: A last question: what happens to the 'original' of a written text?

UE: Certainly at this point the idea of the original disappears. If I go look for the originals of my texts, I cannot find them anymore, unless I've printed them from the outset, since I'm wont to correcting them every week on the computer. But that is not really the problem. Let's say that you write the philosophical masterpiece of your life; even if you'll have lost the original there will always be the latest edition. It will be hard to evaluate your mental evolution, but if your contribution is interesting, that is all right. The problem is with the alterations that I can make to the texts of others. If I download onto my computer the *Critique of Pure Reason*, then begin to study it and to write all my comments between the lines, either I am a good philologist and I can tell which are my comments, or after three years I no longer know what is mine and what by Kant. We'll be like those medieval copyists who automatically corrected the text they were copying because to them it seemed right to correct it in that way, so the risk is that the philological spirit end up disappearing altogether. But here too, the risk exists for the young student who does not realize that he has manipulated the text; it isn't there for the scholarly and academic worlds, which would remain the guarantors of this philological guardianship. In other words, there would continue to be new critical editions of Kant in which one will be sure that the text is his. Anyway, originals are not interesting otherwise than emotionally, unless you become an extremely famous writer, in which case some American university is bound to offer to buy all your manuscripts. But let me tell you the story of an Italian writer, no longer alive, nor that famous, but of solid reputation. One day, a good American university asked him if they could have the original manuscript of a novel he had published, for about $5000 of that time. But he no longer had the original manuscript. So he had his whole printed book typed up, then with a pen he deleted various lines and wrote over them what had been deleted under the pen mark. Officially, then, this is the original manuscript of the author, although it isn't at all – so you see, even with the Internet there can be serious philological mistakes!

Discussion

Let a thousand filters bloom

Umberto Eco asserts that, because the Internet does not have filters, people will not be able to distinguish between quality materials on line and those that are 'the work of delirious occultist crazies'. I disagree.

First, the Internet is replete with filters, though not necessarily the authoritative filters Eco would like. Most associations, such as, say, the *International Society for Philosophy*, provide lists of recommended works. Additionally, many authorities in different fields publish newsletters or weblogs identifying and recommending useful works. The person who relies only on Google may be lost, but nobody relies only on Google.

Second, there is much less of a need for filters than Eco supposes. In a literate society, the vast majority of people are able to distinguish between quality work and that of the less-qualified fringe. People are moreover able to critically assess even the authorities and draw their own conclusions. Filters are perhaps necessary for a pre-literate culture, but we have progressed well beyond those medieval days.

I respect Eco's assertion that the filters he has in mind do not function in the manner of the censor. And no doubt it is not the intent of the publisher who selects manuscripts or the editor who referees an article to prohibit a certain body of opinion from being distributed. But where a filter is placed between the reader and the body of content, then no matter how benign the original intent, the effect is the same as censorship. It is not possible to prevent one's opinions on quality culture, scholarship and criticism from screening out certain points of view, certain means of expression. Free access to information requires disintermediated access to information. That there are certain risks is self-evident, as is the case with any form of self-government. That, however, the benefits far outweigh the risks is also self-evident. For in the question of knowledge as well as in any question of authority, the age-old question arises: who censors the censors?

Stephen Downes

The issue is communication

I don't think Eco implies people will be completely incapable of distinguishing between quality materials and others, but more that the casual visitor will be easily misled. Rather than debates on Kant, think of some of the long-standing 'scientific' debates, such as on the reality of climate change, or the theory of evolution. There are some extremely convincing websites out there that are, on close examination by reputable people, filled with false-hoods, and yet would easily lead the casual visitor who does not venture further into the issues to adopt some rather wrong-headed beliefs. This is happening more and more. How do you fight against it? Censorship is not the answer, I agree; but there has to be some means for people to direct themselves to the sources that will be more useful to them. A filter doesn't have to be for quality or truthfulness of course – American TV networks filter rather severely, and yet manage to broadcast such absurdities as a 'documentary' on how the Moon landings were faked.

The central problem is, to quote the text under debate: 'a society with five billion concurrent encyclopaedias is a society in which there is no more communication'. The simple physical impossibility of an individual reading and comparing every available text on the web means that each of us has to find some criteria with which to select what we will pay attention to. Personally, I have been happy using the *New York Times* web site as my primary filter for news, with occasional glimpses at the *Economist*, Yahoo's news feeds, and a few others. For technical information there are several sites I frequent, but an excellent example of an unconventional filter is the slashdot site – *http://slashdot.org/*. The important thing about each one of these is that it is not a filter of my own design and determination, but I and thousands or millions of others are relying either on an authoritative publisher or a set of editors, or in the case of slashdot a 'rated' community, to filter information for us. Google is much better than older generations of search engines in finding respectable and relevant sites for general information; but it does *not* provide the same functions that these edited sites do.

Eco states that search engines are not what he means by filtering systems, that any algorithmic analysis is insufficient and there is a need for a human 'editor' or 'publisher' who makes deliberate selections. We have some of our own evidence for this in scholarly publishing with the 'virtual journals' – *http://www.virtualjournals.org*. The starting point for these is an automated subject/category search, but then a human editor steps in and selects papers subjectively based on the likely interests of the target audience. These virtual journals seem to have been very successful, and point out exactly the need people have for filters, rather than having to 'critically assess . . . and draw their own conclusions' on everything, as Stephen Downes suggests.

Certainly every organization that tries to establish a filter will be subjected to critical evaluation by each user, and the freedom to select which filters one uses should be fundamental. Perhaps I won't like the filtering imposed by the *International Society for Philosophy*; I certainly hope that other philosophical organizations will step in to provide alternatives. Perhaps in the long run we will even decide we can afford to pay for such things.

Arthur Smith

Peer review is and always was the filter and 'authority'

Umberto Eco says that filtering information is the fundamental problem of the Web. So many have said this, in one form or another. And, faced with the heterogeneous hash on the Web today, most of it trash, even if 'filtered' by Google's link-count economy, it is understandable why people might think that filtering it all is a new problem, unique to the web, and *the* problem. But it is not; it is none of these things: the problem is old, predates the web, and solved.

For science and scholarship, the filter is called peer-review, which is nothing mysterious: it is just qualified specialists (referees), assessing and improving the quality of the work of their fellow-specialists, mediated by a meta-specialist (the editor), before the work is published, with a quality-control 'tag' (the journal name) certifying that it has met the established quality standards of that particular journals.

The system is nothing unique or new; similar principles are involved in certifying the quality of eggs.

What is new is that the economies of the on-line medium make it possible for authors to bypass this filtration if they like, 'skywriting' their raw texts up into the post-gutenberg galaxy directly. What has made this vast vanity press – this global graffiti board for trivial pursuit – possible is simply a new economic fact: it is now so much cheaper to disseminate one's texts on line than on paper that it is within reach of every living soul who can read and write. In the Gutenberg galaxy, the 'filter' against this was simply the costs of publication.

But if, counterfactually, it had been as cheap and easy to print and disseminate paper in those days as it is to stand up on a soapbox in Hyde

Park (or to hold forth on today's chat-radio and chat-TV), then the 'filtration' problem would have been there too.

And the solution. If one is serious about one's inquiries, one will restrict them to the texts of qualified experts, certified by their qualified fellow-experts.

On the Web, we are simply assaulted by the new reality: rather as if the older media – radio, TV – had suddenly been augmented and overwhelmed by billions of new channels, all purveying people's personal (or corporate) phonograffiti. Except there, in the oral tradition, we would not have had the established mechanism of peer review and its quality-tagging to fall back on as our guide. Never mind; we would still have figured out how to choose reliable channels eventually. The Web has the advantage that, as a special case, it inherits the peer-review filter gratis.

Gratis? Not quite. Peers review for free, and always did. And they also write and distribute their papers for free. But someone always had to pay for the *implementation* of peer review (receiving the manuscripts, circulating them to the qualified reviewers, tracking the process and keeping it on schedule), and that cost some money (about \$200–\$500 per accepted paper). But this relatively modest cost was bundled in with many other purely Gutenberg costs (printing, distributing and marketing the paper – and lately also the paper images, pdf, online). All those costs were wrapped into the journal, which was then sold as everything else on paper was sold: for a fee.

Unlike with books and magazines, though, the authors of these peer-reviewed papers never sought or received royalties, salaries, or fees in exchange for their texts. All they ever wanted was as many of their fellow-researchers as possible to read, use, cite, and build upon their work.

And here is the real key to solving the 'filtration' non-problem: As soon as this peer-reviewed (filtered) literature is as freely and fully available online as the unfiltered literature, the 'brand names' will perform exactly the same filtration function they always performed on paper.

But this will alas only work for this give-away literature. For the non-give-away literature, the 'filter' will continue to be a financial one.

Stevan Harnad

Minority satisfied, the world awaits

To suggest that to solve this whole problem of 'unsolicited' information by just using such a thing as 'peer review' is quite ludicrous. Although, yes it will filter some sites and render a small part of the web 'reliable', it will still leave the vast majority of this etherial library left unfiltered.

'But it is not; it is none of these things: the problem is old, predates the web, and solved.'

How can a problem that arose from the net itself predate it? Although the theory of peer review has been around for some time, and yes predating the web, it is not the solution to this problem, as it will still only help those who have access to it. All we will have is the most privileged having access to this so-called quality information.

In my view I believe what Eco is trying to say is that there is no real solution to filter the web and there will probably never be on just because of the sheer size of the internet.

David Klemke

Filtration and education

I agree with Stevan on the fact that the open access of the whole corpus of peer-reviewed literature will be one of the most important improvements of the Web as a cultural tool.

Still, I can see the point that David Klemke is trying to make. Most people, even scientists, do not know how to orientate themselves within domains that are outside their professional competences. These days, I am looking for an on-line course for learning how to design dynamic webpages with Dreamweaver software: even if I use the Web daily for my research, I'm a bit lost in evaluating the authority and seriousness of the offers that I have found.

This is a common experience, and we should take into account these ordinary experiences when we discuss these matters. Filtration and education are not two distinct problems: education is a system of filtering information, as Umberto Eco rightly points out in our interview. But people cannot be educated in any domain, there isn't enough time for this. So we do not have a personal or professional filter for every domain. The Web gives us the new possibility to access information in domains for which we do not have any criteria of evaluation. This is really new: to access the same information before the Web you should already possess a lot of 'meta-knowledge' about how to reach this information and to classify it. Now you can just type 'Astrophysics' with Google and see what you find as a result.

So, on the one hand, the Web allows us to overcome some of the rigidities of educational systems by broadening our chances to acquire knowledge in a variety of domains, whereas on the other hand, we are in a desperate need of more education now, to empower our systems of filtering. Indeed, education and filtration will be the more and more close issues in the future . . .

Gloria Origgi

Divide and filter

In making the implicit analogy between the entire contents of the Web and the contents of a library or encyclopaedia we are conflating things that should be distinguished, and thereby inventing hybrid problems that could be much more sensibly solved by simply partitioning the on-line corpus *a priori* with tags that are no more 'authoritative' than simply indicating the pre-web provenance of the item, if it has one (e.g., journal name).

(That is what I meant to imply with my hypothetical example of what we would do if everyone's every spoken and unspoken thought suddenly materialized as a competing URL on the Web, indexed by Google. The point of the thought experiment was to remind us how and why this is a non-problem in the analog world of written and spoken discourse and mentation, simply because 'babble' is 'tagged' babble by its medium, and thereby 'filtered' from 'scribble'. The 'authoritativeness' of scribble is partly ex officio, because the Gutenberg costs of disseminating one's every verbal and mental rumination in print were prohibitive. On the Web they are not, but does that mean we must now treat all effusions and diffusions on a par simply because they are there?)

First, how did people orient themselves outside their professional competences in the Gutenberg age, when confronted by the contents of libraries and bookstores, of books, journals, magazines, newspapers and pamphlets? For the 'authoritative' material, there were always their 'authoritative' sources, 'tagging' them. Outside one's professional competence one could still make do with those signposts.

So, to a first approximation, the authoritative corpus need merely be made airborne, along with its signposts. This not only restores our terrestrial navigation guides for the airborne incarnation of the scribble, but it immediately sectors the scribble from the babble that is already up there.

Now, on to Dreamweaver software: I ask, timidly, whether, for example, consumer questions should be conflated with scholarly ones, any more than babble with scribble? Does it help to baptize as one generic 'problem' the problem of finding scholarly sources for 'holoenzyme...gracilis...' or educational sources for 'holy grail' or gastronomic sources for recipes for hominy grits?

To a first approximation, sectoring the web (with provenance-tags) according to whether items are or are not refereed-journal items already reduces the noise/signal ratio. The big task is of course getting all 20,000 refereed journals airborne. But am I simply obsessed with refereed journals, or are there not similar *a priori* provenance-tagging solutions for other sectors of the Web, short of having to have heroic scouts pick through it all for us to sort out the reliable bits, or, worse, having to follow the depth of the virtual trails left by everyone making their way randomly through all of it?

I am not declaring the problem of navigating the current Web, *tel quel*, for all purposes, 'solved' by these *a priori* considerations! I am simply suggesting that we may be conceptualizing the problem in the wrong way, and that importing more of the terrestrial corpus, and sectoring the Web, and hence the problem, may be a more promising path to the solution(s) than continuing to treat generic navigation of the current Web as the prototype of the problem.

Gloria Origgi writes: 'Filtration and education are not two distinct problems: education is a system of filtering information, as Umberto Eco rightly points out in our interview. But people cannot be educated in every domain.'

I'm afraid I find the provision of authoritative information to be the primary 'informatic' function, its tagging/certification as reliable (peer review) the secondary one – both of these are done by qualified specialists – and then its imparting to the uninformed (education) the tertiary one. One would hope that the information's (quaternary) use would then be guided by the user's education.

Yes there is an element of selecting ('filtering') the relevant sources in providing an education, but let us not forget that that filtration was performed on relatively refined candidates (published terrestrial scribble) rather than on every piece of babble that automatically became a candidate merely for having uttered a pertinent keyword!

Gloria Origgi: 'The Web gives us the new possibility to access information in domains for which we do not have any criteria of evaluation. This is really new: to access the same information before the Web you should already possess a lot of meta-knowledge about how to reach this information and to classify it. Now you can just type Astrophysics with Google and see what you find as a result.'

And once the full peer-reviewed astrophysical corpus is online, freely accessible, and reliably tagged as such, the user will be in at least as good a position as when consulting the collection of the best terrestrial library on the subject – except that even then merely the keyword 'astrophysics' would not have served him too well. (An encyclopaedia might, after all, be the better choice for that.)

Stevan Harnad

Conclusion: How the Internet has Changed Our Cultural and Scholarly Practices

Gloria Origgi

If we wanted to assess the impact of the Internet on cultural life and research, we could sum it up with a series of unfulfilled promises and threats. Books and paper have not yet vanished from our desks, and we still search arduously for publishers to get our manuscripts into print. Having texts with our names on them meandering freely through cyberspace is still not enough to placate our desire for lasting renown. Linguistic differences have not yet been crushed by the reign of English on the net: there are today 544 million non-English users as opposed to 295 million English users;[1] and despite the expansion of higher education on line, the university auditoriums are overflowing with students, and printed manuals can still be found on the desks and in the book stores. Not only that, but the cost of on-line subscriptions to scientific periodicals has become prohibitively expensive, comparable to the print edition, and universities, research institutions and archival institutions are today differentiated by the economic investment they are able to bear in order to provide their members with access to scientific documentation.

The battle for free access to scientific publications on line is still in progress,[2] but it's enough to consult the *Directory of Open Access Journals* (*http://www.doaj.org*) in order to realize that out of the more than 20,000 scientific peer-reviewed journals, few have gone the route of totally free access. Even editorial projects such as JSTOR (*www.jstor.org*) – an archive of humanities journals sponsored by the Andrew W. Mellon Foundation, with the aim of reducing the costs of storing the old issues of periodicals in libraries, making sure they are preserved and improving access to them – or PubMed Central (*www.pubmedcentral.nih.gov*) – a digital archive of medical and biology journals – is still a compromise between the interests of researchers and publishers. Besides the need to accredit the institution by means of a subscription, JSTOR protects the interest of the publisher of scientific journals by guaranteeing a significant delay between its print publication and its availability in the on-line archive (usually from three to five years). PubMed has been joined up to now by a small number of journals that often publish only a portion of their articles. The completely free access journals are put out by BioMed (*www.BioMed.com*), a publishing house associated with PubMed, and they do not always include reference titles for researchers.

The list of unfulfilled promises and threats could go on at length. The 'pyramidal book', which Rober Darnton envisioned in his famous article 'The New Age of the Book' in *The New York Review of Books*,[3] predicted a substantial modification of the scientific monograph into a hierarchy of levels: the most superficial could be printed and distributed, whereas the digital edition could delve into the subject more deeply, with lower levels including notes, glosses, commentaries and appendices. And yet, the pyramid book has not become a reality; in fact, our use of texts on the Internet manifests the opposite tendency: quick research of a passage on the net, without excessive control of quality, reliability of sources, and the verification of details in critically acclaimed editions (and published in print).[4]

Then there's the other side of the story. No one can deny that the world of research has changed radically since the advent of the Internet. Research is no longer the same; and not only that, but every practical aspect of scientific life – consulting sources, organizing knowledge, the disciplinary system, quality control, teaching, the building of scientific reputations – has undergone a profound mutation which deserves detailed analysis.

How has research changed? Which mutations are substantial, and which are merely an update of our ordinary routines? What are the advantages? What are the risks?

In the last decade, the production, transmission and preservation of scientific knowledge have undergone radical change that is so quick and of such historical import that it has put all our cultural institutions into question. The combination of the Internet and the World Wide Web – that is, the protocol developed in 1990 for the visualization and interoperability of documents on the Internet – has allowed for a massive outpouring of bibliographical data, scientific articles, encyclopaedia entries, world classics, repertoires, hypertexts, etc. in a single active and potentially infinite repository of interconnected information.

This fact forces us to reflect on how intellectual and cognitive activity, 'inside' the heads of researchers and readers, has changed; and it also forces us to reflect on how the information support structure has change, as well as the values that we traditionally associate with the access and consumption of information.

A large part of the research process in humanities disciplines – such as history, philosophy, literary criticism, etc. – involves a process of 'filtering' information already produced with regard to a given topic. We can also define culture itself as the construction and institutionalization of 'filters', or systems of selection and retrieval of information: experts, academies, journals, newspapers and publishing houses are merely the institutional counterparts of the cultural activities of filtering and retrieving information. As Umberto Eco said in a brief essay, in which he explained to his students how to write a thesis, the purpose of a university is less for acquiring information than for acquiring methods and meta-knowledge with which to 'navigate' through culture.[5]

The Internet has effected a profound cultural revolution because it doesn't simply change our access to a corpus of knowledge, but rather changes our filters and methods of retrieving information. In the Google era, one of the principal cognitive activities of knowledge management, that is, meta-memory or the compendium of culturally learned heuristic and methods – from rhyme to indexes – which allow us to retrieve information from the cultural corpus, is performed, at least in part, outside ourselves. Google is a second-generation search engine. The first search engines, such as Lycoos or Altavista, established a hierarchy of results from a search on the basis of a recurring key word in the Web pages. Google, on the other hand, uses an algorithm which calculates the results of a search by using information such as *the structure of the link between pages*; in other words, if a page gets many links from other pages, then it rises in the hierarchy of results. The structure of the link contains an enormous amount of information about what the Web users know. Extracting this implicit knowledge from the tangle of links between Web pages is one of the most important results of IT research in recent years.[6]

The structure of links, produced culturally by the individual choices of Web page creators, is interpreted by the search-algorithms as a ranking of the pages: every link from page A to page B is a vote that page A casts for page B. The hierarchy of results in turn influences the user's choices in a virtuous circle of collaboration between humans and automata.

Google therefore takes advantage of our cognition and together realizes one of our cognitive functions, that of meta-memory, which allow us to retrieve a piece of information from our culture's dense network. If you're not convinced about the division of cognitive labour between machines and humans made possible by search engines and believe that the filtering and retrieving of information is an eminently human and cultural activity not to be left to artificial automata, then connect to *Google News* (*http://www.news.google.com*). *Google News* is an algorithm that filters news from all over the world, using the information contained in the structure of the link between one site and another. The news item with the most 'hits' worldwide rises automatically to the top of the page. Now, compare the first page of *Google News*, whose content is continually updated, with the first page of an international newspaper, the *Herald Tribune*, for example. You'll see that there is not much of a difference. In fact, *Google News* often avoids tendentious articles that may have been included for reasons that go beyond the task of purely informing.

A cultural activity such as that of retrieving and filtering information is achieved thanks to an 'exchange among equals' of information between humans (each webmaster who puts a link between two pages) and automata (the algorithms that read the structure of the links). The co-penetration of technology, cognition and culture is so deep in this case that we are obliged to rethink the very nature of our intellectual activity. In some sense, the artificial intelligence we were dreaming of forty years ago has finally been realized, but on an entirely different basis from what was originally envisioned: not the half-human half-mechanical cyborg imagined by the fathers of cybernetics, but *a hybrid collective intelligence* in which the knowledge generated by the automaton couldn't exist without the ongoing and spontaneous production of culture by the human beings; and at the same time, this production is influenced by the automatic filtering of information.

In which way is research transformed by the new techniques of collective filtering and retrieving of information? Let's take an example: I often write interdisciplinary articles, for instance, between philosophy and cognitive science. In a traditional system of classification of knowledge, I would have to decide *a priori* to which publication I would like my article to go. If I decide to publish in a cognitive science journal, I risk losing the audience of philosophers; and vice versa if I decide to publish in a philosophy journal. But a text in cyberspace – which can be found on my personal website, in the archive of the institution I work at, or in some other digital archive accessible to the public (see, for example, the archive COGPRINT [*http://cogprints.ecs.soton.ac.uk*] for publications in cognitive science) – will be accessible by whomever is interested in the topic by means of a search with a key word. Search engines break the rigid classifications of traditional research – which acted as historic *a priori* directions in establishing what is knowledge and who can access it in any given epoch – and reorganize scientific material in a lighter structure, assembled temporally according to the precise aim of the researcher, and continually updated.

Sceptics will say that I'm painting an idealized image of how a search engine should work in the best of possible worlds, and that in fact the results of a search through keywords depend on the policies of site referencing, which are subject to commercial strategies: the more you pay the higher you go in the hierarchy of results. But try to Google 'neural basis of numerical competence' or 'Adanson, malacology' and you'll see how difficult it is to extrapolate some commercial strategy from the result. This is because doing research, with or without the Internet, means manipulating very improbable combinations of key words, that is, extracting information from the corpus of knowledge from an extremely subtle angle. These knowledge assemblages are rare, relevant for a small community that remains outside commercial logic, and cannot be influenced more than the traditional system of citation. In fact, academic journals often use the practice of self-citation in bibliographies articles published in their own pages in order to increase their quotation ranking, and thus the authority of the magazine.

Of course, this does not apply to the average Internet user who searches 'Manchester, movies, tonight' and gets results influenced by commercial logic. And it applies even less to the freshman student looking for 'Nazism' on the Web and finding a cascade of anti-Semitic or revisionist pages. But although the case of our Manchester user is extraneous to the subject of research, the one of the student serves to highlight how Internet changes not only our way of doing research, but also of teaching and transmitting it. In a world in which information circulates through light knowledge-structures that we can modify and reassemble according to our aims, it would be better to teach students to reason differently. Quite often, the traditionally rigid taxonomy in which knowledge is dissected and transmitted, and which establishes the canon of a culture, does not constitute the most adequate manner of retrieving the information in that culture. The canon, in fact, or the classification and organization of knowledge that allows a culture to identify itself with and pass down a collective memory, has a much broader social function than that of simply transmitting knowledge; it defines the threshold of identity below which a culture ceases to recognize itself. As such, it is maintained not as a cultural artifact for transmitting knowledge from one generation to another, but as a society's 'sacred archive', constituting responses to the question: 'Who are we?' But in an informationally open society, in which knowledge circulates and is constantly reorganized beyond the limits of cultural identities, the various canons are among themselves often dissonant and reveal their inadequacy as tools of cultural transmission. Perhaps it would be better to accustom young post-Internet minds to research heuristics that are more flexible, more adaptable to changing contexts and new situations. Deep down, that's how our cognition works: we retrieve information from our memory in the context of a certain experience, and we can create an unlimited number of *ad hoc* concepts that serve to reflect upon and plan an action in any given situation. (For example, I can develop a concept that corresponds to 'the most important things to save when the house is burning down'; and it will contain a provisional assemblage of disparate objects such as: babies, documents, portrait of grandmother, keys to the safe, etc.). Of course, the transmission of knowledge requires a certain stability of concepts; but if we manage to separate what for this stability is essential for knowledge and what isn't and serves purposes that are noble though not necessary for the perpetuation of cultural identity, we can develop in the future educational systems that are more suited to our minds and the new structures of knowledge produced by our interaction with algorithms. In the coming years we will witness a co-evolution of cultural and cognitive strategies as well as systems of 'knowledge management' that will profoundly change the transmission of knowledge (think only of the educational programme *StarLogo*,[7] developed at MIT Media Lab to familiarize students and researchers with distributed thinking and decentralized systems).

These examples show us how the '*à la carte*' culture provided by the Internet profoundly disrupts the mental practices and institutional roles traditionally associated with the production, conservation and transmission of knowledge. And, as Habermas said, where science and technology introduce themselves into the institutional spheres of society, all existing legitimization is put into question.[8]

Let's take the case of scientific journals, one of the more authoritative knowledge filters. A researcher submits an article to a journal; the editors of the journal send it to at least two anonymous reviewers, who evaluate and critique it, proposing improvements and sometimes dissuading the author from publication. The researcher receives the comments, reformulates the article and, many months later, sees it published in a journal. All of it, obviously, with no remuneration – which distinguishes this class of journals from the magazines one finds on newsstands. The advent of the Internet has brought out a patent absurdity in this market. The researchers are the ones who produce the articles, consume them, and also the ones who guarantee their evaluation for free. Moreover, the universities and libraries are the ones who buy the subscriptions to the journals, allowing for their survival. So why go through journals? Why lengthen the time and increase the costs of exchanging information reserved for a community of equals when it can be achieved at zero cost through the Internet? This reflection has concretized itself through various actions: the movement for free access to scientific journals on the Web that I mentioned earlier proposes to rethink the institutional role of guaranteeing knowledge. The *Open Access* initiative has allowed for the creation of new digital peer-reviewed journals (such as *BioMed Central*, or *Psycholoquy*), the development of free-access programmes for archiving articles on line and for the construction of interoperable archives; and, more importantly, it has encouraged reflection on possible new models of distribution of scientific knowledge. For example, university libraries, whose role is also threatened by the IT revolution, could develop new skills and do the job of scientific journals in filtering and archiving scientific articles. Or a publisher of digital reviews could guarantee profit by making the author (or even better: the author's institution) pay for the service of referring or laying it out in a specific format (the model adopted by *BioMed Central*). Or one could even think of filtering and redistribution systems of information truly different from journals, such as *Faculty of 1000*, a monthly project of selecting the most important articles in medicine and biology proposed by 1000 renowned scientists. Each gets a certain grade, somewhat like the star system film critics use, and depending on where it is published, it can be accessed for free or purchased directly from the site. Surely in all areas of publishing and content distribution, from scientific publishing to recording companies, the rearguard battle to defend acquired rights which we have been witnessing in recent years is not the best way to exploit technological innovations.

Until the end of the 1990s, the Internet developed in a very anarchic and libertarian manner. Unlike the great networks of the past – i.e., the electric grid, or railway and road systems – the Internet is an intrinsically decentralized system: a torrent of information that has inundated all the structures of knowledge management and has put into question rights, norms, mental habits and social roles not only in the world of research but in the general world of production, transmission and preservation of knowledge. The world made possible by the Internet at its inception was perhaps too far removed from what we know; and we have witnessed in the last few years a conservative reaction in which the old forms, the old rights and tradition privileges have been vindicated, often in court (think of Napster). The disappointments of the New Economy have encouraged a return to the old order. Today we find ourselves faced with an important choice: whether to conceive new structures for managing knowledge that are truly the fruit of an integration of cultural practices, institutional roles and technological innovations; or, instead, defend an ancient status quo and risk losing the real image of ourselves as producers and beneficiaries of culture, an image that has been inexorably transformed by the Internet revolution.

Notes

1. Cf. *http://glreach.com/globstats*; Daniel Dor (2003): 'From Englishization to Imposed Multilingualism: Globalization, the Internet and the Political Economy of the Linguistic Code', in *Public Culture*, 16, 1, 2004.
2. See Stevan Harnad (2001): 'Skyreading and Skywriting in the Post-Gutenberg Galaxy', *http://www.text-e.org*.
3. Cf. R. Darnton (1999) 'The New Age of the Book', *NYRB*, 18 March, *http://www.nybooks.com/articles/546*
4. Cf. J. Nielsen (1997) 'How Users Read on the Web', *Alertbox*, October 1997; *http://www.useit.com*
5. U. Eco (1977) *Come si fa una tesi di laurea*, Tascabili Bompiani.
6. Cf. J. Kleinberg (1998) 'Authoritative Sources in a Hyperlinked Environnement', *Proccedings of the 9th ACM-SIAM Symposium on Discrete Algorithms*.
7. Cf. *http://education.mit.edu/starlogo/*
8. Cf. J. Habermas (1968) *Technik und Wssenschaft als Ideologie*, Francoforte.

Index